NB to self subject
Nessus 2 Dejanira
Ovid met 9
8 perlouing from Louis de Boulogne
2 Pan 2 Syrinx
Ovid met 138 I wonder
Self

Matthew

Anne Crosby

Matthew

a memoir

pcb PAUL DRY BOOKS
Philadelphia 2006

First Paul Dry Books Edition, 2006

Paul Dry Books, Inc.
Philadelphia, Pennsylvania
www.pauldrybooks.com

Author's note: The names of certain individuals and organizations have been changed to protect their privacy.

Text type: Berkeley
Display type: Hoefler Text and Bernhard Modern Roman
Composed by P. M. Gordon Associates
Designed by Christine Dunleavy
Jacket image by Getty

1 3 5 7 9 8 6 4 2
Printed in the United States of America

Library of Congress Cataloging-in-Publication Data
Crosby, Anne, 1929–
     Matthew / Anne Crosby.
              p.   cm.
     ISBN-13: 978-1-58988-026-9 (alk. paper)
     ISBN-10: 1-58988-026-9 (alk. paper)
       1. Crosby, Matthew, 1964—Health. 2. Down's syndrome—Patients—
     Biography. I. Title.
     RJ506.D68C76 2006
     362.196'8588420092—dc22

                                                              2005037891

ISBN-13: 978-1-58988-026-9
ISBN-10: 1-58988-026-9

For Dido,
who in all our years with Matthew
never once treated him
as less than an equal.

Eileen Hales Gladys

⊙ = thoroughly corrected feb 08

Contents

Contents

corrections P62, 84, 100, 124, 141, 143, 147
148, photo for 155,

118

307 x 2   310. 311 312, 315
351 x 2   352   353

79 84. 86. 87. 88. 89.

118   125. 127. 128. 131. 133. 134

Matthew

P56 P54

Rose

Our father owned various houses. The one which interested him least was on what he considered a piece of valueless land in West Sussex. Its location pleased our mother because of its healthy surround and relative nearness to a railway station that was on a fast line to London.

The main function of this house was to accommodate children; secretly my siblings and I considered it to be our property. A sandy lane, almost obscured by phalanxes of gorse and several stubby fir trees, branched from a very minor country road and meandered past our house. A short, untended drive stopped abruptly in front of a large clapboard garage. From there a brick path led between vaguely defined, self-perpetuating flower beds to wind around to first the front and then the back door of a rather irrational and impromptu building. Everything behind it was more interesting than anything in front. From our back door, which was divided across as if we inhabited a loose box, a grassy plateau spread to a downward slope that led to a grove of silver birches and a shallow swamp of oily iridescent water studded with large tussocks of grass. One could sear fine cuts across the palm of one's hand by clutching at those blades of grass.

Beyond the swamp, the ground rose a little to meet the bank of a stream, which in places was overhung with water willows. Under the flowing water was ocher-colored sand strewn with round, rusty pebbles; long hairlike hanks of weed swung in the current. A heavy plank served us as a drawbridge, and we used a convenient horizontal limb of one of the willows as a balustrade. Our constant crossing and recrossing had worn stepped paths up and down both banks of the stream. On the other side was a big brackeny, heathery meadow.

DURING THE LONG summer holiday of 1935, toward the end of which I was to turn six years old, I found a friend. She lived at the farthest end of that meadow. We had several times glimpsed each other through the thick hawthorn and hazel hedges that bounded her garden. I envied her the little house she lived in—it was a tiny wooden house only one story high with a corrugated tin roof and a white veranda.

When I walked to the top of the meadow and stood by her hedge, she seemed to divine my presence and would soon appear, large and silent, always buttoned into a clean back-and-front pinafore, which I thought very chic. She wore a bow in her hair and usually carried a doll in her arms. Her smile melted my heart, and though I could not understand the reason for this, it sometimes brought tears to my eyes. Hoping to please her, I would carry in my pocket presents for her doll. My particular treasure at that time was a tin tea set with the face of Mickey or Minnie Mouse printed on every piece. Those tiny plates were more vivid to me than any of the modern art that ornamented our house.

On one visit, I might poke a cup through the hedge, on the next, a saucer or a plate. Each time, I would wave the paw of my toy monkey, and I was often rewarded with a tentative wave back from the arm of her doll. In return for pieces of my tea set, she offered me flower heads through the hedge, each one on a leaf—irises, delphinium petals, oxeye daisies, most often rosebuds.

I came to feel I would do anything to conjure that smile onto her face. We began to make quite a sizable gap in the hedge; I called it a window. I used to ask her to come close, then I would twirl about holding out my skirt and march up and down playing pretend musical instruments, sometimes ending these performances by leading imaginary circus animals up to the hedge and asking them to bow to the grand lady at the window. I soon learned not to have neighing horses or roaring lions, for she was timid; her head would bob down from the window if I made too sudden a noise.

As our friendship progressed, I became aware that she did not understand all I said, and though she loved me to recite poems, she could not follow the words very well. Yet she was familiar with nursery rhymes and would silently mouth the words with me.

Toward the end of August, I had my birthday. I went to tell her I was now six years old and to give her a spoonful of the birthday pudding. I served it to her on the last of the Mickey Mouse plates. As I did so, I realized that, when asked what my birthday wish was, I should have requested not a picnic on the Downs but her presence at the birthday tea. So I said goodbye to her and ran home through the bracken grown taller than myself in the short time I had known my new friend. I jumped the summer shallow stream, then hopped from one tussock of grass to the next and hurried between the birches up to the "loggia," which is what my mother called the pillared and thatched shelter that abutted the end of our house.

My mother had been taking her siesta. Seeing that she was now awake I went and stood by her day bed and asked her if I could change my mind about the birthday wish. I explained I wanted to bring a new friend to the garden to play and have tea.

"What is the name of your friend?" I amazed myself when I realized I could not answer the question.

"How old is she?" I could not answer that question either. I had never considered whether she had a name or an age. "How did you meet her?"

"Through the hedge of her garden."

"Is she well bred?" Unanswerable.

"Well, is she a lady?" Upon recalling how large she was, I nodded. Yes, she was a lady, though in my heart I knew there was something wrong with the description. I suppose my doubt must have shown in the expression on my face, for my mother laughed and said it was too late to rearrange things.

"But if you are still acquainted by the time the Christmas holiday comes, you might like to invite your new friend then."

It seemed as bad as being told "When you are grown up," but I knew better than to protest.

From then on it seemed to me that our nanny had her eye on me and was keeping me occupied. We went to London for a few days, and when we came home, the school trunks were being packed. I did nothing but wander about the house and garden, trying to use my boredom to prevent my last days of freedom from passing too quickly.

TWELVE WEEKS LATER, in the carefree joy of the first morning of our winter holidays, I ran down to the stream and crossed the plank over the now fast-flowing winter water, then raced up the bare meadow. Reaching the hedge, I found I could see through it very easily. My rush to see my friend was checked by a long, cold wait. When at last she appeared, she was wearing a heavy brown overcoat, over which was wrapped her usual pinafore tied round her waist by a piece of garden twine.

She attempted to run toward me, stumbling and clumsy. Not only were we entirely revealed to each other, but our hands could touch through the winter hedge. My friend started to cry; a desperate, touching ugliness filled her face. That was the first time I heard her voice. It came in low bellows. At once I pushed through the bare branches and stood beside her. I gave her my handkerchief, and I patted the back of her doll, which she clasped against her cheek. Just when I felt I could no longer bear her unhappiness and might run away, she took the doll and the handkerchief from her face and gave me a wobbly version of her beautiful smile.

I was so contrite at having neglected her for so long that I was unable to smile in return. I took her woolly-gloved hand and attempted to pull her through to my side of the hedge. I discovered she was very cumbersome and also shy. She seemed intimidated by the prickles and branches. I pushed her head down and pulled more fervently. Suddenly she came bundling through the crackling winter twigs. She stood up and made one of her contented grunting noises that I was to grow to like so much.

On that first occasion of our being together we walked round the perimeter of the meadow across patches of dead bracken into the winter quietness of an area of tall pine trees. There we stood still. I asked my friend the name of her doll. She apparently could not find the word she wanted, so I asked her her own name. She said clearly and loudly, "Rose." I told her it was a beautiful name and asked if her house was named after her—"Rose Cottage." I had often spelled out the painted sign on the white front gate.

She thumped her chest and laughed in a range of sonorous sounds that expressed real mirth. She didn't ask me my name. It didn't seem to matter that I had been longing to tell her that, during the school term, I had changed it from "Finella" to "Anne" so as to be more like other people, and now there were four Annes in our school. We counted the trees we stood under, singing the numbers loudly into the cold air. She took my hand. She was moving so slowly that I was worried that her legs were "bad." When I asked, she shook her head, but she let me lead her back to her house.

I DID NOT pull her through the hedge a second time. Instead we went by way of the field gate; knowing it was against my mother's rules, I walked with her the little way along the road to Rose Cottage. We examined the painted sign, chanting "Rose Cottage" together before I opened her front gate, which gave onto a path tightly packed with closely clipped lavender borders. Beyond the lavender lay wintry, dug-over flower beds and vegetable patches. Her father was our local nurseryman.

I called to him, "Good morning. Please may Rose come to visit me soon?"

He did not turn his head, but Rose's mother opened the front door and shouted, "First you must ask your Mum if it's all right." Then she came down the path and, after stroking Rose's stiff straight hair, led her indoors.

AS WE SAT down to tea that afternoon I took care to appear casual. I remarked to the nanny that it was likely I would have a visitor to play with me the next day. She too declared I must first get my mother's permission. Evening came and our mother summoned her three youngest children: my older sister Moyra, me, and my brother Alan. We went down to the drawing room to listen to *Br'er Rabbit,* a book our mother very much enjoyed reading aloud. Hoping she had forgotten the uncomfortable conversation on my birthday, and waiting until she began turning the pages of *Br'er Rabbit,* I told her I had invited a friend to come to play, saying it airily while standing behind her.

My sister, not taken in by the lightness of my voice, caught the significance of what I was telling and not telling, and went into our family's routine support of any sibling who wanted to deceive. Without curiosity or much sympathy, she set about distracting our mother from formulating any searching questions. She snatched a cushion from beneath my brother, who was already seated in his position as favorite against our mother's knee. He gave an appropriate squeal, and that was that. I knew if necessary I could count on both of them as future witnesses that I had mentioned the visit to my mother and she had not objected to it.

I felt I had a valid reason to disregard the rule about the road. I had an excuse for walking up to that enticing white gate, to open it, and go along the narrow path between the lavender bushes and flower beds. I had a right to mount the three steps to Rose's shadowy veranda and lift the beautiful door knocker, carved in the shape of a hand with painted pink fingernails.

I rapped on the door; Rose's mother opened it. She did not invite me in, and she was hesitant about allowing her daughter to come out. "Are you quite sure your Mum says it is all right bringing our Rose to your house?" I said emphatically, "Yes, Rose can come this very morning."

I noticed that Rose's mother did not make her wear her pinafore over her coat, and had replaced the length of twine with a leather belt. She pinned a handkerchief to Rose's lapel—it had "Thursday" embroidered on it and a tiny rose with one leaf. When we got to the road, we examined the handkerchief together. She was very proud of it. To make conversation, I asked if her doll was well.

This was a mistake. She clutched her chest where the doll should have been and almost turned to go home, but I grabbed her hand and together we marched the little way along the road to the field gate. From there I had intended us to continue down the slope of the meadow, then across the plank into our garden. I explained that we needed to go that way because I was not really allowed to be on the road without a grownup—I was still not quite sure Rose had that status, though she was a great deal taller than I and had a very solid shape.

By the time we arrived at the stream she was already fearful. She stared at the water, stroking my arm and whimpering. I thought such a big person should not mind walking across a plank, and I said so. She looked so stricken that I was immediately sorry for saying it. We started back up the hill. It was slow going. She remained dejected and would not let me pull or push her along. I tried to cheer her by telling her of the nice things we might do at my house. When we reached the road, I proposed— again putting aside my mother's rule—that this time we walk down it to the lane, but Rose only wanted to go back to her own home. Sadly resigned, I accompanied her to her gate and pushed it open for her. I waited till she had gone up the path. Her mother came to the door and I heard her say, "You were quick then. Did you go to the little lady's house?"

I was taken aback when Rose nodded her head, and ashamed that I had led her to nod a lie to her mother. I knew I had mismanaged Rose's treat. I waited awhile, watching her father as he dug a trench along a taut line of string he had pegged across one of his planting beds. I then gathered my courage and went to knock on Rose's front door.

I was nearly in tears as I tried to explain to her mother that we had not actually reached our house, the stream being too difficult for Rose to cross. Her mother came and stood between us, patting both our shoulders, saying, "Never mind now, never mind, our Rosie, you can go again tomorrow if that is all right with the little miss. I will walk you down the road." I felt she was a very kind person and was greatly relieved that I had not spoiled everything "for keeps."

The next day Rose's mum took us as far as the beginning of the lane. From there I led the way to our drive and into the part of the garden where we played. I had taken the toy monkey with me, and now I placed him on the seat of the swing. I pushed gently. When he fell off I propped him against a tree trunk and sat on the seat myself. As I swung into the air and looked down on Rose, she stood so alone and perplexed that I slowed the swing and jumped off. I showed her where her doll should sit beside the monkey, then I gently cajoled her onto the seat of the swing and placed each of her hands round a rope.

I pushed her very softly. I tried to make the kind of grunting noises I thought she might like to hear. At first her back was rigid with fear, but soon I could tell she was enjoying the sensation of swinging. When she had sufficient momentum I let go and walked round to the front of the swing so as to look at Rose's face. She was talking a little to herself, words that sounded like, "Good girl, Rosie, there's a good girl now." Meanwhile she cautiously tipped her foot to the ground and started pushing herself. It took quite a while for Rose to tire of the swing so that I could take her indoors.

AT FIRST ROSE would not climb the stairs. She stared at them aghast, so I put her hand on the banister and picked up one large shoe and shoved it on the stair. I heaved at the other leg, and eventually she gave in and lifted it to the next step. My sister joined us and pushed from behind. The going got easier at each step. We were all giggling by the time we reached the landing and Rose and I turned into the nursery.

She would not take her coat off, but she sat down at the table where my brother Alan was playing with his Meccano set. He took no notice of us as I searched about for toys that might interest her. I got out the toy farm. She could name all the animals. When we finished playing with them, she put the little seated sheepdog close to her face and barked at it. As I packed the farm away she was loath to part with it. "Give it to her," my brother said gruffly, without even raising his eyes.

Suddenly she wanted to go home. Thinking it might only mean she wished to be excused, I took her to the bathroom. She did not appear to need to sit on the lavatory, but the wash basin amazed her. The shiny taps entranced her. She lovingly sniffed the lavender soap, and washed and washed her hands, soaking the hand towels. We ran hot and cold water into the bath and the basin, putting in and pulling out the plugs. We played with the water, grunting and growling companionably in the steam. When we had become too hot and damp, it seemed time to descend the stairs.

There I was stymied. She absolutely refused to go down. My sister stood at the bottom and watched as I sat on the top stair and tried to show Rose how one might descend sitting on one step after another. She hid her head in her arms and leaned against the wall.

Hearing my sister's and my concerted pleading, my mother appeared in the hall below. "Whoever have you got up there... what is your name?" She advanced upon us.

Because Rose did not reply, I said, "She is Rose."

"Well, Rose," said my mother, "downstairs in our kitchen we have glasses of milk and slices of cake. You know what they are, don't you? Now, you be a big, good girl and show these children how well you can walk down a flight of stairs." She took the doll from Rose's embrace and gave it to me to carry. She put one of Rose's hands on the banister rail, tucked the other firmly under her arm, and led her down the stairs.

My mother was as good as her word. She took Rose into the kitchen and told the cook to bring out a glass of milk and a slice of cake. We all crowded round as Rose was made to sit down, given a table napkin, and told to mop up her tears. We watched as Rose sullenly and greedily pushed lumps of cake into her mouth and washed them down with noisy gulps of milk. Her manner of eating and drinking at the same time so impressed my brother that for days, despite threats of punishment, he annoyed our nanny and upset me by imitating it at every meal.

"Now, you two girls must take Rose back to her house," my mother said to my sister and me, and without saying goodbye to Rose, she left the kitchen.

We walked up the road very slowly. I was utterly dispirited and even a little frightened. Holding her doll against her cheek, Rose went into her house without once turning to look at me.

My sister and I ran home; we were late for lunch. It happened to be one of the days when my mother was not lunching out. We took our seats as she ended one of her mocking laughs. She was telling the assembled family that it was droll that I should choose a poor idiot girl to fall in love with. I was thunderstruck; I blushed and kept my eyes on my plate. No one looked at me as I wept.

I escaped from the dining room as soon as I could. I was sitting in the nursery looking out of the window when my brother and sister came in. "Well, I like idiots anyway," declared my brother.

"Grownups are the idiots," my sister added.

"Now, now," said the nanny, and I knew she was going to admonish us with one of her philosophical homilies. One had to pay careful attention on these occasions because she was apt to ask for a summary—"Now, what have I just told you?" Experience had taught us that, though the sense of these scoldings was often obscure, hidden among the plays on opposites were "useful hints" which she expected us to "take to heart."

The homily went something like this: "Two Wrongs don't make a Right! But you, young lady, are going to have to learn that in this family they sometimes do. Lots of things that by Rights should be Wrong are Right in this house. So what if your poor Rosie is not Right in her head, that does not mean it is Wrong to love her if you have a mind to. But it was not Right to invite her here. You ought to have guessed she was the Wrong sort for the likes of your ma. I don't know that you will ever find a way to Right the Wrong you did your poor friend. You would do better to choose the Right kind of friends from now on."

On this occasion she did not try, as she so often did, to even her number of rights and wrongs or rhetorically ask, "Well, am I Right?" or "Well, am I Wrong?" I think we had all lost count.

CHAPTER ONE

A Stable in Delphi

For the three last years of the 1950s, I lived with the man I loved in what was then commonly referred to as "sin." His name was Theo Crosby; he was South African and an architect. It took all that time for us to recognize, tolerate, and finally succumb to the notion of marriage.

In the month of April in 1960, a week after the wedding, we arrived in Delphi. Tired out by our economical manner of traveling, we were resting on two iron bedsteads, which we had dragged across a rough planked floor so as to be beside each other, but more importantly, to be as close as possible to a tiny shuttered window. As I knelt to unpack our rucksack, I peeped between the floorboards and verified what our throats and noses were already telling us: Our room was among the rafters of a byre. Just a few feet below us, I saw the bony backs and stubby manes of two donkeys. They stood motionless, their heads hanging mournfully, as if the slavery of their day oppressed them even as they slept. The fumes that rose from their cooling hides and acrid urine, mingled with the maquis scent of their fodder, were so strong that our eyes watered. We prized the window shutters apart, grateful to find there were no panes of glass between us and a wide view of tree-covered hills made spectacular by starlight.

Since we had boarded a steamer in Brindisi, our travels had day by day become less an embarrassing honeymoon and more a notable journey. It had taken us so far from our usual constraints that I felt almost weightless. I remember thinking how compatible we were going to become. All these years later I know that the few sentences we exchanged while lying on those husk-filled mattresses were the most confiding, the least reticent, we ever achieved, at least until after our marriage ended.

We put aside the brittle premarital weeks we had just endured. We owned up to being unsure and out of sympathy with each other during the first days of our honeymoon, and we agreed that we had once been foolishly enamored of each other and recalled with pleasure our bouts of glorious lust.

There in the now cooling darkness we confessed to feelings of foreboding and our reciprocal fear of having to love not by choice but by contract. We reviewed our now precious era of "living in sin" and found neither of us could recall any actual proposal of marriage. We laughed over this and marveled at the efficient manner in which we had rearranged our affairs, closed the house, taken the dog to stay with one of my sisters, and walked across the green to meet our wedding guests on the steps of Hammersmith town hall.

IN AUGUST of the same year I discovered I was pregnant. When I told Theo, I encountered in him a fastidiousness that I had not come across before. Rather than be made too aware of all the physical changes I was about to undergo, he suggested we be more private, more separate, "until you are yourself again."

As the pregnancy progressed, hoping to break through his shyness, I now and again made awkward attempts to override his rule. While despising myself for imposing on him confidences I knew he did not want to hear, I tried to draw him into discussions that might lead us to talk about the progress of the fetus within me. I did so despite a miserable awareness that my growing size was repellent to him.

Toward the end of the pregnancy I began to imagine my womb was not strong enough. At times, a horrible dropping sensation would seize my belly. I went to visit my so very experienced mother and asked her some tentative questions. She adopted a robust attitude; almost absentmindedly she gave me some commonsensical advice concerning eating, lying on a sofa to read, taking walks, and "of course" rubbing oil into one's skin. Reminding me that she had been through the process of gestation and birth nine times, she admonished me "not to make a meal of the business."

Curiously, each time I steeled myself to visit the doctor, my recurring pain died away. I talked to a close friend who thought that, since my pains disappeared and reappeared, they were probably imaginary. She began to tell me about her own pregnancies, and I hurried away. I tried to outwit the pains, daring them to be real; suddenly they were. Genuine labor pains were occurring too soon, and I slipped into a long and tiring confinement. I was taken to Queen Charlotte's Maternity Hospital, where I gave birth to a son two months early.

He survived only four days in an incubator on another floor. On what turned out to be his last living day, I lay on my hospital bed, dully wondering how he was faring and when I would be allowed to see him. When Theo came to see me he told me that each morning before going to his office he was permitted to sit beside the incubator for a few minutes. He said he could fit two fingers through a small aperture and hold our son's hand. I envied him.

I was startled by a tired-looking clergyman whose shadow fell across my face. He was accompanied by a nursing sister who announced that it was necessary to christen my child and that the Reverend So-and-so needed to have my consent before he could perform this service.

"It is a sensible precaution," that gentleman murmured kindly. "Did you and your husband have any particular name in mind?"

This was the one aspect of my pregnancy that had permitted discussion. We had decided that should I give birth to a daughter I could choose her name, but a son should be named Nicholas Johannes after Theo's father. I told the clergyman those family names. Perhaps because I was depressed and too tired or because I was not religious, I did not think to ask to be present at my son's christening.

Later I tried to imagine that antiseptic little ceremony. I was extremely sorry that I had not been present, not even held our baby before he died.

CHAPTER TWO

The Vegetable Shop

Normansfield Hospital was on the Middlesex side of the Thames, four bridges downriver from ours at Hammersmith. It had been laid out within spacious grounds during the late Victorian era. Its founder was a well-to-do doctor whose intention was to make a good living while honorably caring for and studying a particular type of inmate. Dr. Norman Langdon Down opened a home for "mongoloids," a designation derived from the fact that he, and perhaps others before him, saw their features as resembling those of Mongolians. The doctor gave his Christian name to his asylum, calling it Normansfield Hospital. So renowned was he that present-day carriers of this chromosomal mishap are known as Down syndrome people. However, during the time I am describing, it was not thought pejorative (in England) to use the term mongol or mongoloid. (Even Matthew called himself a "womble," after a little character portrayed in a children's program on BBC television.)

Now that I was married, I felt it my duty to be conscientious in my housekeeping, so despite a not-quite-attributable heartache I had for his son, I stopped buying overripe fruit or fatigued-looking vegetables from the lame man who kept a little stall on the corner of King Street and the old Hammersmith market. His son was a squat, short-breathed fellow who wore densely lensed spectacles, through which he peered and blinked like a nocturnal mammal caught in daylight. I liked the artless way he would try to gauge his customers' attitude toward himself when he broke into his gap-toothed smile. If they smiled back as he weighed vegetables or bagged fruit, he would regale them with a stream of unintelligible words, often causing his father to bark an angry order, "Get on with it, lad." Then the lad, which is how he was known though his hair was partly gray, would quiet his voice to a mutter, which ended with a sweet and sonorous "good-bye" and a childish wave of his fingers.

I forgot my resolve and bought all I could there after the day I ran into the lad a long way down the street from his father's stall. On that day, he had hanging round his neck a blue ribbon that took the weight of a shallow cardboard tray bearing several slices of potato, speared by a little platoon of upright paper flags. He was waving a tin for collecting coins above his head. Despite the dark, wet afternoon and his thin clothes, he looked happy and important. I asked him what he was collecting money for. By way of an answer he rattled his tin harder and called out for all to hear, "Money for mentals, if you please." He lifted the tray from his front and triumphantly thumped himself on the chest. "Money for mongols like me. Money for mongols' place, please."

I could hardly bear it for him, yet I so admired his brave acceptance of himself, his heroic shouting out of that solid word. Better, I thought, to call oneself a mongol than suffer the indignity of being afflicted with a syndrome discovered by some long-ago doctor from across the bridge.

I held out some coins. He grabbed them from me, softening his voice to say sweetly, "Can I put 'em in, lady? Nice putting 'em in that 'ole." He did so with great concentration, one after the other, till the last penny, which he kept in his hand. "Is this one for me?"

I nodded, and he carefully put it in a little worn-out purse before he handed me a paper flag. As I stood pinning it to my coat, he encouraged me with the words, "'S right, best in the middle. Don't stick yourself, Missus."

When I got home I examined the flag. I found I had contributed to "the well-being of the inmates of Normansfield Hospital for the Mentally Handicapped."

When eight years later it became inevitable that our son Matthew was to be put into that asylum, I recalled my brave little friend. His father's vegetable shack had long been pulled down. I wondered if he was now confined in Normansfield. Every time I went to see Matthew, I would scrutinize the faces of any older male inmates I came across, but I never recognized the lad. I like to think he escaped such a fate.

CHAPTER THREE

Mother-in-Law

Seven months later in the autumn of 1961, Theo and I were sitting companionably, eating buttered toast and drinking China tea. The sun shining through the plate glass window made everything on the table glitter. Although I was becoming large with my second pregnancy, there was just room for the dog to sit on my knee while I managed the toasting machine and Theo read his mail.

On occasions such as these I felt myself to be totally married. I was neither glad nor sorry; I wondered if Theo felt the same. As I sat next to him I examined the notion that I would never know nor be able to guess Theo's thoughts or feelings. I picked up a few of his opinions from conversations he held with his friends, in particular the Smithsons, who regularly came to our house on Sunday mornings, more from reading the articles he wrote for the architectural magazine he co-edited, only rarely from talk between us.

The letter he was holding was from his mother. I wondered whether she, after receiving so many of his, might not be more in touch than I with the working of her son's mind. Early in our relationship I had asked Theo what he found to write on those flimsy pages he posted to South Africa every Monday. At the time, I was moved by his simple reply, "I try to do as she asked and tell her everything." I was to receive a more realistic answer to my almost forgotten question that morning at the breakfast table, when he put a few of the pages of her letter in my hand saying, "I suppose this concerns us both." He meant to sound nonchalant, but I heard only timid defiance in his voice. It was the first time I had been permitted to read one of her letters. I learned that even if Theo's conscientious wish was to tell his mother everything, she had been kept in ignorance of my first pregnancy and its sad conclusion.

In my hand I held a what seemed to me a flurried and willful communication: At last a baby was expected; she knew it would be a son; how many years she had waited; now she was ready to come to England. She wrote in capitals the name of the boat she was to take and the date of its arrival. From that day, she wrote, there were only six weeks of waiting till we were all together. The letter ended with a sentence that chilled my heart. I read it out to Theo: "You can tell Anne that I'll take up no more room in her house than a quiet little mouse." Theo smiled and turned away to busy himself with the rest of his mail.

So Theo's mother came to live with us. We went to Waterloo Station to meet the boat train from Southampton. A tiny, deep-bosomed, perhaps sixty-year-old woman (she turned out to be fifty-seven), whose spectacles were decorated with rhinestones, stumbled along the platform toward Theo. He did not stir, so I assumed this was someone else's mother. I just had time to feel relief before she almost fell against him. My heart was torn by her tearful, agonized croon, "Theotjie, Theotjie, my son." Her love for him was at once so evident and so simple that, though I could not have entirely accounted for the sensation, I was deeply sorry for her, even sorry I was there taking up a part of her son's life.

The original impression my mother-in-law made upon my mind when we encountered each other on the boat train platform did not alter—it only crystallized into resolute acceptance. Forever I would have liked that anxious little woman to have stumbled past us into some other son's arms. Despite the immediate, sorrowful affection I conceived for her, I very quickly perceived that she was never going to allow herself to feel comfortable with me. I represented all the foreignness she had been fearing since her one-and-only son had set out for England. Day by day I watched her as she watched me, and more artlessly, her son. I could tell that all the changes that had taken place in him were in her eyes negative, that she attributed each one of them to the loose and carefree influences that radiated from me and my family. I saw she feared what she imagined to be my power. She held herself back from me and my Englishness as if dreading contamination.

I WAS NEARING the date of my confinement and the late-November days seemed interminably long. The tastefully modern reading lamps Theo favored barely dispelled the gloom of the tall living room of our very modern house. At tea time on one dark afternoon, my mother-in-law—whom I was now allowed to call Nicki—was sitting in an armchair that I had placed next to an electric fire. As she fondled the dog, which was leaning gratefully against her knee, her fingers came upon the identification disk attached to its collar. I carried the tea tray into the room and saw that an inexplicable change of mood had come over her. I simply could not account for its suddenness. Her expression was oddly wild; she was evidently near to weeping. "What is the matter? Are you homesick?"

SHE TURNED her head from me and would not reply. I poured our tea, and we drank in painful silence. She could not eat her usual biscuit. Her distress became so palpable that it alarmed the dog, which crept to my side. I leaned toward Nicki and attempted to stroke her hand. She withdrew it sharply and sat in rigid straightness. Eventually I said, "What you are feeling is clearly unbearable to you. Are you ill?"

Nicki opened her mouth just enough to allow a few slowly enunciated, Afrikaner-accented words to escape. "Your dog, Daisy, she gives you away. The dog tells me what my son couldn't."

"What does the dog say?"

"Read what she wears round her neck. She is witness to your sin."

I grabbed the dog and removed the collar. Engraved on the medallion was my name, Anne Buchanan, and since I was living with him when my mother gave the dog to me, this was followed by Theo's address.

"You were here before you were married. You led my son to live in iniquity, at this address."

I tried to soothe her. All the phrases I found seemed to rouse her to further expressions of resentment. Her son had married into a dissolute family. My mother had been spiteful and unwelcoming from the day they met—she was justified in making that claim—my father was a more-than-once-divorced man. I and my way of life were causing her son to lose sight of God. I went to the kitchen and made more tea. I found aspirin and eventually persuaded Nicki to go and lie down.

Then I crept to the telephone and called Theo. I had difficulty in persuading him that what had taken place was not, as he suggested, a mere unpleasantness between an impatient daughter-in-law and his little mother, but a real crisis. I begged him to come home.

He arrived with a bunch of white and pink roses in his hand. Distractedly he brushed his hand across my hair. Then he called upstairs, "Nicki, won't you come down? I'm home nice and early. I have a little something for you."

Hesitantly and perhaps a little shamefacedly, she did come down. Theo gave her a kiss and put the roses in her arms. Then he crossed the room to his drinks cupboard. There he selected a bottle of the sweetest of South African sherries, and in an Afrikaans accent that I had not heard for a long time, he said, "What about a sticky, then, Man?"

I announced that I had quite forgotten to exercise the dog—I would take a nice walk by the river. I put on my coat and patted Nicki's shoulder as I departed.

I came home to find Theo and his mother seated at the kitchen counter quietly peeling potatoes together. I cannot guess how much was said about what the dog's collar revealed, but after that episode, Nicki and I were careful and fair-minded with each other. I know that she was grateful that I took care of her and never forgot how foreign and lonely she felt in England.

When on the evening of December 8, 1961, I went into labor and was taken to hospital, she waited anxiously to hear that at last she would have a grandson. Yet on the next afternoon, when she learned I had given birth to a girl, she did not say she was disappointed. I had ducked telling her that should we have a daughter I wanted to call her Dido. Needlessly so; Nicki loved the name. She merely reminded me that when I had a son of course he would be given Theo's family names. Meanwhile "Dido" sounded just right. She asked Theo if it was typically English; he answered that it certainly was.

AS A FOURTH PRESENCE in our household, the new infant Dido brought us a mood of clemency, of acquiescence. Out of respect for his hitherto undiscovered effectiveness at earning a very nearly adequate income from his architectural practice, Theo was accorded a certain amount of detachment from day-to-day family life. Nicki, as she succumbed to the enchantment of the new baby, timidly took on the proffered role of indispensable grandmother. And I, now that we had a little daughter, was more easily able to accept the restraints of my domestic existence. Each was beholden: Theo to his womenfolk for his many evenings away from home; Nicki to me (unnecessarily) for my total trust in her as a grandmother; and I to her for both the instinctive love she bore the baby and the respites she afforded me. Thus, the Crosby family, if not entirely harmonious, was for a time in synchrony.

CHAPTER FOUR

Matthew's Birth

Just before six o'clock on the morning of May 26, 1964, after a painful night, I went into full labor. At three o'clock that afternoon I was delivered of a son.

On the high birth table under an arc light, I lay flaccid and utterly spent by parturition, only cloudily aware of the midwife and her nurses as they skimmed in and out of the peripheral darkness, executing all the rituals associated with the afterbirth. After I became aware that the new baby had been slithered onto my chest, this pleasant detachment deserted me. By the fizzing and unearthly white light, I examined him. I saw cobalt-blue-colored skin drawn tightly over a delicate, clear-shaped face, which was further refined by a beautiful pointed nose. Pointed, too, a protruding tongue was visible as a shadow between precise lips. I could almost see through the closed eyelids. I held in my arms a strange little neonate who looked not so much newborn as ancient, carved in shallow relief from blue marble. Froglike legs hung against my body; closed fists were pressed to a tiny rib cage. I picked one of them up; the fingers were stubby, the thumb thickly padded. I noticed that the ears, which lay neatly against the head, had deep kinks breaching their rims. In a wave of anguish, I saw that this baby was altogether creaturelike, yet I understood that his imperfections were congruous to his whole, a whole which I recognized as piteous.

Early in my pregnancy, I had made an appointment with our family doctor. I told him I was quite sure I should not be having this baby. I felt there was something terribly wrong. In trying to describe my symptoms, I was unable to make them sound much more than silly megrims. When the doctor dismissed them, rather crudely suggesting that my "problem" was that the baby was not my husband's, I retorted that since he was not prepared to take my pain, loss of blood, and fears seriously, I wanted to consult a proper gynecologist. Reluctantly, he referred me to a clinic at Queen Charlotte's Maternity Hospital. After an examination, it was agreed that "something was amiss" and there might be a need for a termination. I remained in the hospital, and the next morning I was sent to the operating theater. I was told to expect a curettage.

When I wakened from the anesthesia, a young doctor came to my bedside. He assured me that all was now well. I asked in which way "well." He answered that the fetus had been made secure within me, the neck of the womb sewn closed by means of a device known as the Shirodkar stitch, a method discovered by a doctor of that name, who found women of certain Indian sects sometimes practiced this procedure on one another so as to insure a fragile pregnancy would be brought to full term. The young doctor described what had been done to me as a simple but very effective remedy, adding that all I had to do now was lie still in hospital and be patient for a few months.

It was now apparent that, had this fetus not been sewn within my womb, the baby could not have come to full term. I felt nature had been misinterpreted, misused, so that this flawed little being was now paying for the doctors' interference, foisted with a life I felt he had no urge to live. And if the doctors were to compel him to do so, I absolutely believed they would be sentencing him to a vapid and pain-ridden existence. He was a mongoloid, perhaps not even a well-synthesized mongoloid; I foresaw him being perceived and treated as an imbecile. However anomalous he was, I understood he was not that. I envisioned so much suffering for him that I felt compelled to put my hand over his poor blue face.

I desperately wished that from this moment on no other person should set eyes on the baby excepting his father, who was in

Milan putting the final touches to an exhibition he had organized. I saw interference from any outsider as unnatural and intrusive, a violation of, for want of a more accurate word, both his father's and his dignity. And for that matter, of my own.

The lights were being switched off in the now still delivery room. The baby, wrapped in a warm flannel sheet, lay in an oxygen-pumping crib; I, on a table too high for me to climb down from. Very alarmed by the separation that was about to be imposed upon us, I called out that I wanted no measures taken to keep the baby alive. I begged that my baby and I not be parted. Hoping for some kind of support, I asked the sister to send for the pediatric doctor. I was causing such consternation that the nurses were uniting in antagonism. Voices rose to admonish me: I must not talk in this fashion, I was not behaving like a natural mother; a blood transfusion would "normalize" his color, then I would see how sweet he was; it was cruel and unfeeling of me not to want my baby to live.

I tried to find words to put my case. I asked, supposing I were a Seventh Day Adventist, would I not have the right to put my child's fate in God's hands? On religious grounds could I not insist that no doctor interfere? I told them I wanted to be treated as if I were a Seventh Day Adventist.

Even I could hear that my words sounded futile and that I had no hope of making anyone listen to me. The nurses pretended to believe that my mind was rambling, though the sister, after looking at my medical notes, leaned over me and snapped, "You are down as an atheist. Religious grounds, indeed."

The pediatrician appeared, and we were all silent as she examined the infant. I asked if the baby must be made to survive.

"We shall certainly do our best to make it happen."

I retaliated, "Whatever you do to alter his color, you cannot turn him into a normal being. I know his heart is all wrong, and I know he is a mongol."

The doctor forbade me to persist. I felt a needle thrust into my buttock and lassitude overcame me. I was lifted onto a stretcher and wheeled down what appeared to be an endless corridor.

Fillets of late afternoon sunlight fell through the slats of a plastic blind. I was in a room in which almost everything was painted a Naples yellow. I felt the color was meant to pressgang me into false cheeriness. I lay on the bed and reviewed my reactions to the baby. I remembered as a child having watched a bitch snout a seemingly perfect little puppy from her flank. Every time we returned it to her she did it again, until we understood that she sensed some flaw that we could not.

I pressed a bell and asked for a telephone. I was told the rule (at least for me) permitted only one call, to my husband. When a nurse brought the telephone to my bedside, I said I wished to talk to him privately and asked her to leave. An American friend of mine from New York was staying in our house. When he answered my telephone call, I described my baby's and my predicament. I begged him to go to King Street, find the local solicitor's office, and ascertain the exact law respecting our rights. He asked the name of the hospital and the floor I was on. He said he would do as I asked.

As afternoon became evening I dozed. I was brought a tray of supper. Later a nurse came to tell me that the baby's father had arrived. It was my friend; he had had to lie to be admitted. I had been captive in this hospital for five months, all that while receiving regular visits from Theo, yet the ward sister appeared now to believe, such was my waywardness, that another man was likely to be the father of my child. He had talked to a lawyer who told him that, had I managed to bring about my son's death within two hours of the birth, no action would have been taken against me. But, he warned, if from now on the baby were to die by my hand, I would be judged as suffering from acute postpartum depression, and I would be "sectioned," that is, sent to some kind of mental institution for an indeterminate length of time. This warning was of no and every consequence to me. My daughter was only two and a half years old; she had been without me for five months. I was already tormented by the harm our separation was causing her. I had no thought whatsoever of killing my baby; I only wished to prevent painful invasive measures being used to force him to live.

After that time I came to believe that my capacity to think rationally was affected by an atavistic instinct. Perhaps, too, I was affected by an almost eclipsed memory—that of my very powerful mother's mockery of my friendship with Rose.

The next morning a nurse came with the news that my relations or friends had been making telephone calls to the hospital. So far they had been informed only that the baby was unwell; she needed to know what sort of answer she was to give to these inquiries. How was the baby's and my little drama to be distilled into a simple message for outsiders? I had not yet brought myself to send news even to my mother-in-law, who was surely very anxious by now. I chose to continue being evasive.

While I waited for Theo to come, I was kept away from the baby, alone in my yellow room as if in disgrace. Some of the nursing staff were seriously religious, and thus I could hardly resent their disapproval of me. I was reminded of all my years in boarding schools, where my reactions to the more arcane school rules and illogical conventions were seen as rebellious or subversive, usually both. Now I was in another institution, a hospital, where by following a very strong instinct I was again seen as rebellious and subversive. By now I was both frightened by my conviction and frightened of losing it. One of the more kindly nurses told me that such a misfortune could happen to anyone, but I saw it as apt that this baby should be born to me. I decided to pass the time of waiting honorably, and applied myself to making an effort to believe in his survival.

Theo came the following night, suddenly there looking very tall as he opened the door of my room. He was newly sunburned, wearing his only good suit, his wild hair neatly trimmed. Glinting in the switched-on light, Theo's glasses prevented me from looking into his eyes as he held out a bunch of blue scabious flowers and a little punnet of wild strawberries framed in frilly leaves. He walked over to my bed, smiling in a placating manner that made me pity him for what he was about to hear. His arrival at that hour from another country, he redolent of experiences so different from mine, made a strangeness between us that each of us felt acutely.

We kissed formally, and holding his pretty blue flowers to my face, I told him that the baby was very unwell, the doctor so far having said only that his heart was defective. To tell it fairly, I warned him that so far only I believed the baby to be mongoloid, the pediatrician insisting that this was mere speculation on my part. Even so, they had been taking biopsies from me. I then admitted that I was sure so much was wrong with him that I felt they ought not to be trying to keep him alive.

We sat in silence as we waited for the ward sister to bring the baby to the room for Theo's inspection—mine, too, since till now all my requests to see him had been refused. I warned Theo that the baby's skin was alarmingly blue, almost the color of the little flowers that lay between us.

He was wheeled into the room in an oxygen-tented crib, imprisoned from us by the several tubes attached to his body, one in particular, under the cover of a small blanket, to his penis. His face seemed to have a look of deep suffering. His skin, a slightly grayer blue than before, looked aged and flaccid; his remoteness and utter loneliness were awful to me.

How could I have adequately prepared my husband for the shock of seeing such a son? To hide his revulsion, Theo got up from his chair and turned toward the window. For a long time he looked into the darkness of the sky. He tried not to show his repugnance as he turned back to the baby and sat again beside the crib. We talked in short, painful sentences; we expressed a mutual hope that he might be allowed to die. Without conviction, we found ourselves wishing it had been within my power to enable him to do so.

A staff nurse swept in, glanced at the wall above the bed, and then stared disdainfully at us. She wheeled our son from us, enunciating as she did so, "May God forgive you. Have neither of you any respect for the sanctity of life?" That glance she gave to the wall was an unconscious confession, for there hung a little microphone through which, as she sat behind her desk in the corridor, she must have been eavesdropping upon every word we'd said.

After the Birth

CHAPTER FIVE

Tfun days later the pediatrician came to visit me in my yellow room. She seated herself on a chair beside my bed and with assured condescension set about making peace between myself and those members of the nursing staff whom she said I "disturbed." "Your attitude upsets them professionally, you know." She wondered out loud if "your little family might not need an interval of a week or two to acclimatize yourselves to your new situation." She said she was confident that, once he was strong enough to be taken home and welcomed as one of the family, I would learn to love my new baby. And of course my acceptance would enable my husband to come to terms with him, too. She wished to assure me that there was no reason to suppose the baby's "abnormality" would upset our daughter "unless you yourselves cause it to."

I did not want to rekindle our earlier antagonism by explaining that my "intransigence" had not derived from lack of love for my baby, so I let her continue. She told me she and the doctors were agreed that although the baby must remain in the hospital —"He is still so very poorly"—there seemed no need for me to do so. I would be discharged as soon as the obstetrician passed me as fit, but on one condition: I was to undertake for at least a week to return every morning to visit my son in the premature infant unit on the sixth floor.

I realized that she expected me to become "difficult" again— but why would I? I had not been allowed to see the baby since Theo returned from Italy. Now, it seemed, they were willing to fulfill my two most ardent wishes: to at last be able to have contact with my son and to go home and resume my family life.

As the doctor got up to leave she gave a little satisfied pat to a beige-colored folder that she had all the while been clutching to her chest. Later on that day I was able to leaf through the contents of that file. I came upon it as I lay in a blue-curtained cubicle waiting for the doctor of obstetrics to give me a final examination. It had been placed on a table beside the examining couch, as if offered as light reading to help while away the patient's time of waiting.

On the last page, headed with the same day's date, I read that I had been a "difficult and recalcitrant patient who held very unorthodox views"; confirming this diagnosis I tore the page in pieces and dropped them into a bin labeled "surgical dressings only."

An hour later I left for home. As I quit the building I was dazzled by sunshine and realized that it was now June. The sky seemed miraculously far above my head. I was able to see distance again; I could move my limbs and breathe deeply. Theo was there to meet me. As we waited for a taxi I tried to communicate to him my lightness of spirit. I told him our lives would soon regain a reasonable pattern and Dido was ours to enjoy. I held his hand.

For a week, I would leave Dido with my bravely smiling little mother-in-law, and walk to the hospital to sit beside the baby where he lay in his crib on the sixth floor.

At first I was humiliated by these visits. I was unable, as the pediatrician requested, to express milk to be put on ice for the baby's feeds. Every morning I would remind the nurses that I was incapable of doing this. On most mornings they made me try. The nursing staff were either self-righteous or guarded in their attitude toward me. Anyone who was on duty when I arrived would make it clear that she was acting on instructions in not leaving me alone with my baby. I was not even permitted to lift him out of the crib, and they made sure I knew that this was not simply because he was pinned down by the tubes that were attached to his body.

Two weeks passed and the baby did not die, but neither did he reveal the smallest sign that he meant to live. As the nurses became more familiar with me, the tension round the crib lessened somewhat. One morning I arrived to find the baby being examined by a doctor whom I had not encountered before. He greeted me with a smile. I was almost embarrassed by his instant friendliness. He told me that he had read the endocrinologist's report. It confirmed that our son—"Does he have a name yet?"—was indeed a Down syndrome child. "I am interested to know how you immediately recognized his condition, Mrs. Crosby."

I knew I sounded defensive. "Why did they all pretend it wasn't so? I saw that his face was mongoloid, I saw it in his hands, and I saw it on his ears."

He continued, "As you probably know, it is not uncommon for Down syndrome children to be born with faulty hearts, and in your son's case the valves are functioning very poorly. He has other anomalies. The Down syndrome aspect of him might turn out to be one of the least of his problems." The doctor sighed as he got to his feet. We stood together for a minute looking at the baby, whose calm, blue face seemed for the first time faintly purposeful.

The doctor appeared to possess an authority that entitled him to be extremely careless of the pipes and tubes strapped to the little body. He plucked it from the crib and, ordering me to sit down, dumped it in my lap. He waved goodbye and left the room.

No nurse came to remove the baby from my knee, and I did not replace him in his cot till he seemed to be asleep. As in my head I said goodbye, I called him by name—Matthew. From that day on, my visits to the sixth floor were easier. I was greeted when I arrived, I was told how Matthew had fared during the night, I was allowed to hold him.

Again the pediatrician came to talk to me. "Mrs. Crosby, this has been a strain for you." She sounded almost magnanimous. "Your responses to your son's condition now appear rational. We are very pleased by the improvement that we see in the situation. I understand that you've given your baby a name at last, a sure sign of acceptance. We propose that you leave Mark—that is the name, isn't it?—in our care for a while longer. Perhaps you can take a little holiday with your family. Is that possible to arrange?"

CHAPTER SIX

After the Sixth Floor

Theo was expected to visit Milan once more before the opening of his exhibition. Following the pediatric doctor's advice, we left the baby in the care of the sixth floor nurses and went on a family holiday. Before Theo was due in Milan we spent five days at a little sea resort named Bocca de Magra. When we arrived, the summer season had not properly begun, so our taxi driver persuaded the padrone of a small seaside hotel to open some rooms for us.

Each morning we were wakened by bright sunshine. We ate breakfast in the shade of a big umbrella at a table that was placed for us on the sands. We encouraged Dido to set the pace and choose the manner in which we idled those days away. We followed as she ran along the edge of the sea, we splashed in the water with her, lay in the shade of our umbrella, and told her stories. Her father built castle after castle for her. Only when she asked us to help her rake the sand for last year's discarded ice cream spoons were we anything like bored.

After sunset we sat at our table drinking aperitifs and colored fizzy water within the sound of the lapping sea. By the light of a hanging lamp, using olive stones for currency, we whiled away the hour before suppertime teaching Dido the rudiments of gambling. We lay bets on the evening menu and on the numbers and colors of each day's trove of spoons. Through all our later difficulties I did not forget the simplicity of those five days. Never before had Dido had both her parents as constant companions; never had I seen Theo so contentedly familial. Not once did we allow our talk to veer toward serious family concerns.

When the last day came, the holiday did not end. We caught the train to Milan, where for three nights we all slept in a palatial bedroom and breakfasted together in an ornate dining room before Theo set out for his exhibition site. Then Dido and I would spend part of our day in the city's rather broken-down nineteenth-century zoological garden. The place entranced her. The animals lived in houses that had front doors, windows with shutters, and balconies. She did not see these crumbling structures as disguised cages; to her they were neither seedy nor distasteful. She found it marvelous that the giraffe could put her head out of an upstairs window and the crocodile slither down his front steps into a dirty pond.

On our first morning in Milan, Theo handed me an envelope full of Italian money. Waving down a taxi, he consulted the driver, then dispatched us to buy appropriately festive clothes. Dressed delightfully (so we hoped), we would join him at luncheons or cocktail parties, where a fuss was made over Dido and people complimented Theo for his clever designs.

On the last afternoon, a little finale was played out. To the slightly comic sounds of a brass band, we consumed ice creams and sipped sweet drinks. After I had been presented with a bouquet of flowers, a beaming contractor alarmed Dido by crouching before her with his arms outspread. He scooped her up and kissed her; as he replaced her on the ground, he snapped his fingers to an assistant who stepped forward and handed him a cellophane-windowed box. The contractor bowed politely as he passed it to Dido. It contained a midnight-blue toy cat, quite as large as she. Its eyeballs rolled in their celluloid sockets, fierce black whiskers bristled from its plush jowls, and worst of all, a huge felt tongue protruded roguishly from a grinning mouth.

Dido, pink with surprise and gratification, returned a willing kiss to the contractor. Theo was looking on; I saw he was appalled. I was a little surprised that Dido was not intimidated by the size of this electric-blue creature. Theo seized the gift and handed it back to the contractor. After a few moments of bargaining and gesticulating, Theo calmed down and the contractor was smiling. One of the assistants hurried away with the cat under his arm. As tears trickled down Dido's face, again the contractor crouched before her. "He goes to buy a big suitcase for your cat. He takes him to measure."

Theo explained to us that we were to travel to London with the "lesser" member of the royal family who had come to Milan to open the exhibition. "He won't mind my cat, will he?" asked Dido.

An equerry who had been hovering near us observing this little scene stepped forward. With a glass of champagne in his hand and an amused smile on his face, he said, "I shall answer that question. Your father, possibly your mother, and even you, may be going to have your photograph taken with His Highness. How old are you, nearly three perhaps? If so, I am sure you are quite old enough to understand that it would be entirely unsuitable, when this picture appears on the front page of the *Times* or *Telegraph*, that one of your parents seems to be cuddling a grotesquely large cat who is sticking his tongue out at the camera. I am sure your new toy will travel to England quite comfortably in his new suitcase."

A few days after our return to London I pushed an empty perambulator down King Street and along the Goldhawk Road. The hour had come: I was to deliver Matthew from the sterile care of the sixth floor. We had decided on the luxury of hiring a nanny to help look after him during his first week at home, so that I could continue the elusive task we had begun in Italy of reclaiming Dido after the long separation she had endured during my pregnancy. I was sure Matthew's presence was going to trouble her, but I did not at all suppose she would behave badly. I almost wished she might, for I was disheartened by her constant obedience and good manners.

CHAPTER SEVEN

Gladys/My Mother

O n the Sunday before the nanny was due to arrive, Matthew and I were alone in the house when there appeared at our door a small birdlike woman with bright eyes set in a sallow starved-in-childhood face, a canopy of rigid brown curls over her bony brow. She looked touchingly clean and neat; she wore a flowered back-and-front pinafore of a sort with which I was to become very familiar. She gave me a quick, nervous smile, saying she had just popped round to see the new baby. I invited her into the house. She darted past me straight to the cot in which Matthew lay and lifted him up in her arms. I had been trying to coax him to eat, and both she and I were embarrassed by evidence of my efforts and by the disarray of the entire room.

Although we were close neighbors, I had never exchanged more than a smile with Gladys Strong, but I was used to seeing her as our local foster mother on her way to and from the shops, sturdily pushing a large perambulator packed with neatly bundled little babies. Before I knew it, she had settled herself in a chair with Matthew on her knee, taken up the spoon, and was feeding him his meal. I had not been able to get him to swallow properly. In a manner that was at once affectionate and commanding, she held him firmly as she teased and courted him. Then she gently pinched his nose so that he had to open his mouth to breathe; at once she aimed a spoonful of milk straight down his throat, after which she pressed his lips together. She laughed and patted his cheek after each successful swallow.

When the meal was gone, she turned to me. "Not really surprising you haven't shown him down the street yet. Funny color, isn't he?" Then to Matthew, "Too blue-blooded for our street, are you?" Holding him to her, she asked, "Can I borrow him for the morning?"

I was cautious. "Are you sure? It's not his color, I quite like that, you see, but he is a bit fragile. That is why I've not taken him out. There are several things wrong with him."

She answered hurriedly, "Don't say that, he's lovely. His color'll come right, you'll see—probably nothing time, a few good feeds, and our nice London air can't cure." She kissed him. "I won't hear a word against the little love." With sudden formal politeness, she said, "Perhaps you would like to straighten up here a bit. I'll have him at my place. Fetch him this afternoon, eh? I expect I can get him to take from a bottle. It's the best way, never mind what that hospital says." She was wrapping his blanket about him as she spoke. Then she and Matthew were gone. I had not even told her his name.

MY MOTHER TELEPHONED my sister Moyra, who lived in Hornsey, "I propose to take the train to London and stay the night with you."

"Sorry, no room. The house is filled with children's friends."

"But I must check on Anne. I sense a mystery. Why hasn't she brought the new baby down to show me? If she was strong enough to cart him round Italy directly she left hospital, she must be strong enough to drive down here."

My sister went into the family routine of closing ranks and covering up. "I believe they left the baby behind. Anne says they've hired a temporary nanny."

"How wise of Theo to spoil her a little. He is quite right to be proud of her. She's produced a son and heir after all. By the way, is the nanny full-time or a daily?"

"I think Anne said daily."

"Ah ha! Then their spare room will be available. She can have me for the night."

My sister called me immediately. "*She* is coming to visit you. Says she senses a mystery."

Our mother was an unpredictable woman. When I had a piece of personal news, I dreaded having to tell her; I could never foresee how she would react. On this occasion I was so apprehensive that she might create some sort of scene that I sent Dido to play at a little friend's house and begged my sister to be present when she arrived.

As always, she took us by surprise. Once seated in an armchair, sipping her pre-luncheon sherry, she ordered the temporary nanny, who was at once in great awe of her, to bring the child to her.

Putting her glass aside, my mother stood up and took Matthew in her arms. She strolled to the window and stood awhile as if bemused. Behind her back, my sister and I pulled colluding faces. Nonchalantly my mother handed the baby back to the waiting nurse, then smiled benignly as she made this pronouncement: "The last child of this sort who was born into our family was by no means so ornamental to look at, but on the other hand neither was her skin such an improbable color."

As we ate, our mother made to my sister and me a rather dramatic confession. She told us that because they were not able to get married until her divorce had been made absolute, she and our father "had to" elope to Canada. (She did not mention that to lessen encumbrances they first placed all four of her children in the care of a convent.) Soon after they were settled into their hurriedly purchased property, she gave birth to a daughter.

No reference was ever made to this child in letters home, but as soon as they were free to marry, they sold the property in Canada and brought their child to London; there they showed her to no one save a Harley Street doctor. Accepting his diagnosis that she was a mongoloid, our father instructed his lawyer to place an advertisement in the *Times*. A respectable war widow (only wives of officers to apply) was sought—and soon found. She was just as the advertisement required: well-bred and childless. Our mother interviewed her at the Charing Cross Hotel.

Together they drank China tea, ate cucumber sandwiches, and discussed the transfer of the child.

The lawyer was already in the process of purchasing a bungalow in Hastings. This kind woman and the child were moved into it, and she was paid an adequate stipend. My mother remarked that, though she could no longer name the actual sum, she recalled it amounted to more per annum than the allowance the court ordered our father to give her years later when she and he went through their divorce. The woman—whose name our mother said she had also forgotten—was required to foster the child without ever attempting to find out the name of the family she belonged to. Our mother told my sister and me that the arrangement was perfectly suited to both parties. The poor woman had longed for a baby and soon "adored Priscilla." The bungalow became hers when, four and a half years later, Priscilla died.

Our mother said she used to visit Hastings about twice a year, and now and again sent toys and new clothes. Our father never once inquired after his daughter's welfare, and she herself found it only too easy to put the whole matter out of her mind, though she shed a tear or two when she heard that Priscilla had died.

We sat together after luncheon (a meal we called "lunch" unless eaten in our mother's company). My mother laid the baby on her knees as she smilingly recommended that Theo and I set about making similar arrangements for him.

Moyra asked her why, since she was obviously charmed by Matthew, she thought it necessary to send him out of our lives? Her answer was immediate and firm: His existence at home would undermine the marriage, be harmful to Dido, and almost worst, destroy not Theo's, but my social life.

When Dido came home my mother made a pleasing fuss of her, and as was her wont, she was charming and rather flirtatious with Theo. We all dined together, and Dido and I saw her off at Victoria Station the next morning. I was thankful that her visit had passed so easily.

During the day, I felt myself more and more discomposed by her revelations, which I had not yet repeated to Theo. So eager was I to recount them, I could barely wait until he and I were alone together. After I had retold my mother's tale, there was a silence. I watched Theo's face as he shifted and resettled himself in his chair, and the expression I saw there was one of thankful relief. I found this unaccountable until it came to me that he must have suspected that Matthew's defects came from his side of the family. It also occurred to me that the fact that his parents were first cousins had caused him to think so.

I believe it was from this time that Theo's attitude toward Matthew hardened. He remained tender in his treatment of him, but he was implacable and unrelenting in his wish to send him away.

ALTHOUGH I HAD not seen Gladys Strong since the moment she flew into our house to welcome the new baby, she was a force in my imagination. I felt that with her help I would be able to comply with Theo's mandate that Matthew's presence make the least possible difference to our lives.

I knew it was to hide his distress that Theo was absenting himself from home more than ever before. He saw work as his most legitimate refuge. He was convincing himself that he was too busy for low-ranking domestic issues. Theo, who out of sweet generosity was giving my mother a monthly allowance "so that she could buy a few extras," tried to justify his rejection of Matthew in terms of money. He told me that, if I wished to keep him at home, I would have to manage to pay his costs out of the housekeeping allowance he gave me. He evidently needed to perceive Matthew as an indulgence, a luxury, a mere foible of mine. This monetary view of the situation, coming as it did from an extraordinarily intelligent man, so lacked plausibility that Matthew's existence was now a topic too painful for us to be rational about. We simply left it untalked of.

I went to the corner of our street and knocked on the door of the ground-floor flat. As the door opened, I was overcome by a reassuring smell of airing laundry. Gladys Strong stood before me, holding two little babies in her arms. As she invited me in, a reflex made her thrust one of the children into my arms while she dexterously closed the front door with her foot and pushed open another.

We were in her living room; a little girl played on the floor, her toys looking well used and dull. Nothing was scattered or in disarray. On a sofa lay more babies. Gladys bent over and wedged among the cushions the one she was carrying, then sat down to continue feeding the other, an occupation I had evidently interrupted. We talked while she spooned gruel into the mouth of the dark-skinned little girl.

"Been expecting you. That old nurse gone then? Bit ancient for the job, was she? I bet she cost a packet." She held the little girl to her and laughed at me over her head. "Want my help now, do you? 'Spect I can fit him in. Let's start with, say, every afternoon." She asked me to pay her a very reasonable sum of money. As she named the amount, she looked cautious and hopeful, even a little ashamed. I guessed she was asking me more than her usual rate. Even so, I could not understand why she had not asked twice as much. What I wanted from her was the saving of my marriage.

"Oh, we mean to pay you more than that. I cannot tell you how grateful I am for your help."

"No," she said almost huffily, "that's my price. Don't you worry, I'll let you know if I ever have to put it up. Begin this afternoon, then. Don't bring the money till the end of the week. Like to be paid when the job's well done."

PUTTING MATTHEW in the care of Gladys was tantamount to launching him into society, the society of our immediate locality. She had allowed herself to be elected queen of the three streets which converged at our end of Hammersmith Bridge. Standing before the large windows of her flat, she was able to keep an eye on things. On school days, signaling through the glass, she made sure that any children who had graduated from her charge did not run across Bridge Road but instead took the tow path which led them safely under the bridge. She regularly checked the babies whom she put out to take the air in her two shabby perambulators. From her observation post she could wave a welcome to the parcel postman so as to take in everybody's packages.

She ran a little business known as "ordering by post and paying off weekly," which accounted for the fact that so many of her friends wore the same mode of clothing as she, especially the pinafores.

On winter afternoons when school finished, some of the children from the flats were "minded" by Auntie Gladys till their mums got home from work. This was the hour when the suitably respectable old ladies who made up Gladys's court were allowed to come to her front room to pass the time of day, cosset babies, and "keep the kids company." The ladies liked to discuss every aspect of each child's progress, from learning to sip from a cup, sit on a pot, then graduate to the toilet, and in no time take themselves off to school to learn to read and write.

In fine weather Gladys held her court in the public garden at the other end of our street. Never mind how leafy the trees or flamboyant the borders, this pretty riverside park was referred to as "the green." There Gladys would seat herself magisterially on the low wall which surrounded the flagged terrace of the borough cafe. She would spread a rug on the grass for her small babies to lie on and unleash the toddlers to roam, instructing her courtiers to keep an eye on them.

The more affluent old ladies (pensioners, half-price) sometimes sat at the green metal tables of the cafe, to eat a buttered bun and drink a cup of tea. It was absolutely not done to treat anyone else. A few of them hired deck chairs, also half-price, and set about their knitting, which in fact was not strictly theirs, for the wool was usually provided by Gladys, who commissioned little garments for those of her charges whose clothes were inadequate or who wore unsuitably bright garments. (Matthew fell into the latter category.)

"Bless me, what's he wearing today, then, castoffs from a circus? Don't worry, I've got something he can wear to the green. Don't want him looking like the organ grinder's monkey, do we?"

All in the same instant, Gladys could interpret knitting patterns, suckle babies from bottles, and with her foot rhythmically rock a perambulator, which contained only the newest babies—among whom she placed Matthew against a frilled pillow, shaded by a fringed canopy or sheltered under the hood of the pram.

"His poor eyes don't like the sun," or "He feels the cold more than my others, you know." I never knew if Gladys was defending Matthew from the curiosity of outsiders or covering her own slight embarrassment regarding his gray-blue complexion and old-gentlemanish air, both of which persisted long after his birth. When any of her after-school children came across the green, Gladys would imperiously summon them by name: "Now then, Robin, you going to greet your Auntie Gladys?" After the child had dutifully said "Good afternoon, Auntie," she would order him or her to "go and say a nice hallo to Matthew; he's been poorly lately," or "he's feeling more himself today."

I believe Matthew acquired his social aplomb during his early years in Gladys's court; in her care he was taught manners which stood him in good stead all his life. Again and again I heard Gladys Strong order him to "give us a nice smile now" or admonish "just because you don't talk, it don't mean you can't shake hands or nod." When he could only crawl across the floor, she would say, "Matthew'll open the door for you. In his way he's a proper little gent, aren't you, then?"

CHAPTER EIGHT

Dido/Smithsons

While I spent those months in hospital waiting for Matthew to be born, Theo sent Dido to stay with his mother. When my father heard that my mother-in-law was living with us, he wrote me a letter suggesting that I use "some but not all" of my marriage dowry to buy a flat or small house for my mother-in-law. "Being a South African, a Boer to boot, she is unlikely to mind or even be aware of class differences, so she will probably find a small terraced house perfectly acceptable so long as you make quite sure there are no black people within a stone's throw." It was the only advice of his I ever followed. We bought her the top half of a terraced house along the river in Barnes Village, and Theo took care to make it more than acceptable. During the months when she was caring for Dido, Nicki made several dresses for her—old-fashioned affairs in pale colors, smocked across the front. They had white piqué collars, which Nicki laundered every evening. Dido told me that she wore these dresses in the afternoons, when her grandmother took her for walks on the common or to sit by the pond in the public garden. She was also made to wear a little bonnet and crocheted gloves.

I was intrigued by what Dido said. I asked, "Were you allowed to wear mufti in the mornings?"

"What's mufti?"

"The opposite of uniform."

Dido told me there had been special morning clothes, too, all sewn by Granny: pleated skirts and pink or blue flannel blouses, again with changeable collars. On top of these Dido wore pinafores for playing in the garden and when they cooked together.

"Why are all these special clothes still at Granny's house?"

"I asked Granny to keep them. I don't want them any more."

"But your description of them makes them sound pretty."

"They are pretty, but they are for Granny. I am only going to wear trousers now because I might be going to be a boy."

I hardly bothered to guess at the psychology behind this decision, nor did I reason or give an anatomy lesson; she had male cousins with whom she had bathed occasionally, and now she had a brother. We simply went to Harrods together to buy the clothes she wanted. Her father was rather put out. I tried to explain to him that this was a fad, which was likely to be short-lived, especially if we treated it lightly. He could not credit that a not-yet-three-year-old child—"precocious though she is"—was able to make any decision beyond choosing a toy to play with or a story she would like to hear. He questioned why Dido would want to change her whole being. He said rather wistfully that he had become fond of the neatly dressed, compliant little girl his mother had conjured into being. I suggested Dido was not.

Theo was falling into a habit of being facetious or teasing in his conversations with Dido. Although she was often nonplused by such banter, Dido was always at ease with her father. When he came home in the evenings she would go and lean against him as if he were a tree to shelter beneath. After he had poured himself a drink and was seated in his favorite chair, he let her climb on him as if among the branches of that tree.

FROM THE FIRST EVENING of Matthew's presence in our house, Dido assumed a share in the rearing of him. This troubled me. I did not want to exclude her, but neither did I wish him to be a burden to her.

When Matthew was not at Gladys's flat, our most difficult task was feeding him. Dido would alternate between making pretend meals for her toy creatures and helping me. She was neater and more skillful than I at getting spoonfuls of milky gruel into his mouth. Standing beside me as I held him on my knees, she watched his wavering movements and tried to catch his attention. As his restless head veered her way, she would raise one of her hands into the air. His gaze usually followed the hand, and his mouth would drop open. At that moment she tipped the contents of the spoon between his lips. To protect them from his dribbles, which she abhorred, she tucked her fingers under his bib and pushed his chin upward so as to keep his mouth closed.

She did not show particular affection for the baby, and only very occasional distaste. When I expressed my gratitude for her help, she would smile and shrug her shoulders in a very adult manner. Sometimes when the meal was done she leaned over Matthew and gazed at his face. At first I wondered if I ought to account for his blueness, which was beginning to fade to gray, but I discovered that Dido was not aware that there was a normal color for babies. Matthew's curious hue did not alarm her nor did she seem to find him any more odd than the other babies we knew, all of whom bored her.

It was clear to me that Dido's feelings for her brother were benign. She evinced no sibling jealousy, but her every action made me know that she did not see Matthew as a fellow child. She set about supplying his needs as one might those of a small, sick animal. I admired her competence and compassion, but I felt sad for her.

THOUGH THEO HAD no relatives in England, he was deeply fond of a pair of fellow architects, Peter and Allison Smithson, who, he comfortably acknowledged, perceived him as their possession. "Theirs to dominate, theirs to command, something like your family's attitude to you, which makes them almost kin." It was inevitable that Theo should have chosen Peter Smithson to act as his best man at our wedding.

Long before my appearance, the Smithsons had acquired the habit of visiting Theo on Sunday mornings. Few activities were allowed to disrupt this custom; it was resumed directly we returned from our honeymoon. They would arrive in their large motorcar, known as "The Goddess" (it was very modern, a Citroën DS), after our, but not their, breakfast. They came loaded with the accoutrements and educational toys of their two pale, rather mute children, whom they tenderly ushered before them. They seated themselves in their favorite chairs, which they liked to find placed ready for them in our large downstairs room. In keeping with the tradition of the friendship, I helped Theo provide the Smithsons with numberless cups of coffee and a large supply of doughnuts and fruit juice.

I have never encountered a woman who could sit in one position for so long a time as Allison. She was beautiful in the way that is commonly called "statuesque." She had a perfectly regular-featured, pale, handsome face with large dark eyes shadowed by long lashes. Her clear-shaped mouth had a discontented expression, but her smile, which was rare and slow to appear, was most touching and beautiful. With lovely, underwaterish movements, she settled her wide-trunked body into her chair, and there she would remain, expecting to be waited upon by those around her, which indeed nearly always happened.

Allison had surprising graces. She was attentive and respectful to the elderly, however uninteresting their conversation. And she listened peacefully, then talked gently to children.

Peter and Allison were high-mindedly obsessive when discussing their profession. They were also nervelessly ambitious and very intelligent. I saw them as almost disabled by lack of humor. When we had other friends present, both Allison and Peter were apt to leave the room and wander about our house, often opening our cupboards and drawers. Their docile son and daughter played on the floor with their own toys; now and again one of them might clamber onto Peter's knee. He would absent-mindedly fondle the child until he or she slipped from his grasp.

Aside from essential or holiday interruptions, this Sunday morning rite persisted, admitting family members as they materialized. After her arrival from South Africa Theo's mother was included. We added our newborn Dido, who after a year or two learned to play as discreetly and separately as the Smithson children. After Allison gave birth to a second daughter we seemed to be a group that waxed more familial with every visit. That is, until the last comer, Matthew, joined our party.

We were gathered as usual in our large downstairs room where we had placed a cot for him. To stimulate Dido's wayward appetite, I had invested in an electric milk shaker. The Smithson children were longing to try it out. The oldest, Simon, gently took the baby from my arms so as to free me to go to the kitchen and prepare the necessary ingredients. His mother admonished him sharply, telling him to give the baby back to me. Theo rose from his chair and took Matthew from Simon. He sat down again with the baby on his knee. We went to make the milkshakes, after which we rejoined the adults. I put out my arms to receive Matthew, but Theo shook his head. The pleasure I took from this unexpected show of paternal affection was cut short as I caught sight of his face. In contrast to his usual bland mask of amused calm, he appeared utterly cast down.

After the Smithsons had gathered up all their trappings and driven away, Theo, as if hauling up our drawbridge and letting down the portcullis, slammed the yard door which gave on to the street, then even more fiercely slammed our kitchen door. I had never seen him so overwrought. I put Matthew into his cot and opened the French windows, then hastened Nicki, Dido, and the dog out to the garden.

"They told me they are not coming here any more. They have decided Matthew is harmful to their children's psyches. In that heavy-going way of hers, Allison spelled out to me what a brutalizing influence he is going to have on Dido. She doesn't want their children affected in the same way." Theo was striding to and fro in miserable agitation. "I just hope one of their three darlings turns out to have some nasty flaw. Then it will be our turn to feel superior, to crow."

I was amazed by his uncharacteristic venom. "You sound like one of Dido's 'dreaded witches' casting a wicked spell."

"That is what I want to sound like." He gave me a sheepish smile.

While clearing the room of mugs, plates, and all the usual Sunday morning debris, along with my own aggrieved feelings I had an unseemly wish to giggle. Our Sundays unshackled, we might see other friends, take outings to the country, walk by the river.

In the tradition of wishes fulfilled, I was granted the walks by the river, but only because Theo at once replaced one custom with another. From that time on, every Sunday morning, leaving Matthew with Gladys, we took Dido in her push chair and walked across Hammersmith Bridge, following the tow path upstream to Barnes to eat Sunday lunch at Theo's mother's house.

ON THE MORNING following his nighttime return from Milan when he came to the hospital and set eyes on his little blue shadow of a son, Theo, so as to be on time at his office, rose very early and walked over Hammersmith Bridge and went to "pat Dido on the head and explain things to Nicki."

Putting it as delicately as he knew how, he told her that her newborn grandson "was not quite right."

"How not right?"

"Well, his heart for a start."

"What else isn't right? Is he not right in the head? Maybe . . . just look at the family he comes from—Her father four times married. Her mother a wicked woman, your wife growing up not knowing right from wrong."

Theo had allowed Dido to remain seated on his knees throughout this pathetic tirade. It was Dido who described how she and her father had attempted to comfort her grandmother, Dido by stroking the back of her hand and Theo by saying "Now come on, Man. Come on, Man."

"She isn't a man so it couldn't help, could it, Mum?"

Nothing helped. Nicki told Theo she felt her heart would break. Perhaps it did break for she died of a heart attack three months after Matthew was born, at the end of August 1964.

CHAPTER NINE

Normansfield

M atthew spent quite a large proportion of his days and sometimes nights in Gladys Strong's care, only a few steps away from our house. For me it was the perfect distance; for Theo it was not. He still felt bothered by what he considered Matthew's omnipresence. He claimed that Matthew's proximity was continuing to "destruct" our family life.

Theo's suggestions that I "at least look at schools, residences, homes, or whatever they call those nice kinds of institutions" had now become petitions, and I could not ignore them. I felt a little guilty that I had not thought to consult him before accepting Gladys's offer of help, and I shared his anxiety as to how Dido might be affected by a brother such as Matthew, were we to keep him with us (this despite my determination to take such care that Theo might eventually accommodate himself to Matthew's presence, in which case I felt Dido would be no more damaged than if we sent Matthew from us).

So I agreed that I should, as Theo put it, "at least do the research."

In my quest for an institution in which we might safely place Matthew, I read many pamphlets and submitted to various forms of counseling. I listened to doctors, superintendents, a mother superior, and of course, to friends and friends of friends—anyone who had heard of places where residents, inmates, or pupils throve or simply looked cared-for. I traveled to all kinds of schools and homes. Scrutinies took place, not too subtly, of our family's finances, of Theo's standing in society, and of my personality. Questions about Matthew himself were nearly always very brief and left till last. I grew more and more despondent as I learned how Theo and I were likely to fail Matthew by having too small an income and how he might fail us by having been designated by a doctor at our local Health Authority office as "ineducable."

"Ineducable" was also the sentence arrived at by the eminent doctor Thomas Weihs, director of the Rudolph Steiner Schools. I had started my search by consulting him at Delrow House in Watford in September 1965, and I ended it there two years later. On both visits to Dr. Weihs's office I took Matthew with me. The first time I saw Dr. Weihs, Matthew was fifteen months old, still small and weak. Dr. Weihs was tender with him. He sat Matthew on his knee, then hid his own face behind sheets of paper, held colored pencils just beyond the child's reach, hummed little tunes as he helped Matthew beat time. He switched his desk lamp on and off, and he put objects of various weights in Matthew's hands. Finally he carried him over to the window, where he pointed at what there was to see through the glass. The doctor was discovering and demonstrating to me everything Matthew could not take in and did not notice.

He brought my inapt child back to where I sat and placed him on my lap. Matthew laughed and tried to prolong his contact with the doctor by clutching at his sleeve. Returning to his side of the desk, Dr. Weihs gathered his papers and possessions away from Matthew's grasp. He sat quite still and, in what seemed a more pronounced than hitherto German accent, gave me a rather severe reading of Matthew's case.

"I do not believe your child is likely to achieve the emotional maturity of even a four-year-old. His learning will be very slow because I think he will forever keep the mentality of a small child. In this sense, he is indeed deeply imperfect. However, there are things that are interesting about your son; there are compensations. Please do not think it a contradiction if I tell you that notwithstanding all his limitations and anomalies there are signs of an elusive intelligence of a relatively high order. For those who find good ways of communicating with him, there will be responses and rewards."

I returned to Delrow House in 1967 not because in the intervening two years Matthew had managed to develop so wonderfully that I thought Dr. Weihs would be willing to reevaluate him and perhaps place him in one of his Steiner schools or settlements. No, I made my second visit to Dr. Weihs's rooms because I wanted to consult him as to the practicability of myself one day founding some sort of little school around Matthew. By this time I had decided there were really no fit places for so-called ineducable children.

I told Dr. Weihs of Gladys and her good care of Matthew, of her skills (she trained as a nurse) and her dependability. In more suitable words I repeated her tentative suggestion that "if Mums and Dads like your Theo and you would be willing to cough up a bit more than my usual prices, I wouldn't mind taking on two or three more nice little dopes like Matthew instead of all them *ordinary* babies. I get on fine with him, don't I?"

Extrapolate or interpret as I might, after our second visit to Delrow House, Dr. Weihs's reiterated verdict that Matthew was ineducable was no longer to be denied. By the time I returned home and was able to coax Theo into discussing the subject, I was so well reconciled to Dr. Weihs's prognosis that I was able to repeat to Theo his advice that the best remedy for all of us would be to obtain a place for Matthew in Normansfield Hospital, a renowned institution that was local to us, and which had the great advantage of being government funded.

the I gave Theo the letter of introduction that Dr. Weihs had written to the director of Normansfield Hospital. This letter and my acceptance of Matthew's imminent exile brought such relief to Theo that I was moved to make the initial telephone call the very next morning. The first words I heard after I dialed the number of the hospital were indicative of the surreality which dogged me in all my dealings with that place.

"Normansfield Hospital speaking."

I asked the woman who made this statement if my husband and I might come to look at the hospital. She asked our reasons for wanting to do so. My own voice chilled me as I heard myself tell her that we wanted our son to become a patient there.

"You are being transferred to the office."

During the ensuing silence, I imagined this transfer taking place. I drifted in thought along an eerie corridor, as if viewing the scene from above. I spied a transmuted Matthew, no longer connected to me, just one among many whose identities were indecipherable and of no consequence. A whole band of ageless children were performing in a perfunctory way. They sat at tables and ate, holding their spoons correctly. They held each other's hands as they were escorted to and from dining to other rooms and then to dormitories. Now they were being led along a gravel path perhaps to a religious service. All of them were tamed and reduced to torpidity, unaware that people who loved them were hovering above, hoping and waiting for a greeting. Only Matthew, while keeping step with his companions, managed a tiny signal, a flutter of his fingers, the merest residual trace of his usual enthusiastic wave.

A chilling voice sounded from the telephone earpiece. For a moment it augmented my daydream, then swept it away. "This is Sister So-and-so speaking. Am I to understand you want to place your son in our care?"

"Can I have a word with the director?"

With icy guardedness, the voice explained that Dr. Langdon Down was far too busy to receive telephone calls.

"All applications for an interview must be submitted in writing. Your husband should write explaining your reason for wanting an appointment with the doctor. If you have any letters of introduction, they should be included in the envelope. And please, will you remind your husband to put your telephone number on the top left corner of his letter and include a self-addressed envelope." The doctor, she added, was only able to spare alternate Wednesday afternoons for interviews with parents, guardians, or relatives of prospective patients, so we should prepare ourselves for a lengthy wait. Of course there was a waiting list.

I do not know why it did not occur to me to disregard the requirement that it had to be Theo who wrote that letter. In fact I composed it, but I dutifully asked him to copy it out and sign it.

Horribly promptly we received a reply. It came in the form of a succinct message delivered to us by telephone. Would we please attend the hospital at two o'clock on the following Wednesday afternoon?

Where were our promised weeks on the waiting list—or for that matter our self-addressed envelope—the time Gladys and I needed to reconcile ourselves to Matthew's departure?

The order had sounded so peremptory that Theo dared not indulge his usual practice of making a return call to rearrange the date and hour to suit his own schedule. So on that day, he came home at noon and together we motored against the beat of cold hard rain across Hammersmith Bridge toward Richmond Park. As we made our way round the park's perimeter, the deluge was so heavy and the grazing so flooded that to avoid the wide sheets of water both deer and sheep were standing abjectly along the crown of the road. They seemed unable to muster any further instinct of self-preservation, so that our car almost nudged them out of the way.

Upon reaching the town of Kingston, we recrossed the Thames and drove downriver again till we saw the stone gateposts and curving drive that took us to the portico of Normansfield Hospital. The grandeur of the place at once caught Theo's interest.

I had made us so early that we had half an hour in hand. Theo was eager, despite the bleak weather, to look at the hospital buildings. Buttoning our raincoats, we left the car and rushed to stand for a minute under a great cedar of Lebanon before making another dash past a conservatory toward an overgrown laurel walk. This gave dark, forbidding shelter to a narrow gravel path; to me the place was unpleasantly significant, because it so resembled my daydream. As if he had pushed aside a curtain of rain, an elderly gardener with a sack draped round his shoulders stood in front of us.

"You are trespassing."

"We have an appointment here this afternoon. We are just looking at the grounds."

"Doctor won't like that, Sister neither. You go up the porch steps like you ought to have done first off."

A uniformed maid answered our pull on the bell rope. She led us across a high-ceilinged hall and took our sodden coats from us before she opened the door to a reception room. After she closed it, Theo was overcome by nervousness. Taking off his spectacles, he polished them again and again, then cast about for his favorite solace in times of stress, something to read. He had to settle for a fundraising brochure and a few leaflets that were laid out upon an enormous veneered sideboard, a piece of furniture that surely indicated the room's original use. He picked up a high-backed wooden chair and placed it under an almost unlighted chandelier that hung from the center of the ceiling. There he settled down to read while I pressed my face against a windowpane to try through distorting slants of rain to examine the forbidding building which stood at right angles to the one we were in. I glimpsed rows of ground- and first-floor windows, every one barred.

Dr. Langdon Down arrived noiselessly. He stood in the doorway holding out his hand for us to shake. He wore a crisp white coat over a well-cut tweed suit. A gold pen and pencil protruded from his breast pocket, a shining stethoscope dangled across his old-school tie. His rather portly figure, fluffy white hair, and rimless spectacles made him the very picture of a paternal and affable doctor, an impression which was at variance with his cold, schoolboyish face.

He shepherded us through an office lined with filing cabinets into a less practical looking inner sanctum. There he directed us to chairs, as he went to stand behind a large and well-polished desk whose surface was burdened only with golfing trophies and framed photographs, arranged around a Morocco-edged blotter. In a pleasant and confiding voice he embarked upon a practiced narration, starting with the story of his grandfather's founding of the hospital and finishing with an appraisal of his own "modest" achievements. During the brief time we had been in his presence, neither of us had uttered more than a few words. Even so, the doctor had somehow deduced that it was Theo's rather than Matthew's or my need which had brought us to his institution, and his oratory therefore was addressed to Theo.

"It is wise to put a child such as yours into professional care as soon as may be...This type of patient always fares better among his own kind...Here your son will, if we find a place for him, quickly grow used to the company that his type is capable of enjoying...The memories of these little people are mercifully short...I have found that it is the mothers who quite mistakenly object to placements. Of course, they soon come to realize how much better off everyone is."

My initial conviction that our newborn but dying infant son should not have had life forced into him had by now been so refashioned and modified that it was a mere bruise, a black patch in my mind. I was no longer sure which should have happened, Matthew's death or his life. But I did know through and through that it was my task, my responsibility, to make his life as easy and satisfying as I possibly could. Thus this interview (or was it a confrontation?) with Dr. Langdon Down was a torture to me. The doctor seemed to personify the threats and dangers that were likely to beset Matthew once I allowed him be removed from my safekeeping.

I sat there hearing and watching Theo being seduced by the doctor's promise that should Matthew join his "little community" we would be entirely relieved of an unnatural burden. It seemed it was a part of Dr. Langdon Down's power that as he gave a flourish to this last sentence the room became luminous. The rain had ceased moments before, and now sunshine poured through the windows. On Theo's behalf, certainly not my own, I felt a fleeting sensation of a smile after tears. The doctor walked to the door and switched the electric light off.

"Mr. Crosby, I believe it might interest you, as an architect, to see how my grandfather laid out this hospital. I just have time to give you a tour of our premises before my next appointment. Do follow me."

In the hall the maid was waiting, our wet coats over her arm, and in her hand an umbrella for the doctor, although the sun continued to shine. Again, but this time led by the doctor, we splashed along that gravel path toward the outbuildings, which, he explained, had once constituted a model farm, but were now converted into playrooms—paid for, I was later to learn, by the local authority.

Although it was not long past three o'clock, we found the buildings locked. This, according to the doctor, was because the working day was over. "The patients who attended this facility tire easily so are now back in the main building, enjoying an hour or two's recreation before being given their high tea." He smilingly encouraged us to peep through the window and envisage Matthew's future presence within, where he might one day play, have lessons, and eventually be taught some kind of light employment.

So it was that without setting eyes on even one of the inmates, not being made cognizant of bleak, crowded day wards or urine-smelling dormitories, Theo was permitted to feel he had inspected Matthew's future refuge and seen it to be entirely satisfactory. The doctor took this conjuring trick to a conclusion by discreetly escorting us back to our motorcar by way of a path that led through a rose garden, from where we saw only the unbarred windows of what I suspected were his private quarters. When it was my turn to receive his curiously limp handshake he granted me a final glib sentence.

"First, Mrs. Crosby, let us be sure that we actually can put your son's name on our waiting list before we arrange for you to meet Matron, who, I am sure, is more qualified than I to answer all those motherly questions that I know you must be aching to put to me."

BY THE SECOND MONDAY in October 1967, when Matthew was three and a half years old, I had bought, assembled, name-taped, and packed what seemed a surfeit of required clothing to accompany him to Normansfield Hospital. I also put in the motorcar a box of his favorite toys and heaved into the remaining space his blue pedal-car (which I thought resembled a prototype Morgan). He sat his constant companion, a velvet lady pig, behind the steering wheel. It was almost unbearable to sit beside him, witnessing the pleasure he was feeling as we drove toward the hospital. He liked being driven through the park and he was delighted that we had his car inside my car. "Two drivers, Mum." His puzzlement when I was later required to take the box of toys and the Morgan back home gave me such a feeling of betrayal that I could not properly look into his eyes as I knelt to kiss him goodbye.

CHAPTER TEN

Incarceration

On the day I was sure I was pregnant with Matthew, I ceased being able to paint. From that day and for a long time after, the pattern of my life was altered in so many essential ways that I could hardly distinguish this particular loss.

Not until Matthew was immured in Normansfield Hospital and Dido enrolled in kindergarten was I often enough alone to try to paint again. On a late October morning when the light was very clear, I set up my easel and re-opened my paint box. In their established order along the top rim of my palette, from left to right, starting with a blob of flake white, I squeezed from their tubes a line of warm colors, from light to dark, through the cadmium yellows, ocher, cadmium red, and raw and burnt umber. Starting again from the white, this time down the left of the palette, I laid out a line of cool colors through viridian green, cerulean, cobalt and ultramarine blue, to ivory black. This familiar sequence of actions should have brought about something akin to the quickening of my olfactory senses.

I had already prepared a canvas of a specific size and made sure my paint brushes were usable. I now poured turpentine and a drop of oil into a dipper, and from it I filled a sable brush. I had mixed a cobalt-blue-colored ink, with which I started putting marks on the canvas. From that moment I began to doubt the subject of the picture, "The Waking of Somnos," based upon a tale told by Virgil and again by Ovid. I tried to concentrate upon the geometric aspect of it. The shapes were to look flat and verify the subject, but I simply could not muster that degree of interest which would have enabled me to achieve this balance.

I had taken the trouble to clear away any obstacles that I might have been tempted to use as excuses not to resume painting. I had cleaned the house, done the laundry, answered letters, and even sewn my way through the mending basket. Now I was determined not to let lack of conviction stop me from putting something on that very white canvas. I had the notion that painting was a justification, a way of accounting for myself to myself. I wanted to achieve this small work of art so much that I strove for almost three hours, battling to relate shapes and tensions back and forth across the picture plane. In doing so, I managed to destroy both the meaning of the subject and the flatness of both shapes and canvas. When I stepped back I saw only falseness in my efforts.

My only remedy was to wipe the canvas clean. I scraped the colors from the palette, washed the brushes, folded the easel, and gathered all the paraphernalia to do with painting and stowed it in a cupboard under the eaves of the roof, a part of the house that I considered exclusively mine. As I went into the kitchen, I felt as if I had just initiated the closing down of my essential source of abstraction.

I opened the glass doors that gave onto our garden and moved a chair to where the light fell upon the table. I fetched a pad of paper and a pencil, and from the larder a half-drunk bottle of wine, some bread, cheese, and celery. I sat down to eat my lunch. I wanted to explore this loss, and to speculate as to its duration. I planned to help myself do so by drinking wine. Ahead of me lay an empty afternoon, because the sister at Normansfield had ordered me not to visit Matthew more than twice a week. She claimed my constant presence was preventing him from settling in.

I conceded, but only on condition she keep me informed as to the state of his health. As much as my actual presence, my repeated telephone inquiries must have ensured that I remained a thorn in her side. If my call was answered by one of the younger nurses, I usually received a straight answer: "Yes, Matthew is dressed and downstairs," or "No, he is to remain in bed for the day." But the staff nurses and sister were capable of implying, if not telling, lies.

"Mrs. Crosby, there is absolutely no need for you to come and see your son today. He is bright and cheerful, and as you know, he is in Doctor's very capable hands."

"Are you keeping him in bed?"

"We leave that decision to Doctor."

"Surely it has been made by now?"

"That I couldn't say."

So I would drive to the hospital. Usually a blind eye was cast in my direction as, carrying toys brought from home, I passed through the hall and mounted a baronial staircase to make my way along shabby inner corridors toward Matthew's dormitory. If I found only his velvet pig on his pillow, it brought me no relief. I would need to see for myself that nothing dire had caused his absence. Resolution born of anxiety would drive me down the stairs again to try to make my way to the women's day ward, where the littlest children spent most of their time.

It was rare that any but members of the hospital staff penetrated the locked doors that led to that awful ward. Twice I managed to elude the vigilance of the staff and find a way into it. On the first occasion I tried every doorknob till I turned one that opened. I walked into a vast, well-lighted, overheated room. Three of its four walls were lined with either stationary wheelchairs or maroon-colored, mock leather sofas upon which were seated (some strapped) the most gruesome-looking older habituées. Weaving and milling around the central space and making a great variation of noises were ambulatory patients, all of whom wore overalls and bedroom slippers. Among the crowd I glimpsed children of both sexes. Some were surprisingly playful and undaunted, while others stood, sat, or even lay on the ground, bobbing and rocking. The nurses who were busy among these poor creatures seemed serene and authoritative. There was not a person present who gave any sign of being affected by the stench, yet I could hardly breathe. Within minutes I was rescued by Matthew himself.

HE CAME TROTTING to my side. I leaned over and hugged him, and he took my hand. I was impressed by his aplomb and the ease with which he led me through that alarming throng. As we passed them by, a few women clutched at him, but he managed to duck artfully away. He sidled up to a portly, white-haired staff nurse seated at a table. She greeted me in a rich Irish brogue, "Well, if it isn't little Matthew's mam, and aren't we seeing him less peaky today? You would be wanting to spend a while with your boy then? You may as well be benefiting from God's fresh air"—I asked myself then why were her patients not doing so?— "Now, you follow the garden path round our building till you find the front door. I will have your little fellow taken to one of the visitor's rooms. You'll be seeing him there." Before I properly understood what was happening, this grandmotherly nurse had slipped from her chair and opened a door just wide enough for me to pass into the garden. With an affable smile and a surprisingly strong arm she had evicted me from her domain. I found myself standing on a worn patch of grass thankfully breathing the air she had prescribed.

I knew the two visitor's rooms by heart. Both were lit by an acid light that came through panes of Pre-Raphaelite-styled stained glass windows, each depicting images of bare-bosomed maidens carrying or pouring liquid from bulbous vessels. I had examined the crusted ornamentation of the ceilings and debated with myself as to whether the tiles surrounding the paneled fireplaces were or were not too musty in color to be genuine de Morgans. On tiptoe I had studied mottled photographs: "The Langdon Down family entertaining patients at tea on the lawn," "Dr. Langdon Down (evidently the original) with his staff and patients at croquet," "Taking a Stroll in the Grounds," "One Happy Family." It was not always easy to divine which were the patients.

There were days when I had to wait in one or the other of those rooms for so long that I feared my allotted time with Matthew was all but wasted away. A clean, demure little Matthew would at last be ushered through the door. We then did our best to play. I unpacked a meal, which I fed to him from Dido's plastic tea set and which he ate with a certain daintiness. He scribbled so hard in Dido's coloring books that he usually wore away the fat waxen crayons he delighted in most—the pinks and purples and gold-colored ones. I had to replace these frequently.

But often he was listless. Then he would lean against me, pulling at my watch strap or buttoning and unbuttoning my cardigan. There were times when he whispered, "Dancing." Then I stood up and took him in my arms as I tried to hum a Strauss waltz or some blues melody from Jelly Roll Morton. I stepped and spun about the room, but my efforts to achieve gaiety made us sad. Matthew might weep, but I dared not for fear of never ceasing.

Every now and again we came across other families in those visiting rooms, every one of them more staid than we. They spoke in hushed voices and seemed to close their knees together and draw in their feet to maintain a defining distance between themselves and us. I could never bring myself to cross the carpet and ask even one of the many questions that were on the tip of my tongue: How long did it take for your relation to settle here? Does he or she manage to remain healthy? Smile and laugh as before? Show symptoms of fear or unhappiness? Have friends?

As if caught in the midst of some naughty pursuit, we were always startled when the nurse opened the door to tell us our time was up. We rarely managed a proper embrace in her presence. I had to drive home with the image of Matthew walking away, waving the fingers of one hand over his shoulder in an effort to signal a final goodbye.

WHILE SIPPING MY WINE in the noonday sun, I made myself put aside my self-centered concerns about painting in favor of more pragmatic questions. I reached for the piece of paper and wrote:

1. Matthew. What can I do to get him out of that god-awful Normansfield? Why should anywhere so wretched exist? What measures can I take?

At this point my writing bit deep into the paper.

2. Dido. Must Matthew be denied so as to safeguard her? Is that what she needs?
3. Theo. Is his attempt to cut Matthew out of our family prudent and farsighted? Does he believe we are all so fragile?
4. Anne. Suppose I allow Matthew's banishment to continue, how shall I contrive to remain an adequate mother to him? Will I be condemned to a semi-clandestine relationship with him? Surely not relinquish him altogether?

As I drew a tipsy line under this list, I drank off the last of the wine, which had by now induced in me an annihilative boredom. I remember first pitying myself almost as much as I did Matthew, and the next instant seeing myself as making a drama out of circumstances which many other families would simply accept.

By the time I went to meet Dido at her school gate I had acquired an aching head and just enough wisdom to know I needed advice. I thought I knew whom to consult. But there was the question of whether Theo would countenance my taking our seemingly healthy daughter to such a doctor. I wanted us to be counseled by Dr. Donald Winnicott, a child psychologist whose book I had recently read.

CHAPTER ELEVEN

Dr. Winnicott

Dido and I went to see Dr. Donald Winnicott in May of 1968. As we drove toward his house in Chester Street, I tried to account to her for our forthcoming interview. "You and I are about to see a sort of doctor."

"Are we sort of ill, then?"

"No, he is interested in children and part of his job is to advise their mothers—and fathers if they have the time, of course—as to how they might arrange their family life." I felt I had made a poor job of the explanation.

Dr. Winnicott opened his own front door to us, then stood aside and motioned us past him into a narrow hallway. He was a small, somewhat anxious-looking man, perhaps in his late sixties. We watched him make sure he had fastened the door and shot all the bolts. He pointed in the direction of his consulting room; he followed us and closed that door very quietly, then seated himself in a low upholstered chair without armrests. Despite the mildness of the weather he reached forward to light a gas fire, waving me to a taller but equally comfortable chair. Finally, looking cozily at Dido, he flapped and gestured comically with his hands to signal she was free to do as she liked—climb onto a third chair, sit on a stool or on the carpet, even roam about, which she chose to do. She very soon came upon a cardboard shoebox into which were crammed a little community of well-used dolls and shabby woolly animals.

Till now the doctor had not addressed either of us, but had worn what I saw as an exaggeratedly passive expression. "Ha ha, you've found my friends. Shall we invite them over here?" His voice was academic-sounding and gentle. Dido carried the box to his side. He picked out a girl doll. "Perhaps this is you?" A pause. "Is it you?" She shook her head. "Shall we sit her against the stool and tell her she is now your mum?" Dido laughed. He glanced toward me. I had already divined that I was to remain silent. "Now let's find out which is you." Dido picked up a sailor doll. She and the doctor continued to peer into the box, "Anyone else there, I wonder? . . . your daddy?"

"He's gone to the office."

In an almost inaudible voice, "Anyone else?"

A slow nod from Dido.

The doctor put his hand in the box and stirred; seemingly carelessly he withdrew a dented little celluloid baby, along with a grayish rabbitlike creature. Dido, head on one side, appeared to be debating with herself. She pointed to the doll. "Matthew."

"My goodness, he looks thoroughly unwell, and all naked, too. Shouldn't we wrap him?" The doctor twitched a somewhat grubby handkerchief from his sleeve and dropped it onto his knee furthest from Dido. She looked up at him, he nodded, so she reached for it. Together they wrapped the tiny doll. "Now, for a nice warm place; my pocket, perhaps? I wonder if there is room for him in there."

Dido, who was normally a diffident and distant child, put a hand into his jacket pocket and left it there for a few seconds.

"Warm enough? Any room?"

"Your matchbox and some crumbs in there."

The doctor proffered the wrapped doll. Dido hesitated. "Perhaps it's not the right place? Maybe further away?" He unceremoniously tipped the remaining toys from the shoebox to the floor on the farther side of his chair. "Now he can have this nice bed; where should we put it?"

It was a rhetorical question. One of his feet was delicately shunting the box toward the fireplace. "In an altogether other place, maybe."

Dido helped guide the box. When she had placed it satisfactorily far from the two of them, she arranged the handkerchief about the little Matthew doll till he was entirely hidden. She then returned to the doctor's side and once again slipped her hand into his pocket. He let his arm encircle her as he lightly patted the pocket. The two smiled at each other. There was a silence.

I assumed we had reached the end of our session, but it was not so. Causing Dido to retrieve her hand, the doctor shifted his chair so that he now faced me. "Where does Dido's brother live at present?"

"He is in what used to be called an asylum."

The doctor very gently nudged Dido so that she stood in front of him, facing in my direction. He put a hand under each of her elbows and, as if making an offering, said "Here is the important child, the bright and whole one. We can safely say the other is The Throwaway Child."

My eyes at once filled with tears; they spilled down my face. I found my handkerchief and tried to blot them. Dido watched me with dismay.

"We must let your mother cry, Dido. What I have said is very hard for her to hear, but I notice it did not take her by surprise."

I felt I had been taken by surprise. Ashamed of displaying so much feeling, I reassembled myself.

"You have a wonderful child. She is standing right here. It is seldom I get the pleasure of meeting a near perfect child. Thank you for showing her to me."

CHAPTER TWELVE

Dr. Mac

Shortly before Matthew entered Normansfield Hospital, a compassionate little woman doctor was commissioned by one of the National Health Authorities to assess the mental and physical powers of every patient there. Since Matthew was not well enough to spend time in the nursery building where she was conducting her clinic, Dr. MacSorley had not had a chance to examine him. So on a cold February afternoon she came to see Matthew in his ward. Both Matthew and I were squeezed into his cot, he languidly tapping on his xylophone, I singing nursery rhymes to his beat. I was always able to hear Sister's sharp tapping shoes in time to climb out of the cot. Dr. MacSorley, allowing herself to be guided by the sounds we were making, had strolled peacefully along the corridors, an approach I later learned to be typical of the manner in which she dealt with most circumstances. As we looked at each other over the rails of the cot, I felt almost as constrained as Matthew literally was, for he was strapped in.

She gave me an apologetic grin and in doing so threw me a metaphorical lifeline, which I did not fail to grasp. Then and there this most unmethodical doctor set about an examination of Matthew—an assessment which neither of us felt it necessary to complete—coincidentally embarking upon an unending interview with me.

Over the ensuing weeks I paid several visits to Dr. MacSorley's clinic in the nursery building, where Matthew was now well enough to play. Her first move was to allow me to surreptitiously watch him. Seeing him in the playroom acted upon my mind in contradictory ways. At first I was horror-struck. To my eyes Mat-

thew in no way resembled his peers; I wondered we had ever allowed ourselves to be duped into consigning him to such a bedlam. Eventually I let myself perceive both him and his peers in
a truer light. I noticed his and their playfulness. Now that summer was come and he was less and less ill, it was evident that
these hours were a joy to Matthew. Two conscientious women
gave all their energy to the task of entertaining, at times even instructing, as many as twenty little individuals whose ages ranged
from Matthew's four years to nine or ten years.

I witnessed momentary transformations taking place. Children's contorted and mouthing faces calmed to near tranquillity
as their shaking hands poured water from one jar to another. I
saw purpose overcome dreadful clumsiness, as rigid fingers
swirled colors onto sheets of old newsprint or dragged at bright
modeling dough; intractable limbs glided in dance. But most
touching—though strange to my ears—was the growling and
humming of hymns.

> *All things bright and beautif-ool . . .*
> *All creatures great and smaaall . . .*

or

> *There is a green hill faaar awaaay . . .*
> *With th' outa city waaall . . .*

Without making it clear to me that it was part of her assign-
ment to test the intelligence quotients not only of her Normansfield patients but also of their siblings, Dr. MacSorley asked me
to bring Dido to see her. Until she put this request, we had been
somewhat circumspect with each other, I defensive, she unhur-
ried. Caught unawares, I lost my politeness and retorted, "Good
God, I couldn't possibly allow Dido to even glimpse this jail we
have flung our poor Matthew into. Anyway, how could you suppose her father and I would not have noticed if our daughter
was in any way feebleminded?"

The doctor's smile persisted. "Perhaps it might interest her father to know the level of his other child's intelligence? Wouldn't that knowledge be a useful guide for her future education?"

She assured me there was no need to bring Dido to the hospital; the tests could be done at her other place of work. "Why don't you come to see me there? We could talk. I feel we have interesting things to say to each other."

She prevailed. I ~~quickly~~ formed a habit of dropping in to chat with her in her room at the Institute of Child Psychology on Notting Hill. Of course I allowed her to assess Dido. Her tests revealed a surprisingly high intelligence quotient. When I told Dido this was so, she asked, "Aren't I anything like him then?"

A windup gramophone and a stack of children's records were ever at the ready in her shabby and crowded Institute, where walls were scribbled upon, floors littered by torn books and broken toys. Every shelf and table was heaped with file boxes, folders of case histories, and piles of children's paintings. Cups of tea and biscuits were offered at any hour in ~~this place that witnessed so much suffering. With~~ the sounds of that gramophone as a background, listening to a distressed mother's plaintive voice, or a sad or belligerent child's whine, Dr. MacSorley, who had been a refugee from Nazi Germany, could be said to be happy. She exuded peace of mind.

She also plotted. She plotted against Normansfield Hospital and, in a more committed way, against any government department ~~dealing~~ with health or education which she saw to be remiss in its duties. For Dr. Mac—as she was known at the Institute—and her confreres were sponsoring a cause which I readily espoused. As the law then stood in 1968, education was not mandatory for the subnormal. The doctor and her associates were aiming to get this law altered, which in fact they managed to do within a year, so that regardless of his or her potential, every child in the land ~~had a~~ right to be schooled.

DR. MAC DID NOT so much give a sympathetic ear to my verbal agonizing about the inadequacies of Dr. Langdon Down and his cold-hearted institution, as train me to take my grievances away and resubmit them to her in the form of orderly and verifiable criticisms suitable as grist for her ever-grinding protest mill.

This pertinacious woman led me to take action after action, each one more committed and public than the last.

"Should you not make known your disquiet to some of the individuals who are on the hospital board?" She supplied names.

"Why not follow with a letter to the local Health Authority?"

"Now perhaps a copy to your member of parliament?"

"If it could be arranged, would you submit to a short interview before a microphone?" (She was perfectly aware that it could be arranged, since she herself had been in touch with Broadcasting House.) The scope of her plans expanded between each of our meetings, so that the short radio interview became an intense forty minutes before television cameras, during which I was to be exposed to (mostly antagonistic) questions from a large audience of fellow parents.

DR. MAC FED ME the information that Dr. Langdon Down had diagnosed more than sixty percent of his patients as so irretrievably incapacitated that there was no purpose in prescribing any activities or amusements for them. He was sure "that kind of thing would only disturb their equilibrium."

Dr. Mac would at times extend the hours of my meetings with Matthew in her part of the nursery building in return for my cooperation. The price sometimes seemed high, for each time I was there she forced upon me further glimpses into the emptiness of the lives of the adult patients whom she was now busy assessing. She worked her stratagems upon me so that, though not yet inured (I never would be) to their harrowed bodies, I was able to accept their mental limitations. I also learned to mask my sympathy and to usually see them as very gallant beings.
more often than not

She urged me to dream up any sort of contrivance or toy that might possibly stir a neglected mind or limb. "You are an artist, are you not? So now you create in another meadow." Concern on their behalf led me to try to imagine interesting objects for them to use or play with, but very soon I came to realize that any such object must make almost no physical demands and thus would probably require some sort of *mechanical or* electrical knowledge I did not possess.

Was it at Dr. Mac's instigation or did I decide to make use of my connection with Hornsey Art School? However it was, I consulted Stuart Brisley, who ran a basic design course there. Echoing Dr. Mac, I "wondered" if he could present his third-year students with this "challenging" design problem. After Mr. Brisley came to talk to Dr. Mac, I noticed that he too was acting as she wished. He went back to his art school and persuaded the principal of the college to make a telephone call to a relevant National Health authority (name and number supplied by Dr. Mac) to obtain approval for a "very constructive little field study" to be carried out, of course, at Normansfield Hospital.

The artful Dr. Mac even managed to inveigle some impressive official to write a *subtly* faintly threatening but obviously flattering letter (I was shown a copy of it) to Dr. Langdon Down, to assure him that were his hospital made available as a venue for "this very constructive project" beneficial publicity would *surely* follow. *?* I was told that when, at the last minute, he spotted my name attached to the proposal, Dr. Langdon Down made an attempt to ban Stuart Brisley and his students from entering his grounds, using the pretext that they might overexcite his patients. He withdrew his objection when he was told that a BBC camera crew was proposing to accompany them. I suspect it was Dr. Mac who contributed this piece of fiction.

Although the BBC began recording my program in January, 1968, it was not broadcast until the following September. During the ensuing days, 280 letters were sent to the BBC, causing them on several mornings to dispatch one of their black motorcars to transport me to their beehive-like building at White City, where the assistant producer of the program and I read every letter, then tried to compose fitting answers to each one. Some of the letters were written by the siblings of mentally or physically handicapped people. As I read these I had the depressing sensation that I was being made privy to Dido's future sorrows. Whether lovingly or resentfully told, too many letters gave intimations of blighted childhoods, and too few claimed any benefit. A number of parents put to me my own question, "How much harm are we doing our child if we banish him or her from the family?" Quite as many wrote that same question in reverse, "By keeping our retarded child at home, what harm are we inflicting upon his or her siblings?"

Those letters made me ashamed I had made use of the fragile workings of our family as a model upon which to base a public discussion, with the equally fragile hope that wider consciousness and government awareness would result. I now wondered if those who wrote and even those who didn't had perceived my performance as a betrayal.

Aware that I would never have had the temerity to expose us in this way if Dr. MacSorley had not urged the absolute necessity of it, I asked her to share the responsibility of replying to the letters.

"I must not interfere between you and your fans, my dear."

Yet, directly the broadcast was finished, she had rushed to the telephone to make a triumphant critique. I heard her glee. "Our program went rather well, don't you think? Most stirring. You are my good dog among the pigeons." If excited, the doctor was prone to emphasize her meanings with misquoted aphorisms. "A few short minutes of discomfort; such a cost for such a desirable effect. The Nation's conscience has been aired. Questions will be put, you mustn't doubt."

How could I doubt? She had for weeks been putting pressure upon me, and I in turn had less mercilessly and with better grace put pressure on a friend who had a seat in the House of Lords. He had given his word that our cause would be "aired."

Dr. MacSorley, short in stature, warped by arthritis, speaking in a markedly German accent, crowed, "I believe I lack what is called charisma." (She did not.) "So I exercise my other talents. Often I choose not to myself act, but to promote and to prompt."

DURING ALL THE promotions and promptings I submitted myself to, I never lost sight of the arrangement Gladys Strong and I had envisaged, that of starting a home around Matthew.

An aunt of mine who had lingered in a small, private, and very comfortable asylum for many years had finally died in her sleep and left me a sum of money. I saw this to be a wonderful piece of symmetry. I could simply transfer her money so that it would pay for her grandnephew to live in an asylum, too, an altogether humbler establishment, put together by Gladys and me. We needed no remote country house, no strong-armed keepers and nurses disguised as chauffeurs and domestic staff—just a certain sum of money and a modest house for Gladys and her extended family to live in.

My father claimed my poor aunt had not been in her right mind while making her will; he threatened to take his case to court to prove that it was family money and should have reverted to his sisters and himself, rather than be willed to me. In settling the matter—out of court—my inheritance was so shrunken that there remained barely enough to buy the mortgage.

In June of 1968 I had gone to talk the matter over with Dr. Mac. "Ah! We must discuss. You must tell me about your father."

"My father?"

"Yes, his attitude toward his daughter and, more important, her attitude toward him."

"I'd rather we talk about how I am to gather enough money to set up the home."

"Oh, that is a detail, but we settle it first. Then you tell."

"What should I do?"

"You ask for it."

"Whom do I ask?"

"Everyone. You beg."

And that is what I did. I composed a begging letter. I suffered a certain amount of trepidation before I showed it to Theo. To my surprise he willingly endorsed it. He took it to his office to correct my spelling and have it printed, and sent it ~~out~~ to almost everyone we knew and a great many of his clients.

I did not realize how uneasy asking people for money made me until I was trying to account to Gladys for having written such a letter. In the event, I simply confronted her with it.

"Oh, that's all right, Anne. If all them people can afford it, then they ought to cough up. Like at church. It's good for 'em."

I was relieved to hear her words, for like everyone else in her court I hated being in what she called her "bad books." But from then on, Gladys began to perplex me. All of a sudden she appeared desperately bored with our scheme. To re-enthuse her I would report to her the sums of money we were raising. After the television broadcast I was able to tell her that the attention and publicity it occasioned was bringing in a new wave of donations. I assumed I was reassuring her. When I suggested we might go together to look for a house that suited our purpose, she gave me a dismissive smile that was peculiarly hers, and with it a glance that seemed to pass by me to rest on an object more interesting. "We'll have to talk it over sometime. I'll let you know when I've got a moment."

"I thought we had done most of the talking."

"Well, that's all right then."

It was a painful exchange, and I knew I had been in some way insensitive toward her. It was Theo who understood the cause of Gladys's reaction. "She has cold feet, my dear. I don't blame her, and you should not. I suggest you look in another direction to start your home for Matthew. Unless, of course, you do the intelligent thing and drop the whole project." He said those last words facetiously, meaning "I am of course half in jest, but the other half..."

I answered him that I could not possibly drop this idea, for two reasons. We had already accepted a deal of money from friends and strangers, and I believed that he and I could not be comfortable together unless we were able to ensure that Matthew was made secure and happy. Theo rose from the stool in front of his drawing board, stepped from the circle of lamplight which always revealed his expression in fine detail, and joined me in the gloom of the shadowy evening. Then he did something he rarely felt moved to do. He swung me around and gave me an affectionate kiss.

CHAPTER THIRTEEN

Letter to Dr. Langdon Down

1 October 1968
To Doctor Langdon Down and the Chairman
of the Board of Directors of Normansfield Hospital
and to whom else this may concern:

I am writing to you to say that I have come to the conclusion
that my son Matthew Crosby should not remain at Normansfield Hospital...

As you know, Matthew has not been at all well in the time
he has been in your care. During his first three and a half
months in Normansfield he was gravely ill in a way he never
was at home. He had a fever, coughed constantly and his
breathing was irregular and shallow. This is what I observed;
you told me nothing.

I am not entirely blaming your hospital for all his illness.
Matthew must be constantly exposed to a variety of germs in a
large community such as yours. What I am objecting to is that
you and your staff do not take proper care of him. He sleeps in
a room with twelve beds, nine of which are occupied by adult
females. You say he has to sleep here because only in this ward
is there a night sister. What about the days? Matthew has been
desperately lonely while confined in this room. Matron told
me it is too far from the day ward downstairs to be constantly
checked by your nurses.

Occasionally when I visited Matthew, there have been others
who were ill. One young woman in a bed near Matthew's cot
continuously retched and choked. I was warned not to lend
her a toy or an object of any sort in case she tried to put it

down her throat. Another patient had several fits while I was there. Yet another lay crying and making hooting noises. When I went to look for help I was told that for these poor creatures the presence of a nurse made little difference; I suppose they might have been unaware of the pitiful noises they made or their strong odor of urine, but Matthew was not.

This was the only kind of company Matthew had all the time he was confined in bed and it had a horrible effect upon him. He has been very melancholy. For days at a time he refused to be roused. When I came to see him he would not allow me to let the side of his cot down. Against Matron's orders I persisted in doing so. I was sure that although my nearness made Matthew cry I was helping him to stay alive.

Last time I was there a large half-naked woman came into the room. She called out, "Baby, baby," and tried to pull Matthew from his cot. I had difficulty keeping him from her; I scolded her and sent her away. What if Matthew had been alone?

Nobody who is ill is allowed toys or playthings beyond one doll or stuffed animal. Sister told me that the majority of the patients are too severely handicapped to make use of toys, but to Matthew they are a necessity; give him a tea set or his telephone and he will play.

I provided these things and many more kinds of toys but you told me they had to be sent over to the school because of the rule that forbids possessions in the main building.

I believe this lack of personal property is a key criticism of Normansfield. Matron tells me it is not possible to be tidy with "things lying about." Obviously not. The therapist at the school said she had tried sending toys up to the hospital but they only got broken. She said possessions lead to jealousy and bullying.

You consider it sufficient that there are "therapeutic gadgets and things to do" in the school and occupational center, but is that sufficient? Some patients are not able to make the journey of two hundred yards or so down the garden to that building. Those who can, spend at most four hours of their day there and then return to your two large day wards, the one for men and the other for women and children.

For a few, you say you organize dancing one afternoon a week, films on another day and sometimes swimming. The older people sing hymns. But I happen to know the majority of your patients spend their lives doing nothing at all. When the weather is good the children are let out to play in a pen in the garden. It is not enough. The little children share a day ward with ninety-six adult female patients. I am not surprised Matthew suffers fears; a great many of these women are very alarming; even their smells are oppressive. It would seem reasonable to take the children away from this place and give them a nursery of their own with a sister whom they could recognize as the protective figure they need so badly. Cots could be kept in this nursery so that those who need to rest or have days in bed would not have to be left alone upstairs.

Surely there are trustworthy adult patients who could help here? I have noticed that a large part of the manual work, the cleaning and even a little of the nursing is done by adult patients.

I am only writing about what I have seen in the time Matthew has been with you. I am not making these criticisms on Matthew's behalf only. I cannot forget the other patients who live in Normansfield Hospital. I cannot bear to imagine Matthew's future taking place there. At present he is only four years old; the staff find him comparatively charming and make a fuss over him, but as Matthew gets older no one will want his hugs and kisses and one day he will graduate from the women's and children's ward to that horrible all-male day ward where there is a terrible lack of affection and, I have heard, a certain amount of bullying. For Matthew to survive he would have to come down to a very crude level. Once he acquires the thick skin you recommend, he will be unfit to live anywhere but in Normansfield's male north wing, and that, as I see it, is a life sentence worse than prison.

Sincerely yours,
Anne Crosby

why big letters

THOUGH THEO MADE no objection to my writing this letter, he declined to put his name to it.

CHAPTER FOURTEEN

Simmonds Smith

The reverberations from the television program had all but died away, and I was well on the way to detaching myself from the mostly painful recollection of it when there came one last consequence. The assistant director of the program telephoned to tell me that a very smooth-talking fellow had just left her office and was on his way to our house. She had not discouraged him because she was not sure that what he had to say would not interest me. That evening when Theo arrived home, he found this lightly built, orange-mustached man sitting in his chair helping himself from our decanter of whiskey. For the better part of two hours I had been listening to his talk; first I made him tea, then I cooked Dido's supper, and still his words flowed. I decided to abandon him. I took Dido upstairs to put her to bed.

Our visitor jumped to his feet and offered Theo his hand as if welcoming him to his own house. "Major Simmonds Smith, Royal Marines. I have been trying to persuade your delightful lady wife that you should throw your lot in with ours."

I expected Theo to deny having a "lot," but he simply fetched a glass for himself and sat down. I was later to discover that all sorts of intelligent and upright men responded to Dave Simmonds Smith as Theo did that evening. While I prepared dinner I could hear the major retelling all he had told me. He laughed as often, gestured with the same boyish enthusiasm, and made the same self-deprecating jokes. "I want to buy a large house with extensive outbuildings and a bit of land; I have my eye on the very place, a great bargain. I am going to start a residential community for retarded children. My wife and I would offer these kids a lifetime of care. I open every speech I make with that promise, and I'll be damned if I don't keep it. You know, when we've got going, those words will be our motto: a lifetime of care, yes, a lifetime of care."

Once more I heard how he and Madge "like to go on the road" appealing for money. "I address all sorts of groups—trade unions, Rotary clubs, Women's Institutes." Again he wiped tears from his eyes as he reminisced about his little Down syndrome son who had recently "passed away, a great little trouper." This time he added, "Given half a chance, I'd like to adopt another child of that ilk."

Though I perceived him as having genuinely empathetic feelings for the mentally handicapped, I also saw that Major Simmonds Smith was too much of a showman. As the evening wore on—and on—he became exaggeratedly at ease in our company. He seemed driven to boast of his somewhat specious qualifications; he even disclosed his love of trickery. Though his affection for "those whose lights shine less brilliantly than ours" sounded authentic, he caused me to wonder if he was willing to exploit them, as he made waggish remarks about charging fat fees for private "patients."

By the time we said good night and closed our yard door upon him, I was ready to altogether dismiss the Major's dreams and his "heartfelt" request that we invest in them. As I cleared the table and Theo set about washing the dishes, he began to talk. "You know, I was no more taken in by your visitor than you were, but I did not dislike him." I wanted to remark that I had not disliked him either (I was most surprised that this was so), but I was too impatient to hear what Theo was about to say. "Rather than your timid plan for making a 'home,' as you put it, 'round Matthew,' I prefer Simmonds Smith's rather self-promoting scheme. It meets a greater need and reaches nicely into the future. I think we should combine the two. Your caution will temper his flamboyance. We should search out other parents of children like Matthew, ask them to help us form a board of governors. I see a role for myself in all this. Someone will have to keep a watchful eye on the Major; I shouldn't mind directing the man's energies. Neither you nor I have his gifts. We're neither able nor willing to perform and exhibit ourselves to raise funds. But I believe I am capable of persuading charitable institutions and certain large companies to support our cause. The vital thing is that the Major feels a genuine fondness for the subnormal. It sounds as if he and his wife really want to work among them. Could we consider such a way of life? We should be grateful to him and we should work with him."

I knew he was right. Major Simmonds Smith's arrival was fortuitous if not miraculous. I confessed to Theo that I was daunted by the largeness of the Major's scheme, the amount of discussion, the meetings and the organizing.

In his semi-jocular way Theo offered me a generous bargain. "Oh, none of that will bother me; it might even be interesting. I think I would enjoy setting up a project of this sort. You know me, I much prefer the abstract to the intimate. I never was one for the hands-on approach. As you more than once remarked to me, I enjoy being an *éminence grise*. So, my dear, if you can cope with Matthew, I will take on Simmonds Smith and his palace of varieties. Is that a deal?"

I was full of gratitude, and year after year I had reason to continue being so. I believe Theo was grateful to me, too. Certainly we each kept to the bargain we made that night. Though he never once complained, I cannot believe Theo enjoyed those endless board meetings, the often fruitless dealings and ceaseless correspondence with authorities. He might have derived satisfaction in the early days when he was painstakingly designing and supervising the construction of the special housing, the classrooms, and the workshops. For the rest of his life, Theo worked and fought for what he once defined as "the depressing cause Matthew landed us with."

Now there are several MacIntyre Schools. To the end, Simmonds Smith remained as we first saw him, boyishly enthusiastic, beguiling and sentimental. Eventually he became bored and was careless with our funds and given a handsome sum in exchange for his absence; his resignation was accepted with less regret than relief.

THE DOWN PAYMENT and initial mortgage payment were I believe mostly paid for by Theo and myself, simply because we were in possession of the money we had begged for and I was able to sell a cottage I had bought for my mother, who was a victim of Alzheimer's disease and was living in a nursing home.

By this time, the Simmonds Smith family had already moved their two adolescent children, all their furniture, a couple of young helpers, and six handicapped lads into the home. One of the first tasks the Major and his "gang" tackled was the planting of a large, hand-painted notice declaring Westoning Manor was now to be known as MacIntyre School.

CHAPTER FIFTEEN

Matthew's Absence

For the duration of Matthew's eighteen-month incarceration in Normansfield Hospital, Gladys Strong did her utmost to maintain a distance between herself and me. Perhaps she blamed me for giving in to an arrangement that led to Matthew's being wrested from her care, or was she acting in obedience to one of her obscure professional edicts? I could not ask her directly since Gladys abhorred explanations, considering them symptoms of weakness. She had a maxim to justify this particular prejudice— "What I don't know can't kill me." Comprehending Gladys was one's own responsibility. She liked to end her sentences with any of her favorite sayings, "Seeing is believing," "What the eye don't see the heart don't grieve over," "Time will tell," "Well, we all end up in the grave, don't we."

On the morning after I delivered Matthew into the grasp of Normansfield Hospital, I walked round to see Gladys. She blocked her doorway, standing like a little sentinel.

"I came to tell you how ... well, I came to thank you ..." There I stopped, recalling that, even more than explanations, she eschewed "thank you's."

"Must get on; got a new little boy to look after." She managed to load these few words with heavy meaning; it was as if she were nodding and winking. I turned from her. She saw the action as entirely suitable. "Bye now. Might run into you some-day ..." Her words were dismissive. She had set the pattern. We were not to consort.

To each one of Gladys's arcane rules there was an almost-offered exception. She would acknowledge our connection if we met, not in the vicinity of our home streets, but further afield on neutral territory, at the market or in the Cooperative. In these sorts of places she might draw up her perambulator for a few minutes and allow me to give her news of Matthew. She liked to cut me short and put pertinent questions regarding his weight, how he was dressed, and whether his manners were as "nice" as ever.

The weeks of his absence lengthened to months and my answers grew not, as Gladys tried to command, more satisfactory to her ears, but less and less so, until at last she needed to fend off my news with another of her devices. First asking me, "How is our little boy doing?" she quickly answered her question by declaring, "He'll settle in no time now, you'll see," or, "He'll be as right as rain soon; any place suits him . . . Likes all sorts, he does . . . Makes a friend of anybody . . . He's not particular . . . That little charmer won't lack for nothing once they get to know him properly . . . Be twisting those nurses round his little finger when he's well and gets to be his old self again . . . Soon be making a little world of his own, I expect you'll turn up one afternoon only to find he don't need you no more."

Spring was turning to light summer, and Matthew was still suffering long bouts of confinement in his melancholy dormitory. He and I had to celebrate his fourth birthday there with only his velvet pig for company. Among the other cards and properly ephemeral presents I carried to him was a lush card from Gladys and all her family. Matthew made me repeat its trite little rhyme to him over and over again. Then he kissed the card and murmured their names, "Auntie Gladys, Uncle Fred, Our Lil n' Our Kev." Those were quite a large proportion of the words he admitted to being able to say, for he had reverted to a life of mime.

I lay in wait for some weeks hoping to catch Gladys and tell her of his reaction to her card. Those accidental occasions when I might have exchanged greetings with her were becoming rare. More than once I saw her flit away from me round a corner or down a side street.

On other occasions my antennae made me aware of her proximity and at the same instant her avoidance of me. By now I was trying to suppress a recurring and selfish compulsion: I wanted to confront Gladys, make her understand my accumulating desperation.

At last, I came upon her just as she had finished her Sunday morning job of cleaning the windows of her flat. There she stood on the pavement, wearing the pink version of her apron, her head tipped to one side as she scrutinized the surfaces of glass. I was overcome by my need to catch her attention, so I went and stood beside her. After we had both uttered our obligatory politenesses, asking after each other's health and talking about how the sunshine showed up spots on the windowpanes, I plunged into the subject of Matthew, essaying a description of the foul-smelling, eerie dormitory in which he spent so much of his life. After a few sentences Gladys's expression made me know that, like Theo, she suspected me of wild exaggeration. To keep my precious contact with her, I tried to alter the tenor of my words, but too late. She had interrupted me.

"You put too much thinking into it." To Gladys, that was just as suspect as explaining, which was nearly as wrong as fibbing. "It don't do to make yourself feel so bad. You'll see soon enough you've done right. After the dust settles, you got your little girl still, haven't you? This way you are keeping her pa sweet, too."

Just so. I badly wanted to keep Theo sweet. I stood quite still. And while I listened to her every word I felt on my cheeks the little breezes that were disturbing the new leaves on the plane trees. I focused on those trees, one by one, down to the end of her street, where they met the silvery twinkle of the Thames at high tide. I realized ruefully that Gladys's remonstrances were in essence the sentiments of every friend whom I had made privy to Matthew's suffering. The only words that came to me as I left her side were, "I expect you are right."

There was no point in telling Gladys I had wanted some other sort of talk from her, words that would, aided by the sharp, unveiling quality of the morning sunshine, help me to know what I ought to be doing. Behind the varying degrees of sympathy shown by my friends, I believed there existed a residual awareness that I had once wished Matthew be allowed to die. That awareness would at times be made known to me (or imagined by me) by oblique references or studied avoidances. My ripostes, rarely spoken but shouted within my head, went like this: "Yes, I did want Matthew dead, but that was before he began to live. I wanted to prevent him from becoming a mere creature needing to be fed and housed. I wanted nobody to do what I am already allowing to be done. I wanted Matthew dead rather than so little alive as he now is in Normansfield Hospital."

So often, there I would be, sitting among "our set" of friends, in what I had come to see as obscene comfort, perhaps nursing a glass of lightly iced alcohol or consuming some ornate meal in their intelligent company. Among these friends, I once in a while had a quite pointless urge to justify those first hours of mental clarity, but more palpable was my overwhelming shame that I was with them and not where I ought to have been.

Gladys's wonderful merit was that she was still capable of seeing Matthew as "all right," just as all right as he was from the moment she set eyes on him. I understood that she liked him more than she was ever going to like me, and I loved her for it. Not until March 26, 1969, was I able to bring Matthew back to her.

"Not before time, I'd say. He'll want his old cot back. Little Sharon isn't stopping long. Only till her mum's had her baby. So she can make do on the sofa."

"I'm sure your prices have gone up since Matthew last lodged with you."

"Maybe." She honored me with what she would have called a "savvy" grin.

BESIDE THE FACT that I had failed to induce Theo to sign the letter I wrote to Dr. Langdon Down, I had difficulty in persuading him that Normansfield was so shamefully run.

It was not until the autumn of 1968, when he read the journal the students had kept during our toy-making venture, that Theo began to credit all I had told him.

Meanwhile, the Strong family spent their annual holiday on the Isle of Wight. After their return, Gladys came to see me. "Me'n Fred have worked out what with the dosh we'd get from selling our old flat we could afford to buy one of them nearly-near-the-sea boarding house set-ups. Make ourselves a living doing Bed and Breakfasts. Fred's plumbing on the side. Kids like it down there. Schools nice enough, specially the one for little dopes. Went and saw Medina House, that's what it's called. You could write to 'em. I'd be taking little Alex if we do go. Might as well have your Matthew. Gets on nice with Alex, don't he? Make it up for me ducking out of our other arrangement, eh?"

CHAPTER SIXTEEN

Isle of Wight

Matthew was finally removed from Normansfield at the end of March 1969 and returned to Gladys's care. By the end of August the Strong family had sold their London flat and were ready to move to the Isle of Wight, taking Matthew with them. I had allowed myself to become so used to his renewed presence at the end of our street that I could hardly bear his being torn away.

Once Matthew was gone, there was no satisfactory way for me to keep in touch with him. Talking on the telephone for any but practical reasons was to Gladys analogous to throwing money over Hammersmith Bridge. She permitted me this extravagance less than once a week.

"Hullo, Gladys, how are you?'

"Well as can be expected, thank you."

"And the family?"

"Likewise."

I knew better than to ask her if her husband had found a job. She let me know that every word I said must conform with her concept of what kind of talk was appropriate to the telephone.

"Don't do to be personal. Can't be sure operators aren't listening."

I took a risk and asked about her new role as a landlady. "How is the Bed and Breakfast doing?"

"Early days yet."

If I could not soften her up with any other kind of preamble, I would introduce the subject that nearly always loosened her tongue, the weather.

"Don't talk to me about the weather. I was told it was meant to be sunny beside the sea. Well, it's not like that here. Our Lil doesn't like getting her shoes wet, and our Kev's fussy about the muck sticking to his bike. Then there's the guests. They want to stay indoors when it rains, get under my feet worse than the children."

"Ah, the children, how are they settling into their new schools?"

Gladys knew my anxiety on this subject concerned only Matthew, and sometimes she held out on me.

"Expect I'd have heard if anything was wrong."

Toward the end of my calls she sometimes relented and we talked about Matthew.

"Is Matthew's schoolbus picking him up regularly?"

"Little devil, he doesn't give a tuppenny damn, climbs on that bus without a wave goodbye. Can't say his manners are improving in that Mediana school."

She would never allow me to take my telephone privilege for granted. "Well, goodbye, Gladys, it was good to talk to you. Shall I call again next week? Then I might have a word with Matthew."

"We'll see. Bye for now."

IN MY IMAGINATION I pictured Dido and myself loading the motorcar with our picnic basket, warm rugs, bathers, macintoshes and little presents for the children who resided with Gladys in her guest house, Sun Set. I saw us setting out from London and, in a leisurely fashion, driving southwest to Portsmouth to take the car ferry to the Isle of Wight. There we would find our way to Sun Set and enroll as paying guests to spend the first of many weekends in Matthew's company. I hoped it was going to be salutary for Dido to visit him on his ground. I thought he might gain a little stature in her eyes since it would be his right to act as host in his new home.

I imagined the three of us taking the sea air together, idling along the promenade and visiting Shanklin Pier. I pictured us sunning ourselves behind the glass screens of ice cream parlors or buying sandwiches and fizzy drinks, then carrying them on tin trays across the pebbles to a spot where we would spread our rugs and have a family picnic.

Though the reality was not quite as enchanting as I had dreamed, Dido and I did make one or two journeys to the Isle of Wight, but I made the first visit alone in mid-October, anxious about a baleful hint Gladys had made down the telephone wires.

"Good evening, Gladys, how are things going?"

No answer.

"Are all the children flourishing?"

"Hmm."

"How is the guest house progressing?"

I heard a sigh.

"Oh, dear, aren't people coming to stay?"

"Well, they come sometimes, but I don't know about staying ...I suppose they might if..."

"If what, Gladys?"

Her silence was an accusation. My anxiety caused all sorts of placatory phrases to flutter in my head. I heard myself saying brightly, "It sounds as if you have room for me. May I come and visit?"

"Please yourself."

"Then I will come on Friday." I mustered all my courage and added, "I would like to speak to Matthew."

In tones of exasperation, Gladys answered, "I don't know why you bother." I thought she was going to put the telephone back in its cradle, but then I heard her say, "Here, catch hold."

Matthew must have been standing very near, for I realized that all through our conversation I had been faintly hearing his whistling breath. I wondered if he always hovered hopefully by when Gladys and I had our laconic telephone talks. I was nearly sure that I had heard the noise of his breathing during other conversations.

"Hallo, Matthew, it is your Mum speaking...Are you being a good boy?...Well, are you being a bad boy then?...Do you want me to come visit you?..." I knew that Matthew's silences were of a different quality from Gladys's. "Are you nodding your head, Matthew? I can't see down the telephone, you know, you will have to tell me your answers."

"Yep."

"Is there anything you would specially like me to bring?"

"Yep."

"What is it?"

"Car."

"Oh, dear, I was thinking of coming by train this time. Could I bring something else?"

"Yep."

"What should it be?"

"Little bit of car."

Even when I was standing beside Matthew and could watch his face, I was rarely able to gauge from his expression how much of his funniness was intentional. He did not expect others to perceive his jokes; he made them for himself. I delighted in his habit of giving no sign that he meant to amuse. If any part of Matthew's intellect was developing well, it was his cultivation of private and gentle jokes. As he grew older and the dimensions of his humor widened, he did learn to relish sharing his funniness, though he never depended on the flattery of laughter.

"Perhaps I can bring you a toy motorcar instead."

"That'll do, Mum."

I journeyed on the train, took the ferry boat across the sea, then rode in a bus round the coast of the Isle to reach the little town of Shanklin. I walked along a street in which every other dwelling seemed to be a guest house, advertising itself by a fanciful name: Linga Longa, Peace be w'ye, The Repose Boarding House. I came to an uphill road where the houses were set less close to one another, and eventually came at a gate marked Sun Set. As I climbed the steps and rang the chiming bell on Gladys's front door, I was still going over her words, or rather the meaning behind them. I wondered in what manner Matthew's presence was having an effect on her clientele. I was alarmed that my affection for him could blind me to any offensive qualities he might have. Gladys's training had always been stringent; she was meticulous about his manners and cleanliness, and she dressed him neatly. I had never perceived any symptoms of aggression or crudeness in him. It was not possible to consider him noisy. He moved timidly and he rarely talked; he only answered questions, and then he used words as economically as if he were sending telegrams.

At that time Matthew was not yet six years old and still small; his legs were thin and unsteady. When he attempted to run it was as if an unexpected gust of wind had seized him and blown him diagonally from the direction he wanted to take. Perhaps people feared his clumsiness? I did not believe guests would flee on account of that sort of fault in so young a child.

As she opened the door I was at once aware that Gladys intended to widen the difference between us. I was no longer to be a friend whom she invited into her kitchen. She ushered me down the hall into the visitor's sitting room, where I was left to wait while she went to make up a tea tray. When she brought the tray to me, there was but one cup on it, and she would not sit down. I was left sitting alone on a new bouncy sofa to contemplate potted plants and tourist brochures.

After I had drunk my tea and eaten two demitasse biscuits, I boldly carried the tray into Gladys's kitchen. I was not sure whether Matthew was home from school yet; he was not. I felt guilty that I had suspected Gladys of keeping him from me. I suggested there might be time before he and the other children returned for her to show me the house. She insisted upon carrying my bag as we mounted the stairs to my room. By the time we had admired all the new wallpapers and the excellent plumbing which her husband had installed, and laughed a little at the slightly erotic swirling shapes that were molded into the pink glass panels that encased the new shower, we were a little more comradely, though I knew that I would not safely be her friend again till she called me by my first name, as she used to. I was unpacking my belongings when I heard the melody of the door bell. I leaned over the banister, but there was no sign of Matthew. I settled down to write in my journal. Time passed, and no one called to say Matthew was home, so I put on my jacket and went to tell Gladys I would go to meet his school bus. As I put my head round the kitchen door I saw Matthew, a napkin tied round his neck, sitting among some other children waiting for his tea.

"There you are, how lovely to see you."

Matthew did not move. Instead his eyes rolled toward Gladys with an expression that was at once loving and obsequious, rather like an obedient spaniel; he seemed to beg for permission to jump up and greet me.

"All right, go and kiss your Mum."

He struggled to free himself from the table and tumbled toward me. I glanced at Gladys over his head. She looked tired and angry. "I was going to send him up to you when he'd eaten his tea."

I did not concern myself over whether I was breaking one of Gladys's rules or eroding her discipline. I simply took his hand and led Matthew from the kitchen. In the passageway I recognized a coat hanging on a peg as one Dido had outgrown. I unhooked it, and seizing Matthew's push chair, I tumbled us out of the door and down the front path. As I tried to harness Matthew into the push chair he gave me the widest of smiles. Then as if he were a rag doll he relaxed all of his body and fluttered his eyelids. This comical piece of acting released us from our constraints. I took a deep breath and decided we should make for the beach.

The early May air felt surprisingly benign as we swung down the hill and turned into a bungalow-lined road that led us toward the sea. The horizon suddenly appeared magnified and made luminous by the light of evening. Everything close to us seemed to possess a last minute of opalescence. The tide was far out, but the tiny plop of lapping waves was very audible along the empty sands. I parked the push chair, then took off our shoes and socks, hiding my wallet among our outer clothes. I carried Matthew to the very edge of the sea. When I set him down on the cold wet sand, he seemed ignited by a wild hilarity. He pushed himself from me and zigzagged into the shallows, then staggered back to where I stood. I reached for him, but he eluded me and veered toward the glittering pools that surrounded humps of weed-covered rocks. There he stood for a moment, then back he came, flinging past me. This time he was following a thin line of shells and fine weedy debris left by the tide. Watching Matthew's erratic gait, I wondered he had not fallen. I was amazed at his stamina. When his strange celebration ended, he was alarmingly breathless.

"Matthew, dear, stand still a minute, you must catch your breath." He appeared unaffected by the raucous noise coming from his chest.

He smiled, "Engine going fast." He pulled my hand down and cupped it over his ribcage. I could feel the heavy, irregular beating of his heart and a mocking echo repeating those thuds in soft reverberations all down his torso.

"Does it hurt?"

"Hurt?" he repeated vaguely, while his foot stirred the sand.

"Is it a bad feeling?"

"'S big." He measured with both his hands from under his chin down to his navel.

"Is it horrid?"

He looked up and gave me an almost imperceptible nod. I stood with my feet in the sea, awed by Matthew's acceptance of an "engine" that must often make such alarming and painful thuds.

The sea lost all color as the light left it. I turned and found Matthew standing a little distance behind me. "Aren't your feet cold, Matthew?"

"Yep, here," he said, pointing to his stomach. I recalled that I had rushed him from the house before he had a chance to eat his tea.

"You are hungry."

"And toilet," he almost shouted, clutching at himself.

"You can pee in the sea, Matthew, the sea won't mind."

He looked at me with shocked consternation. "Oh, Mu-um."

But in the end his need was so urgent that he had to. Hastily he took off his trousers and handed them to me. "Don't look," he ordered and marched away. I started to walk very slowly toward the push chair. When he caught up with me I asked, "Did you manage that?"

"Yep, rainbow," he said smugly. I was surprised by his use of the word. "Washed hands in sea."

I believe Gladys and Matthew were at one in their conviction that the mastery of the art of personal hygiene was a perfection entirely worth devoting themselves to. Matthew remained so faithful to Gladys's teaching that the times we spent together were often punctuated by forthright, almost boastful, announcements that he needed to pee. (He dealt so easily with bowel movements that I was rarely notified.) The rituals, subsequent to both necessities, of washing his hands were his rewards, his specialty—his field of study. I often wished they weren't.

The last of the daylight was leaving the rim of the horizon as I carried the now very tired Matthew across the stones to his push chair. I dressed him and tried to make us both look tidy enough to go into the town to find a suitable place to buy supper.

Drawn by the festive air of the colored lights strung between the lampposts along the seafront, I wheeled the push chair toward the pier. As we drew near I had to steer in and out of the spring holidaymakers who leaned against the sea railings or walked arm in arm up and down the promenade. When we found ourselves abreast of a neon-lighted, music-blaring fish-and-chip shop, Matthew's fatigue left him. He sat upright in the chair and clapped his knees together as if coming to attention, then with an almost devotional gesture tipped his head back and sniffed deeply. I tried to pass quickly by but he strained to be released from the push chair.

"I suppose that is the sort of place where you would like to eat your supper?"

A vigorous nod. "Isn't it too noisy for us?"

"Nope."

"Too crowded?"

"Nope."

I had meanwhile spied a discreetly lighted, altogether more seemly little café a few paces down a side street. "I know of another place which probably serves bigger plates full of fish and chips and then lovely rice pudding." (At home in London that had been his favorite dish.) "There will be no big rowdy boys to barge into us."

"Like 'em."

"You would like the friendly grandmas and grandpas even more." Before he could disagree, I hurried to say, "There are nice ladies who will bring our food to the table. They are waiting for us to come and eat supper in their warm café."

"Oh, Mum."

Trying not to catch even a glimpse of Matthew's expression, I wheeled his chair about and left the esplanade. I hurried him down the side street and sure enough, the place I had chosen had a friendly air, so I unstrapped Matthew from the chair and ushered him through the door. While I stood at the threshold scanning the room for a vacant table, Matthew sauntered between the two lines of stalls, peering at the occupants. When I caught up with him he was pressing himself against the heavy thigh of an elderly woman. She looked up at me and asked, "What's he saying then?"

Her friend forestalled me. "I think he wants to know if you are a granny."

"Yes, darling, I'll be your granny," she answered, hugging Matthew to her.

Before I could restrain him, he was climbing onto the bench beside her. "Sit there, Mum."

The woman who was sitting on the opposite side of the table obliged him by sliding along her bench so as to accommodate me—I had no choice but to sit down.

Matthew was by now staring at his new friend's plate. His eyes followed her fork back and forth as she put food into her mouth. All at once, like a stalking creature seizing its prey, he shot both of his hands forth and simultaneously seized a fried potato from each of the women's plates. Under any other circumstances, I would have been delighted by such coordination—I did not know he could be so dexterous—but now I was mortified. I could feel my blushes burning even to my forehead. Both women burst into laughter and Matthew giggled with them. Putting an arm comfortably about his shoulders and giving him a companionable squeeze, the larger woman said, "Poor little mite, has his mum kept him from having his dinner all this long evening, then?"

Matthew looked up at her and half closed his eyes, letting his long lashes rest on his now pink and glowing cheeks. As I sat and watched him, half hearing the murmurous exchanges between Matthew and the women, salient words such as *cod, haddock,* and *little cherub* reached my ears. I wondered if Matthew could possibly be aware of his charm, or had he momentarily closed his eyes because of the bright lights? Perhaps those long and seemingly affectionate stares he was now bestowing upon each woman in turn signified that he was having difficulty in focusing? I resolved to ask Gladys to have his sight tested. Meanwhile, I was impatient for the waitress to bring a menu so that we could order our own meal. By the time she got to our table, Matthew had purloined so many morsels of food from his new friends' plates that I felt it only proper to offer them a pot of tea and a choice of ice cream in recompense. The women accepted graciously and became very affable as they took up the fan-shaped wafers and supped their pink ice creams.

All at once it was time for them to gather their belongings and to put on their coats.

"Come rain, come shine, dear," said one flourishing an umbrella.

"Landlady bolts our door at nine, little Cinderellas, that's us."

I got to my feet, too, and tried to think of appropriate words that would express my gratitude for their jolly and affectionate company. I did not get the words out.

"Made our evening, he has. Wonderful company, aren't you, my pet?"

Matthew hardly allowed the kisses that were being bestowed on his cheek to interrupt his task of collecting mounds of fish with his fingers and cramming them into his mouth, but he waved vigorously as they left the booth.

"Matthew, I think you were too familiar with those two ladies. You should not have taken food from their plates."

"Best friends," he said. Then with a gesture worthy of a conjurer he thrust his arms out so that his clenched fists almost touched my face. Pleased that he had surprised me, he slowly uncurled his fingers. In each palm he displayed a half crown.

"Matthew, how ever did you come by such a large sum of money?"

"Grannies." He looked very demure. I was appalled they had tipped him and so much! That amount would have bought a night's keep at their boarding house or a day's meals and amusements on the promenade. "You must never take money from strangers."

"Grannies."

Resolving that I would, as soon as possible, put the money in a charity box, I took two pennies from my purse and offered to swap them for his half crowns.

"Yep, they better."

When I was helping him back into his push chair, I saw that he had not bothered to pick the pennies up from the table.

MATTHEW WAS ASLEEP by the time I found our way back to Sun Set. Gladys had left her front door on the latch. As she came to help me unbuckle Matthew, it was obvious that her attitude toward me had undergone another change. Her apprehensive expression made me feel remorseful. Without considering her feelings I had swept Matthew out of the kitchen and away to the beach. It was apparent that I had caused her to suffer an uneasy evening. I wanted to apologize but she beat me to it.

"Don't heed me, Anne, I haven't been acting right for quite a spell. I'll get over it. Hope you aren't thinking of taking your Matthew off my hands. I can always manage him, you know, a sight easier than me own family, truth to tell."

We were climbing the stairs as she spoke. "There now, young Matthew, you aren't too tired to take yourself off to the toilet. I'll be along to make sure you've washed your mug and cleaned your teeth."

Tactfully she conceded me the right to tuck him into his bed. He went back to sleep so quickly that neither of us received a kiss good night.

The next morning I was wakened by Gladys's daughter, Lil. She was standing by my bed carefully pouring a puddle of muddy looking tea from a saucer back into a cup.

"Mum says to tell you, more in the pot but you'll have to come down for it. Breakfast in the kitchen and she hopes you don't want it cooked like all them fancy boarders do."

By the time I entered the kitchen, only Matthew was seated at the table, a cat on his knees. I took a seat beside him. Gladys was occupying herself at the stove.

"Our Kev is at football practice, and our Lil has taken little Alex round to her friend's house."

"And Fred?" I had not seen her husband since my arrival.

There was a prolonged crashing of dishes in the sink. "Gone back to his mum, hasn't he? Found a job, temporary, he tells me. Didn't find enough work here, so he says. Didn't see him trying very hard."

She came over to the table and slammed down two cups of hot water. She stirred a large amount of powdered coffee into them both, then pushed one cup toward me and sat down. Warming her hands around her cup.

"Won't be able to stand that company for long, will he?"

Gladys's habit of ending her sentences with a question was more pronounced when she was upset.

"Oh, Gladys, I'm so sorry. How could anyone have guessed there would be too many plumbers on this island?"

We sat in sad, amicable silence. Both our thoughts were taken up with the anxiety Gladys's husband was causing her. "Here I am forgetting me manners. Hope you didn't want tea. Your toast is keeping warm in the oven. I'll fetch it over."

She dashed from her seat. Another clatter at the stove and she was at my side, this time a bright and brave smile on her face. In a folded tea cloth she presented me with a plate that was too hot to touch. On it lay four neatly cut triangles of toast. I offered one to Matthew.

"Don't you dare, that's your Mum's breakfast. Had yours long ago. You put that old puss cat down. I don't know if your Mum wants to come, but me and you've got to go and do our Saturday shopping."

While I sat sipping the powdered drink and toying with the pile of margarined toast, I considered Gladys's honest exposure of Fred's paltry retreat. I was convinced that her vision of life in a holiday resort was now over. She had revealed to me all the fragility of that dream, and I wondered how I was going to put it to Theo that there would soon be a need for another set of changes.

She would have to return to London if she wanted to reclaim Fred. The excellent school Matthew now was attending? And the beneficent sea air as against his being in London once more? Anyway, in the light of what was expedient for Gladys and her family, my preference was of no consequence. As far as I was concerned, she might live where she pleased as long as she kept Matthew by her side, even next door to the dreaded mother-in-law. If that was to be her last ditch, I depended upon her offering Matthew a place in it.

I watched Gladys as she stood before the looking glass that hung above the mantelpiece. She took a rather grubby hairbrush and dabbed at the front of her hair before she applied a few strokes of the brush to Matthew's head. Placing the brush back on the shelf, she reached for her handbag, snapped it open, took out a lipstick, and standing on tiptoe stretched and pursed her lips as she painted them. She squatted to Matthew's level and took his face between her fingers and thumb. He too made comical grimaces as she gently touched the lipstick to his lips. She dropped the lipstick back into her handbag and lifted Matthew to see his reflection in the glass. As she placed him back on the floor she murmured, "You taking yours, then?"

Matthew nodded and crossed the room to a wooden orange crate that served him as a toy box. He dragged out a shabby, maroon-colored handbag, much like the one Gladys was now slinging over her shoulder. I was more and more intrigued by what was evidently their Saturday morning ritual. Their last little ceremony was to stand beside each other as they each gripped the sides of their clothing and in unison performed lascivious wriggling movements. I realized Gladys, at least, was pulling down her girdle. My laugh made her sheepish.

"Forgot you was there. Matthew and me, we must look a right pair. He likes doing same as me, the saucy monkey. Does so want to be like, don't you, Matt? You don't mind him having my old handbag? Keeps his bits and bobs in it. Go and show your Mum, then. Don't think it's sissy, do you?"

Indeed I did not. I was touched by Gladys's concession to Matthew's need to be "like," as she put it. I could see what she meant when she said she could manage Matthew a sight easier than her own family. Inside the bag I saw nothing but torn-up newspaper.

I took a deep breath. "Gladys, I think you want to give all this up." I hurried through my next words. "I am speaking for

Theo as well as myself. If you and Fred are considering return-ing to London and could bring yourselves to accept our help, we could afford..."

Gladys gave a little sigh of relief and turned toward me. On her face there was a smile that was at the same moment honest and sly. "From the telephone box like, so as his mum couldn't sniff out our business, me and Fred had a talk last night after you'd gone to bed a bit along those lines. We were sort of con-sidering asking you..."

A few weeks later, Theo received a typed letter from Fred Strong. The postmark told us that he was back on the island. His notepaper heading bore the Sun Set address and spelled out all his credentials as a plumber. In excessively formal sentences he emphasized that it was his principle never to borrow money, but he named a modest sum, assuring Theo that it would be enough for a down payment on a house "anywhere in London." In return for our help he offered to move his family to a locality of Theo's choosing "so that young Matthew can settle into the right school." He ended his letter by spelling out his plan for re-paying the money, adding that "Matthew's weekly cost will be de-ducted."

I went again to the Isle of Wight as Theo's emissary. I handed over the last of my dowry to Gladys, and in return accepted a signed and witnessed acknowledgment from Fred.

"Me and you know it's your money and my know-how. Good letter, wasn't it though? Poor old Fred, has to save his face, doesn't he?"

A week or two later Gladys telephoned me. "Turns out Fred's already found us the right place. It's in Isleworth. A very nice school for the likes of Matthew nearby. Yesterday Fred and our Lil coped here so as I could do the day trip to London and give it the once-over. It's a bit near Heathrow. Good house, nice quiet road, can't say the same for the sky, though. Don't suppose a few noises from up there matter much. Anyway, Fred's a dab hand at double glazing."

CHAPTER SEVENTEEN
Isleworth/David

The years from 1970 to 1974 were relatively tranquil. Theo was earning what he called "a real living." The Strong family—Matthew with them—were cozily ensconced in the house in Isleworth, just in time for Christmas of 1970. Seemingly none of them were bothered by the noises in the sky. At the start of the new year, Gladys was once again practicing as a licensed foster mother. Schools had been found for the two Strong children, and Matthew was about to attend the Linden Bennett "school for little dopes"—Gladys's definition—in the adjoining borough of Hansworth. It was plain to me that Matthew was content in his role of appendage to the Strong family. He loved Gladys and saw himself as part jester and part sibling to the babies she fostered. The limitations and regularities she imposed upon him gave his life an understandable pattern such as I never could have achieved.

WHEN I DROVE the five or so miles to visit Matthew, both he and Gladys found ways to remind me that I was only a visitor. I could never divine quite how much of a support or an interloper I was. When I arrived, Gladys always asked me to come indoors "for a bit"; she would let me know when that bit was up. "About time for you to take his nibs off my hands, then?" or "You want to go for a nice ride with your mum, don't you, Matthew?" At that point, he and I would either set out on a short exploratory journey or drive to one of his preferred destinations: local churches, playgrounds, garden suppliers, hardware stores. When Gladys granted us enough time, Matthew liked being brought back to our house in Hammersmith, there to have a meal or to play awhile before he suggested we visit any one of my friends: "Time to go 'n see so-and-so, eh Mum?"

On every school day unless he was ill or she wanted him to stay at home, Gladys never failed to have Matthew ready for the "special bus." It happened that two other children who attended the same school lived close by. One was an altogether lopsided little black boy and the other a large motherly girl whose harelip and belligerent look were delightful to Matthew. In her company, a natural courtesy caused him to adopt her manner of speaking so that the bus driver assumed, till Gladys enlightened him, that Matthew, too, had a cleft palate.

Gladys described to me how the children took it in turn to choose which of all the front gates on her road they would stand behind while waiting for the bus. She told me the owners of the houses had learned to accept this odd trio of interlopers and the bus driver was expected to drive his bus very slowly till he spied them.

I asked Matthew about his school. "What is it like there?"

"Dunno."

"What do you do at school, Matthew?"

"Go toilet, sing 'Hallo Jesus 'n his father God a men,' do pictures, do sewing, do dancing, go toilet some more, wash hands, eat dinner, lie down a bit 'n play." As an afterthought he added, "Dinner's nicest, 'n Jerry."

I did not know the names of his two traveling companions so I asked, "Is Jerry a girl or a boy?"

"Nope."

On suitably warm Saturday mornings Matthew liked to be dressed and ready at an earlier hour. This was because the milkman allowed him to ride on the milk float all the way up on the one side of the street and then down on the other. Matthew enjoyed ringing or knocking on doors and being encouraged to sing out, "Milko!" He carried the empty bottles back to the float to put them in racks. Sometimes the milkman let Matthew help steer. Gladys told me that on one occasion the milkman tried to tip Matthew and Matthew's feelings were hurt. Overhearing his protests, Gladys hurried out. Matthew managed to explain to her, and she to the milkman, that Matthew did not want a tip from the milkman because the rides were the greatest pleasure of his week. Matthew and the milkman shook hands.

FROM MY JOURNAL
Tuesday 17 June 1971

Yesterday Gladys telephoned to announce that she was keeping Matthew "back" from school. "You know he picks up bad habits there. Best to let him stop at home a day or two, give him time to mend his ways, don't you think? You can have him one of the days if you want."

"What sort of bad habits, Gladys?"

"What happened Saturday, to give you the idea. Alex was away with his Mum. Me and Matthew took Ali down the shops. I had Ali in the pram. No room for Matthew, what with all the shopping. He was dawdling a bit—I thought it was just his legs was tired—till I caught sight of him in the shoe shop window glass. You know what your boy was doing? Only dragging one leg, flopping his arms about, holding his head funny and dribbling out of his mouth. Acting like the worst lad at the school, he was. Sees too many of that sort, he does. I'm not having him acting handicapped and showing me up in my own high street like that."

Gladys decided that it needed more than two days of corrective absence from school to properly brace Matthew so that he would resist the baleful influences of his schoolfellows, so I drove to her house twice to bring him to Hammersmith for the day.

"Keep your eye on him, mind, don't want no more of his Mickey Mouse antics, now, do we, young man? You've got to remind him it's not funny to act like a retard. Not kind neither."

As Matthew and I arrived at our house we could hear the ring of the telephone. My friend David Sylvester was on the line to confide to me all over again how much he longed to live alone. He told me that today he was going to do something practical about it. He needed me to chauffeur him round his neighborhood. He had obtained a list of likely houses from the local estate agent, and I was to help him choose one that would suit his family.

"Why don't you take Pamela? She is the one who has to move into the house."

"I want it to be a fait accompli; in effect I am giving her a present, aren't I?"

I wondered if she would see it in that light. I warned him that I would be bringing Matthew along.

"I'd like that very much."

Matthew nodded and smiled. He had been sharing the receiver with me, pressing his head alongside mine, apparently listening with great attention, though he may only have been doing his duty by the telephone. He respects it, is enamored of it, delights in its ring. He sometimes likes to test its persistence by picking up the receiver as late as possible. We occasionally miss calls because of this game. That upsets him, and he blames the instrument.

David, his wife, Pamela, and three large daughters live in a confined ground floor flat in Wandworth. It contains one spacious room in which David displays precious objects. A large Roman head stands on a formidable sideboard. Several Benin bronze bells are arranged (and rearranged) around it. A broad table is crowded with David's latest purchases, which vary as he does deals with auction houses. A few of his treasures remain constant among them, a polished African parcheesi board and a narrow, sickly white marble Egyptian arm.

There is almost no space on the table for David and his visiting secretary to do his writing, yet two ponderous chairs await them. Artistically repaired Persian carpets hang from the walls and a precious but threadbare rug covers most of the floor. Three Ashanti chieftain's stools stand beneath the shuttered windows. On the wall just inside the door, eerie and dominating, David has hung his portrait by Francis Bacon. Who would dare perform mundane secretarial tasks beneath such a picture? It would be as unsuitable as allowing daylight or his children to invade. Honored visitors must remove their shoes and, once over the threshold, submit patiently as David catechizes them to the point that he has their total endorsement of the room's appearance.

The next largest room is the marital bedroom, which serves as a sitting room, homework room, and a room in which to watch television. Adult meals are eaten from one's knees while one is seated on a huge double bed, and a great deal of quarreling takes place behind its closed doors. There is a little sideways slice of a kitchen, its walls hung with glass-covered scribbly ballpoint drawings torn from one of Willem de Kooning's yellow pads. The remaining room belongs to the children. It is dark and filled by a two-tiered bed and another beside it, which leaves just enough space for a chest of drawers and a wardrobe. Certainly David needs to buy a house for his family.

Matthew and I arrived at David's flat exactly on time. Matthew likes to ring David's doorbell, and even more he enjoys the noises made by the sequence of lock turnings, burglar alarm mutings, and drawing of bolts that David must go through on the other side of his front door. I reminded Matthew about the grand room. He must only peep in. Luckily it is the kitchens of other people's houses that interest him. Today David's wife was gone to her job as a teacher and his daughters were at school. As he opened the door to us, we saw that David was wearing a peculiarly short and ornate dressing gown. Matthew stepped boldly in and almost attached himself to David, that is, he stood as near to him as he could and regarded him with immediate and intimate affection. It is curious that Matthew seems to know instantly whom it is he will love. David is somewhat the same. We waited and waited for David. Now and then he emerged from the bathroom partially dressed to make an urgent phone call. He was extremely patient when Matthew insisted he dial the numbers and listen to the voices too. David, at last fully dressed, picked up his briefcase and keys, re-alarmed the flat, and trebly locked the door from the outside.

Holding Matthew's hand, David padded down the path and climbed into the motorcar. His bulk filled the front seat. From the back, Matthew leaned his head on David's shoulder and stroked his arm. I drove following David's directions. We picked up keys and a list of houses from the house agent's office.

David was not brief in his cataloging of the shortcomings of every house we saw. Matthew and I had to pretend to be Pamela and three big girls as we tramped up and down stairs and in and out of cramped bedrooms or tiny sitting rooms. Matthew tilted his head, the better to watch David; I wondered if it was not merely his glasses that made him seem to concentrate on what David said. He took David's hand. David was very polite to Matthew, which Matthew graciously reciprocated.

Seated in the motorcar once more, David gave way to his woes. Huge sighs came from him, then a long silence. I did not dare start the motor. Matthew pulled a toy motorcar from his pocket and leaned from the rear seat to run it to and fro, lightly and comfortingly, across David's broad shoulders. At last David asked in a rhetorical voice, "Well then, do I or do I not buy one of those houses? Do I sacrifice most of my capital to accommodate my family? Does this mean I am finally parting from Pamela?"

I cannot guess what motivated Matthew to lean forward so that his mouth was close to David's ear, then to say, "'Sright, Davie, you do it. Good boy."

The following day I was allowed to have Matthew again. When I rang Gladys's doorbell he was waiting on the other side. He had prepared a joke. As he opened the door he said, "Where's Davie?" Then with a glint in his eye which I saw even through his spectacles, he stepped round me and bent down as if making a careful search for something—or in this case, someone—very small indeed, perhaps only the size of an ant. He looked up and gave a shout of laughter as he broke into a caper, flapping his arms and slapping his knees, "Davie not here, Mum."

David says he is glad Matthew has decided to call him Davie, it is the name his mother uses when she feels affectionate toward him.

I HAVE WONDERED if the moves David subsequently made were not in some part due to Matthew's firm instruction, for he bought a house—though not any of those we viewed—and he kept the flat all for himself.

FROM EARLIEST CHILDHOOD, Matthew possessed a propensity that appeared to cause him a kind of pleasurable anguish. He had, as the French say, "antennae" that made him particularly conscious of distress. Tongue-tied by fear of intruding or not being able to express his sympathy, an almost clown-like, sorrowful expression would spread across his face as he made timid gestures to convey his awareness and his commiseration. He seemed for a short while to suffer an exaggerated apathy. His head would droop, his hands caress his knees until he found the courage to stroke the arm or shoulder of the small child, the friend, or even a stranger. He might lean down so as to be able to look upward into the person's eyes. From this position he did his best to entice a smile to their lips; sometimes he resorted to pulling comic faces or pretending to cry. If he found he was failing to distract, then he would turn away and hang his head. I witnessed this empathy overtake Matthew many times. Toward

the end of his life, perhaps too fancifully, I came to see his awareness of people's grief as a reminder of what he needed us to feel
for him.

WHEN SHE WAS twelve and Matthew nearly ten years old, Dido,
who had been suffering pains in her legs, was found to have a form
of arthritis. In the spring of 1974 an operation was prescribed;
Theo and I sought second and third opinions but the operation
was unavoidable. After lengthy surgery an infection set in. Dido
became mortally ill and remained so for months on end. Again
and again, she was operated upon, but still the infection did not
quit her body. Unless Theo took my place, I rarely left her side.
She and I lived in St. Charles' Hospital together, my bed beside
hers; we hardly noticed day from night, our respites came with
her opiates. Her father and I waited desperately for the doctors
to predict her recovery, which at last began to happen.

In all this time I was unable to pay attention to Matthew or
help Gladys in her care of him. Although she seemingly accepted
the necessity for this, telling me, "You can leave off bothering
over him while your Dido's so poorly," eventually she must have
found taking full responsibility for Matthew too much of a burden, for as was her custom, she composed a letter for her husband to send to my husband. In it he asked Theo to name the
likely date of Matthew's removal from his wife's care.

I had not, as Gladys later suggested, forgotten Matthew, but
was seeing him as if from a distance and through the torment of
Dido's plight. For the first time in their lives, he appeared the
stronger of the two, the one whom I could put aside for a while.
After those awful episodes of pain and fear, vestiges of this view
of Matthew remained with me, for I found I had acquired a facility for consigning him to a separate part of my mind where the
weight of him was at times light, and from then on only rarely
unbearably heavy.

I telephoned Gladys to tell her Dido was beginning to recover, "Oh, Anne, I feel that awful. Course you've had other

things to think about. After we sent that letter I said to my Fred, 'Just imagine if it was our Lil.' That did it. You leave your boy with us till Dido's herself again; by then it's likely he'll be brassy enough to enjoy boarding at your old MacIntyre School." On Theo's behalf I offered to pay more for his board, at which Gladys snorted and rang off.

CHAPTER EIGHTEEN

Miss Stromwell

rather In. dido holiday activity did not morning which Doctor mac... entirely approve of but which Did... managed to enjoy.

As I arrived to meet Dido at the end of her school day, her teacher, Miss Stromwell—who had a reputation for great insight and Nordic thoroughness—took me aside to tell me that she had discovered Dido could not hear properly. This teacher often gave me the sensation that I was in the company of a sad and clever little overweight girl. Her large blue eyes stared as if bravely from a fine broad head, which seemed to require more support than her invisible neck gave. This babyish appearance did nothing to contradict her forceful profile.

With distressing tact she questioned me to elicit what I was sure she already knew, that Dido had a mentally handicapped brother. Hardly had she drawn this from me before she launched into what I guessed was a prepared speech. She suspected Dido was not so much physically deaf as unwilling to hear. Miss Stromwell had noticed other symptoms in the child, "an air of isolation, of melancholy, even." Dido, she said, rarely played with the other children. She preferred being a spectator, so much so that her companions had named her "the judge." I hoped it was meant hypocoristically. I wondered if Dido needed deafness and, if so, what for. To ward off boredom? I had not noticed any defects in her hearing, but I supposed the closed-down expression that I knew so well could be mistaken for deafness. Miss Stromwell, as she expatiated on the psychological implications of having a sibling such as Matthew, was so earnest in her statements of the obvious that I was tempted to become as deaf as Dido. I promised to discuss her concerns with my husband.

Dido was waiting for me in the motorcar. In her imagination, she was not alone; two eagles, Goldie and Silver, were perched on the backs of our motorcar seats, and through the open window she held the leading rein of Flyer, her amazing white steed. Not in the least interested in the reason her teacher had delayed me, she cautioned me to drive carefully so as not to injure Flyer.

A few afternoons later, Dido brought home a note from Miss Stromwell; in it, she in effect asked herself to tea. She "wished so much to meet the rest of her little pupil's family." Recognizing the euphemism, I sent an answering note, telling her that Dido's father seldom came home before seven o'clock and Matthew was at present living with a foster mother in Isleworth. Miss Stromwell was not so easily put off. In a next note she asked if I would take her to Isleworth to visit Dido's little brother one day soon. She felt it would be helpful in her understanding of Dido.

I told myself that her motives were surely decent. I asked Dido if she would like Miss Stromwell to come to tea with us.

"I suppose we've got to do what she wants, she's the teacher, and we're the only ones she has not been to tea with."

"I do not have to do what she wants; you do, but only while you're at school."

"Oh, well, she can come if she likes, and see *him* too, if that's what she's asking for."

I warned Gladys that we would be bringing Dido's teacher to meet Matthew. She was surprisingly conversant with such proceedings. "Wants to meet Dido's little brother, does she? Dunno what good it will do anybody. I'll remind Matthew to be a good boy."

So later that week, we suffered a strained little tea party. Dido obligingly displayed the symptoms of a deaf, withdrawn child. She ate almost nothing, and she scowled a little as she passed plates of sandwiches and slices of cake. Like Gladys, I had issued a reminder concerning good manners, in Dido's case meaning she should not quit the table till the ceremony was over, and even if she brought her imaginary eagles to the table (how could I stop her?), she was not to feed them morsels of food.

"You hurt their feelings, calling them imaginary," was all she said.

After we had eaten our tea, I drove us the few miles to the Strong's house. The door knocker was freshly polished, and Matthew opened the door to us. He wore his best blue velvet shorts, a clean blouse, white socks, and his new sandals. Altogether he seemed a little too perfect. As if he'd been rehearsed in his role, Matthew conducted us to the front room, where "Auntie Gladys" was waiting, a beautiful Asian-looking little boy in her arms. For once she was apronless. Clearly she knew just how this encounter should be conducted. She asked Miss Stromwell to make herself at home, then explained that though Matthew was not much of a talker, he understood everything. "That's right, isn't it Matthew?"

Matthew nodded. It crossed my mind that the two of them had made some sort of pact. "Now shake hands with the nice teacher."

Miss Stromwell and Gladys were seated on either side of the fireplace, and, as if we were their audience, Dido and I, somewhat removed from the scene, sat on the sofa. Placing the baby boy in front of Matthew, Gladys gave his two hands into Matthew's, and nudging them along said, "Show our Ali to the teacher, Matthew." With Matthew's support, Ali took a few steps forward and teetered in front of Miss Stromwell. All of us became aware of her agitation. Matthew's reaction was instant. He turned his little friend around and steered him back into Gladys's arms.

Miss Stromwell collected herself and said vaguely, "How sweet, wherever does he come from?" She beckoned to Matthew, who gave her a brief glance and pressed himself against Gladys's knee. "Go and be nice to the teacher," she said. This time she gave him a shove. As if at a puppet show, Dido and I watched Matthew sauntering toward Miss Stromwell. With one hand she stroked his hair while leaving the other hand lying on her lap. Both Dido and I tensed as he picked up the hand, and unclasped the fingers.

After giving us a roguish glance, he let drop from his lips a great gob of spit; it landed in her palm.

A shudder went through her, accompanied by a tight little scream. Almost giggling, Gladys plumped Ali on the floor, saying, "The saucy little monkey, how did he think up a trick like that?" Meanwhile, Matthew appeared oddly gallant in his stance, as if he had just carried out a necessary duty on his little friend's behalf.

Gladys left the room, in no time returning with a soapy washcloth and a clean towel. As if Miss Stromwell was one of her "kids," she took her hand and washed it vigorously, then handed her the towel. Without any degree of conviction, she said, "I'm sure Matthew's very sorry he did such a naughty thing." I noticed that this time she didn't ask Matthew to verify her statement, nor did she make him apologize. A look of admiration had flickered across Dido's face as she sidled from the room.

I expected Miss Stromwell to resume her role of gracious ~~helper~~ teacher, *who was usually so* always ready with a psychological explanation, but all such refinements were gone. Her expression made me prudent about giving Matthew his goodbye kiss. I deprived him of it in the hope that Miss Stromwell would remain cordial toward Dido, *during her fifth* but the look she gave my daughter as I climbed into the motor- *morning of constructive play* car where she had taken cover made me doubtful.

After delivering Miss Stromwell to her *little* house and seeing Dido into her bath, I telephoned Gladys to ask her to give Matthew a kiss on my behalf and tell him I was sorry for not having done so. "Oh, he didn't notice, he's as right as rain. Enjoyed it all, I shouldn't wonder. Couldn't find it in my heart to scold him, could I? ~~Calls herself a teacher, then?~~ Dido all right, is she?" I said yes, but ~~in fact~~ I hoped to find out by keeping her up until her father came home so that I could hear her version of the incident. She did not mention it.

Calls herself one of those child terrapins does she I would let my Juline anyway near her

CHAPTER NINETEEN

Mount Tabor House

Before Theo and I dared believe that the first MacIntyre School was properly established at Westoning Manor House (the place Dave Simmonds Smith "had his eyes on"), yet another establishment was offered to us.

A group of Anglican sisters had for many years dedicated their lives to the care of a congregation of mentally handicapped people living at Mount Tabor House, situated in the village of Westoning. These elderly sisters were now fervent in their wish to discontinue this duty and be allowed to spend their remaining years under the roof of their mother convent on the south coast. Their mother superior came to visit the MacIntyre School at Westoning Manor. After the briefest of inspections, she left again. A short while later, she and her bishop sent us a joint letter offering an astounding bargain: Mount Tabor manor house, its stables and outbuildings, its lodges and grounds, would all be ours on condition we also accept and care for its present inmates, who had been living there for so long that they could remember no other home.

So in 1971, our new board of governors became the owners of Mount Tabor House, a pretentious, turn-of-the-century property, which with the exception of its fine mahogany doors, the staircase, and a large collection of red fire buckets was painted throughout in green and cream. Before she departed, Mother Superior put together for our guidance a folder of notes and reminders, which I read with great interest. It contained very astute summaries of the characters and foibles of every one of the seventeen "poor souls" whom the sisters were to leave behind. Each summary had attached to it a succinct little addendum which rated the degree of support we could expect from their relations. Not one un-Christian sentiment was to be found in that document, yet by the time I finished reading it I had been made aware of everyone's shortcomings.

Mother Superior told our board of governors that she had exacted a promise from "every soul" who was to be left in our charge that they would recite their prayers night and morning and always attend mass on Sundays, a pledge which she expected them to honor and us to facilitate.

Before the Anglican sisters took over Mount Tabor House, it had been known as Wingrave Manor. In 1975, when Matthew was first put there, I would pass through the wintry village of Wingrave to reach the house, now and again to find Matthew more than usually frail and gray-faced. On my return journey, again through the village, I might in a state of superstitious sadness appreciate the renaming of the Manor. Mount Tabor, a place where prayers were perhaps listened to, seemed vastly less doom-laden than a manor house called "Win Grave."

By the time Matthew joined MacIntyre School, the entire interior of Mount Tabor House had long since been repainted. The very few "Souls," as they had come to be known, who were still there slept in rooms of their own. A large television set was installed in the once "silent room," and the fire buckets were gone forever. (The sand they contained proved irresistible to the children who came to live in the manor house.)

The Souls missed their old disciplines, the early rising, the prayers and hymn singing, the exact folding of clothes and making of beds, and the year-in-year-out repetitive chores. Not wishing to exploit them, our newly engaged staff were reluctant to allot tasks or issue orders, so the Souls persisted as best they could, murmured prayers and hummed hymns as they washed, polished, swept, and laid tables. It took months for them to teach us how to administer to their needs. There was a great deal of pouting, weeping, and door slamming until one day Mother Superior paid us a surprise visit. She scouted around and quickly grasped the situation. In no time she set things in relative order, a less disciplined and more lackadaisical order than that of her time, but an organized system which satisfied the Souls and suited our more modern scheme of things.

Most of the Souls had welcomed the presence of little children, but a few strongly, even spitefully, objected to their intrusion. These, on the advice of Mother Superior, were rather forcefully promoted to Westoning Manor, which was now recognized as the senior part of MacIntyre School.

None of the Souls made old bones. This troubled me. The news of each death seemed a very sad defeat until Dr. Weihs assured me that a short life was usual among the mentally handicapped.

After many months Dido was well enough to go back to school, albeit in a wheelchair. This event prompted Gladys, who evidently had spies in our street, to telephone and remind me, "There's the question of Matthew. Truth to tell, Anne, he's not really family no more. We can't always take him to the places we want to go. It makes Fred feel he's got to keep explaining your Matthew's not ours and all that. Anyway, what's the use of your going to all the trouble of arranging that MacIntyre place of yours if you don't think it's good enough for his nibs. I'll miss the little blighter, but it's time for him to go."

CHAPTER TWENTY

Prison Officer

On a dark October Sunday afternoon in 1975, Theo and I once again found ourselves forcing our motorcar through a spectacular rainstorm to reach a place where we intended to confine our son. The drama of this much longer journey was intensified by Matthew's actual presence. When we made that first visit to Normansfield Hospital eight years before, Matthew was our worry, he filled our consciousness, but he was not with us. Driving to Normansfield and back so many times seemed to have inoculated me. I managed to conduct us through this second distressing expedition with a certain detachment.

Though his appearance might have led an outsider to guess his age to have been eight or nine, Matthew was now eleven years old. He was going away to boarding school clothed in a proper boy's outfit: gray shirt and shorts, knee socks that even garters could not clasp to his thin legs, and heavy brown shoes with laces. He proudly wore a goodbye present from Gladys, a newly knitted gray cardigan. In putting together this outfit, it was as if she and I were hoping to armor him, to protect him from we knew not what.

We splashed our way around London to reach the M-1 Motorway, which would take us to Buckinghamshire. As we drove along, Matthew repeatedly slid from where he sat in the back to crouch against my driving seat, from there to whisper his fears of the bad weather hotly in my ear. When Theo reprimanded him, he would reseat himself and make another effort to be brave, until his anxiety became so urgent that we had to stop under the canopy of a petrol station where, with his rag doll (later to be known as "Boy") around his neck, Matthew tum-

125

bled out of the rear door of the car and tugged frantically on the front door handle. Theo turned it for him, and he clambered onto his father's lap and pressed his face against his chest.

I had to steer more and more cautiously against the oncoming headlamps, whose beams were being fragmented by teeming rain. All the while Matthew was either squeezing his eyes shut or leaning toward me urging me to "stop the weather." I tried to make him understand that I did not possess the power to quieten storms, till in desperation he bellowed, "Can't see; can't see through noisy rain. You stop it *now,* or Dad have to."

Theo from his own state of nervousness answered tartly, "I leave all that sort of cleverness to your mother."

As a last resort Matthew tore off his spectacles and fumblingly tried to stuff them in my pocket, a precaution he took only when he felt he was under unbearable duress. Perhaps in the belief that his action might aid the windscreen wipers, he spread the fingers of both hands as widely as he could and agitated them to and fro. Theo let him continue this frenetic mime for a few minutes, then gathered Matthew's fingers into his own and firmly tucked all he could of him into the shelter of his overcoat. Although Matthew soon fell to sleep, Theo persisted in gently singing an African lullaby till we arrived at our destination.

As we turned onto the final byroad, we left the storm behind us, and our way was suddenly illumined by rays of a cupreous sunset. Repetition had reduced Theo's little song into an incantation, a mantra against whatever each of us was anticipating. Had either one of us, during those minutes, been foolhardy enough to make a sympathetic gesture or utter a few commiserating words, a great sadness might have overtaken us. Having learned to accommodate each other's private anguish and thus achieve a fragile accord apropos Matthew's banishment, we seemed to have forfeited the art of comforting each other.

A YEAR EARLIER, my cousin had dispatched a removal van of overlarge family furniture to the new MacIntyre School at Mount

Tabor House. I had helped distribute carpets, a dining table and chairs, a huge sideboard, sofas, chests of drawers, and all sorts of bedroom furniture about the gloomy Victorian rooms. So though I had not yet been introduced to the new headmaster and his wife, I felt quite familiar with the place where Matthew was going to live. As we stepped through the front door into the hall, it was evident that changes had occurred. Two of the lofty paneled doors had "No Entry" notices tacked to them. Screwed onto a wall was a large board to which were pinned typed lists of rules telling of meal- and bedtimes, bath rosters, folding of clothes, forbidding running or talking in corridors, forbidding leaving doors open, and a reminder as to the purpose of the doormat. Was it expected that any little inhabitant of Mount Tabor House was able to read one word of this officious nonsense? Gone from the long settle were the piles of coats and jackets; no Wellington boots lay on the floor; no longer were "lost and found" toys displayed on the mantelpiece. The three of us stood beneath a branched wooden chandelier that had been robbed of all but two electric bulbs.

Matthew was not cast down. Standing beside his new suitcase, he pulled at Theo's coat with one hand and swung his doll to and fro with the other, singing, "Supper soon, supper soon." Suddenly and silently the headmaster and his wife materialized. Before any courtesies were exchanged, the wife's hand shot forward and nabbed Matthew's suitcase. He laughed and tried to push her hand aside. She let go her hold as if she had been scalded. Meanwhile Theo was removing from under his arm a rather ostentatiously expensive bottle of brandy. This time it was the headmaster's hand that shot forth. For a few seconds we were all as still as a tableau: the headmaster and his wife with their expressionless faces; Theo, his shoulders drawn up, an embarrassed look on his face; Matthew, still with a firm grasp on his suitcase, gazing questioningly at me; and I, intent upon not revealing the aversion I felt for the gruesome pair who stood before us.

After what probably was a mere moment, Theo made a shrug that seemed to release us all. In an unwilling, ambling fashion he obeyed the headmaster, who, while holding his newly acquired brandy bottle in one hand, was gesturing toward a door labeled "Private" with the other.

"Your son should take off his coat and come through here." The wife opened another door, that of the playroom. Inside I saw most of the ambulatory residents waiting, one behind the other, in a rambling line. The wife noticed my amazement. "We are teaching them to stand in an orderly line while they wait for the second supper bell." As she spoke, that bell clanged, the line began to drift across the hall and through the dining room door. Dropping both his doll and the handle of his suitcase, Matthew reached for my hand. "Come on, Mum, Muffin Man." He placed his arms around the waist of the last little girl. Feeling sheepish, I trailed after him.

The wife and I joined the children who were standing, each behind a chair. The table was set with colored drinking beakers and small plates upon each of which lay one thick slice of white bread, a small cube of cheese, and a large pickle. Three or four water jugs stood along the length of the table. I heard my voice sound very loud, "Good God, this was never meant to be Dotheboys Hall, neither is it a jail. These poor children should not be eating prison rations."

"Quite a usual Sunday supper I'd say, bearing in mind it's the kitchen staff's night off. The grace, please."

A young helper folded her hands and opened her mouth, but I did not wait to hear her pray. I called Matthew, who, in imitation of his companions, was pressing his hands together. "Come on, I am sure we can find somewhere we can buy you a reasonable supper even on a Sunday."

The helper attempted to quell a nervous giggle as she bustled Matthew round the backs of the now occupied chairs. I put my arm around him. "We had better find your father."

We came upon Theo in the hall. With Boy under his arm, he was standing beside Matthew's suitcase scanning those absurd lists.

We walked down the front steps and got into our motorcar. Guided not so much by beams cast from our headlights as by clear moonlight, we made our way from Mount Tabor House through the village of Wingrave, easily deciphering the signposts which pointed to the town of Leighton Buzzard. Moonshine seemed to magnify the narrow roads. Hedges and trees, occasional groups of buildings, and a church were transformed into either snow cold images or dense black silhouettes. Every field we passed was made immaculate by moonlight. This beautiful stillness sent Matthew to sleep and calmed Theo and me. We decided that after eating together we would return to Mount Tabor House. While I saw Matthew to bed, Theo would tell the prison officer or his wife that I would be returning on the next and all the following days till I was confident that Matthew was quite comfortable at Mount Tabor House, and I decided that if he was not I would simply take him back to London.

As I cruised the car round the deserted town of Leighton Buzzard, our serenity was somewhat diminished by our not finding even one eating place whose owner dared defy the Sabbath. At last, glancing down a tiny alley, we saw a lonely neon sign twinkling the words "Light of India." Before I had properly parked the car, Matthew was skipping through the doorway. As always he had wakened in a mood of cheerful expectation. He was entirely justified on this occasion, for we walked into what at that moment felt like a little Aladdin's cave for hungry thieves, filled with gold chairs and red plush banquettes, tables covered in crisp white damask, and little electric candles. A smiling proprietor and two waiters tugged napkins from their shirt fronts as they rose from their seats. We had interrupted them as they were eating from their own bill of fare, and the smells were delicious.

Matthew commanded, "You choose, Dad." He spread his arms in a gesture that was meant to embrace every table. His father seated himself on one of the upholstered banquettes and Matthew squiggled in beside him.

I sat on a gold-painted chair across the table from the two of them. An odd little festivity was initiating itself. Theo picked up a wine list, and doing as his father did, Matthew leafed through another taken from an adjoining table. A waiter came and, for no reason, handed the menu to Matthew rather than Theo. Matthew in his assumed role of host ordered, "Rice 'n nice smelly stuff like you eated, please, big glass of beer Dad."

The mood was set, gaiety prevailed. Theo slapped his menu closed and laid it aside. Using language almost akin to Matthew's, the waiter announced, "We have ready a dish specially right for the young gentleman; not too strong, plenty in goodness."

Giving Theo no time to answer, Matthew replied, "Right," adding, "Beer Mum 'f you like."

The food we were so ceremoniously served was a feast. Dish after little dish appeared on our table. With the blandest expression of humorous obsequiousness, the waiter served Matthew a rather different meal from ours, finally bringing him a glass filled with jelly, decorated with a tiny paper parasol.

Upon our return, we were once more made to wait in the hall of Mount Tabor House and again taken unawares by the noiseless approach of the headmaster and his wife. By sighs and frowns they signaled that we had kept them from bed. This taciturnity seemed to activate in Theo a mock imperiousness I did not recall seeing before. It was his turn to wave toward the door marked "Private." The headmaster submitted. As if in retaliation, his wife gestured toward Matthew and me. We meekly followed her up the staircase, along a corridor to a dormitory door. Children were fast asleep in all the beds save one, upon which lay Matthew's suitcase with his rag doll propped against it. Matthew tiptoed into the room and embraced the doll with such comical exaggeration that it crossed my mind he was tipsy. At dinner he had sipped from both our glasses, importuning us with such remarks as, "Ah, tickly cold," or "Like goldy brown taste; more, please." After I hurried Matthew to a bathroom and helped him prepare for bed, he lay down and at once fell asleep, the paper parasol and his glasses tucked under his pillow. I fervently hoped that when he woke in the morning he would remember my promise that I would come back after breakfast.

To the acute annoyance of the headmaster and his wife, for five consecutive mornings I simply turned up at Mount Tabor House and remained within reach of Matthew throughout the day. I was not offered so much as a cup of tea or coffee, not even a chair to sit on, though of course I seized that for myself. The explanation shamefacedly whispered to me by members of the staff was that they had been instructed not to make me welcome because I was a spy.

I would become so hungry that after Matthew had eaten his school lunch, I swept him away to the Light of India, where Matthew always managed a "little something."

The prison officer and his wife were justified in their accusation, more and more so as those five days passed. I did spy. I listened to complaints and witnessed meannesses till I became so enraged that I resorted to removing from the notice board and taking home the most revealing of their abominable injunctions.

> If certain members of our staff wish to spend their off duty evenings in the local public house they must not expect to find their dinner waiting for them when they return.

> It is considered that every member of our staff is offered adequate nourishment during meal times. Hot drinks or snacks will no longer be available.

> Despite warnings, certain members of our staff have persisted in helping themselves to bread, milk and other supplies whenever it pleases them. From now

on we feel obliged to keep the larder and pantry doors locked.

To our kitchen staff: Supplying residents with milk and biscuits at midmorning is to be discontinued. It has been noticed that this practice interferes with their appetites for the main meal of the day.

To all night staff: Too much milk is wasted on evening drinks. Would you please water down the residents' nightly cocoa and allow only one petit beurre per person, Thank you.

AFTER I RETURNED HOME, I drove to see Matthew three, two, then only one day a week. I watched Theo's disapprobation of the prison officer and his wife waning in the same ratio. He defended them, saying the school was being managed with proficiency and economy. This remark rekindled my rage. I reminded him of those purloined notices and the coldness of my reception at Mount Tabor House. I don't know if he showed the notices to his committee, but I was pleased by the importance he and the other governors attached to the lack of hospitality the prison officer and his wife had shown me. Toward the end of his probationary period, the headmaster was told that he did not possess the temperament needed for a school such as MacIntyre. Before new applicants were interviewed Theo added to the list of requirements that there should be a policy that all parents, at all times, must be made welcome by the school.

CHAPTER TWENTY-ONE

Princess Anne

On the last but one day of the prison officer's reign, Princess Anne paid an official visit to MacIntyre School. This improbable happening took place at Westoning Manor, which meant the princess was not granted any light relief from our more engaging residents, the little children.

This somewhat daunting honor befell us by chance. A regimental colonel, upon learning that one of his captains had become engaged to marry Princess Anne, at once issued an order that every soldier in his regiment have docked from his pay a certain sum of money to be put toward the purchase of a suitable wedding present. While the officers in their mess and the soldiers in their dining hall were debating suitability, the colonel learned that imposing such a levy was against army regulations. We were told that every soldier of the regiment, commissioned or otherwise, refused to be reimbursed. Instead they voted their tithe should go to a charity of the couple's choosing.

The princess's fiancé, Captain Mark Phillips, had a sister who was mentally handicapped. I speculated as to whether Dave Simmonds Smith had a hand in this, for how else would MacIntyre School have proved to be the newest "Forward Thinking Lifetime Care Home for the...," etc.? I felt only he was capable of ensuring that our school was the recipient of the regiment's wedding gift.

Two days before the great event, Theo told me it was he who was to greet the princess and show her around, and I was to accompany him, "Generally look after her, you know, powdering noses or whatever."

"Surely, ~~not~~ all the way around, I know so little about how the place works."

I need not accompany her

"Well, be there between set pieces, so to speak."

"Why me?"

"Because you are my wife and we thought you'd be good at it."

"But I'm not the right sort, don't wear the right clothes, don't even go to hairdressers." I sounded idiotic.

"For God's sake, she knows the sort of place she is coming to. She won't be expecting glamour. Wear that linen-suit thing. I always see it as your classiest outfit."

A motley welcoming committee headed by Theo and myself watched as the helicopter blasted its way down from the sky to land on the side lawn of Westoning Manor. A group of full-dress soldiers hauled a little staircase to its door. A brass band struck up a gladdening tune. A few dozen military men, plus the regimental band, had arrived hours earlier to set up a marquee and to "altogether make ready." The door flew open. One after the other, an equerry, the princess, and a lady-in-waiting were handed to the ground. Theo walked forward, and somebody whispered to me to follow him.

Everyone shook hands, though ~~I~~ resorted to my long-ago boarding-school instruction and curtsied. As I straightened up, I found the equerry standing near me, holding out his hand. On his palm lay a solitary waistcoat button. The lady-in-waiting called, "Oh, dear, there is sewing to be done. Where shall we go?"

The princess, whom I had always identified as the only truly royal-looking member of the royal family, at close quarters impressed me further. She appeared both Hanoverian and, in an odd way, beautiful. She made a sweeping gesture, which evidently included me. "On the other side of the helicopter?" She was already leading the way; I trailed after our august but perhaps not entirely stately guests. The equerry, possibly not exactly an equerry but certainly a major general, on account of his unfashionably cut suit, probably was at least sixty years old. I watched his shrewd, smiling face as he stood to attention in front of the lady-in-waiting, who had taken out her "hussif" and bent to sew the button to his pinstriped waistcoat.

The princess was laughing. "Isn't she skillful? Mind you, she has plenty of practice, has to carry that equipment of hers wherever we go. More than once, got me out of a hole, haven't you, old bean?"

As I stood there it came to me that among these three there was a wordless understanding, a humorous pact, absolutely within the bounds of good-heartedness, and of course, rigidly safeguarded by decorum. They were about to treat this day's ceremony, as they very likely had others, as a lark. Allowing me to perceive this, as they did, meant I was to some degree to be included. Thus my way was clear, and my inadequacy dispelled. The four of us rejoined Theo who was looking nonplused and impatient.

To the waning beat of band music, we were led by a posse of board members and senior staff through a series of clean and tidy classrooms, teachers and residents feigning various occupations in each one. Everyone behaved perfectly, save one covetous girl who made a lunge toward Princess Anne's hat. The princess made a neat skip and simply walked on. My cousin, who had at one time coached her at lacrosse, had told me of Her Highness's swift reflexes. I now saw what she meant.

Prompted by the lady-in-waiting, I occasionally found myself having to whisper to Theo that we should move on. After a brief inquiring scowl he became almost too eager not to dawdle. The princess smiled gratefully.

The tour over, Theo swept the four of us from the hut-like classrooms back to the manor house. Once in the hall he made a hurried and self-conscious bow toward Princess Anne. "I'll leave you in the capable hands of Anne." He then turned to the equerry and invited him to visit the downstairs cloakroom.

"Whoops," said the princess.

"Oh, it's my name, too. I am supposed to escort you to..." Too late I recalled the instruction I had received before my en-

she told us an anecdote

counter with her aunt, Princess Margaret: "It is required that you employ the title Your Highness initially. Thereafter you may address her as M'am."

"To the Latts, thanks."

I got them as far as the upstairs landing only to discover I didn't know where the lavatories were.

"Never mind, she who finds, sings out," suggested the princess. She set off, the lady-in-waiting a few steps behind her. Almost at once one of them sang out.

We stood contemplating the most minuscule lavatories I had ever seen; there were no doors across their partitions. "Designed for first-timers," suggested the lady-in-waiting. We all giggled.

"Needs must," called the princess. We were still giggling as the three of us found ourselves leaning over the equally tiny washbasins.

The lady-in-waiting apologized for having hustled us through the tour of the school, but the princess claimed the fault was hers. Her gardener who was in love with her cook and that morning fallen from a royal cherry tree and broken his arm while filching blossoms for his loved one. Forgetting she would need her motorcar shortly, the princess sent him to hospital in it. Thus, in effect, it was the gardener who had caused the late departure of the helicopter.

I realized the day was in danger of continuing as unpunctually as it had begun, so before joining the assembly below, the lady-in-waiting and I hurriedly went over the list of people whom I was about to introduce to Her Highness. As we descended the staircase I explained why I hoped to deprive the last two on the list, the prison officer and his wife, of this honor—as it happened, I failed, for they introduced themselves.

While the residents and the soldiers ate sandwiches and drank ginger beer on the lawn, the band played within a marquee, where we sat on gold-painted chairs at damask-clothed tables, being served slices of rare beef with horseradish, mashed potatoes, and peas. I was placed next to the major-general-cum-equerry. We talked comfortably about this and that. As he sawed at his meat, he lightly asked me if there was anything the regiment might do "to cheer your protégés on," at the same time demonstrating the correct and at once obvious solution to an old problem concerning dining table etiquette. A drift of mashed potatoes and peas had slid from his plate. I managed to answer his question, and at the same time keep an eye on his solution. "Judging from the good time our residents are having out there on the lawn among the men you sent ahead, you might arrange that they come again, perhaps the brass band, too. They could march up and down a bit, even let some of the boys"—I dared not include the girls—"join in."

"Enjoy that, would they? It seems they are not so very unlike our soldiery." Meanwhile he was eating most decorously, placing morsels of meat onto his fork, then from the tablecloth adding potato and peas. I mustered the courage to ask him if his response to the mishap was prescribed procedure or merely his personal solution.

"I find it easiest to stick to Nanny's code of conduct on these occasions." We finished our meal and listened to speeches companionably.

CHAPTER TWENTY-TWO

Wednesdays

Until Dido was old enough to go to boarding school, I brought Matthew to the London house only if I was able to arrange a holiday for her elsewhere. After Matthew went to live at MacIntyre School, I had to wait months before anyone there dared trust that a visit home would not upset him, so I made it a habit to spend one day a week with him. We talked on the telephone.

"I shall be there on Wednesday, Matthew."

"Which 's Westday?"

"Monday, Tuesday, Wednesday; that day."

"Right, Mum, Westday."

Once I needed to alter our arrangement. "I cannot come this Wednesday, Matthew; but I can come on Tuesday."

"Which day is that?"

"Monday, Tuesday, tomorrow."

"Right, Mum, can have Westday, Tuesday . . . Tuesday won't mind being after him."

This kind of answer made me take the precaution of asking him to fetch a member of staff. I then explained that although Matthew would probably persist in calling it Wednesday, I was coming around eleven o'clock the next morning. I would nonetheless have found myself worrying all the way to his school if I had not made doubly sure Matthew was expecting me by calling him before I started out. "We shall see each other later on this morning, Matthew."

"Yep, Westday, Mum."

"No, today, Matthew."

"Yep."

Just to be sure, I telephoned his housemother and asked her to remind Matthew I would be there that very day. Somehow she forgot to do so. At the school I had to look for him. I went into his classroom and searched among a very diverse group of children. At the farther end of the room a male teacher was lounging in an armchair, holding a writhing little girl in his arms. He was evidently helping her to read a letter from home. He twitched his head in Matthew's direction. I spotted Matthew kneeling on the floor, head bent and mouth open, dispensing little teaspoonfuls of paint powder into their matching colored beakers. I was pleased that he seemed so at ease in his surroundings.

I watched him take a glass jar in his hand and rise to his feet. As he caught sight of me all his serenity left him. He dropped the jar and burst into tears. The cry he gave was inexpressibly forlorn, a drawn-out call from the heart, "My Mu-u-um-mm!"

I made my way between the little tables to where Matthew stood, but when I opened my arms to pluck him from the glittering shards of glass that surrounded him he stepped back from me as if in fear.

His teacher rose from his chair and strolled over to us with a mock sigh, as if to say, "another jar broken." He suggested Matthew go and fetch a dust pan and brush. In a jocular voice he added, "Step carefully, you clumsy young fellow."

A tall, awkward girl grasped Matthew's hand, and they left the room together. While they were gone, I told the teacher I wanted to take Matthew for a ride in the car.

"Not a bad idea," he said as he drifted off. When Matthew and his friend came back, the girl was carrying a dust pan, and Matthew followed her, flourishing a brush. She gently took it from him, murmuring "I do it, I do it," and stooped to the floor. As I invited Matthew to come out with me in the motorcar, this sweet-faced girl looked up, blinked several times, and whispered, "Goodbye, Mum and Matthew, back soon."

Not until we found his dormitory did Matthew let me comfort him. I washed his face with his face flannel and I cleaned his spectacles for him. We both drank a little water from his tooth mug, then he gave way to a weak little giggle. "Better."

"From now on I shall do my best always to come and see you on the same day every week and I shall talk to you on the telephone just before I leave home. Which day shall it be?"

"Monday, Sunday, Friday; Westday's horrid weaving. Westdays you come."

I was pleased that Matthew could machinate to avoid a boring afternoon in the weaving room. I saw it as evidence of intelligent wiliness, so I laughed and hugged him. "Much better to be with Mum than to weave."

"Clever girl, Mum," he said offhandedly.

Although he could chant the days of the week in their right sequence for Dido, he would not do so for me; he assumed his sheepish, idiotic look whenever I asked him to.

On one of our Wednesday outings, Matthew told me he needed a diary. We found something that perfectly matched his requirements. "No pictures, lots of squares and numbers"; it was an office calendar. While we sat waiting for lunch in one of Matthew's five-star eating places (I had known him to award twenty), he expressed his appreciation for this present in an indirect way. He took a ruler and pencil from his briefcase and carefully drew several lines and arrows over the first page of the new calendar. After scribbling and erasing here and there, he leaned back in his chair and said in a satisfied tone, "Better." He pushed the calendar toward me.

"What's better?"

"Paper days; changed 'em to right."

"I can't quite see what you mean; tell me how they go."

"Number one day, Saturday, television football match. Number two day, Westday, me 'n you. Three day, Monday, shopping with John." He named a favorite teacher who at that time was endeavoring to acquaint his pupils with the principle of spending one's money on essentials. I was told that Matthew enjoyed these shopping days with John immensely. He would hold one ridiculous object after another high above his head and in a piercing voice that distracted the other customers, call out, "This one sensual, John?"

"Last day, Sunday, cold dinner, clean our room, boring."

"What happened to Tuesday and Thursday, Matthew?"

"Not there any more."

I asked him if he wanted me to help tidy up the scribbles on his new calendar. The question quite scandalized him. He stretched the fingers of both hands across its pages and asked, "Want to spoil it, then?"

Now that my Wednesday visits were accepted as routine, Matthew and I found they served all sorts of purposes, the most banal being the overhaul he received each week prior to my arrival. I would find him waiting for me in the large playroom, looking almost dapper. Renewed cleanliness had always brought about a certain smugness in Matthew, his recently washed hair billowing around his clean pink face, his nails nicely trimmed, clothes fresh from the laundry, and sometimes his shoes polished. He often had a clean handkerchief in his pocket, occasionally accompanied by a carefully folded list in a houseparent's handwriting, but obviously supplemented by Matthew. "Tooth paste, new socks, a hair brush. Don't forget Hugo's birthday." Then there would be a line or two of indecipherable loops and pot hooks. "What does this writing say, Matthew?"

"Things I need."

"What sort of things?"

"Haven't decided."

An understanding we never put into words now existed between us. When an injustice had occurred or some fear which he could not overcome was oppressing him, or if he was bothered by the loss of a necessary possession or the breakage of a toy, then he would lead me upstairs to his bedroom. There we would embark on a game that we both depended upon to bring his problem to light. It was a game that had grown from Matthew's habit of hiding any clothes that were torn or stained.

I would ask politely, "May I sit on your bed for a minute or two, Matthew?"

"Cert'ly, Mum."

I would then plump the pillow and smooth the covers so as to make myself comfortable; during this process I might discover strange lumps. "What can these be?"

"Hiding there."

"Oh, dear, is something wrong?"

"'Spect so, look 'f you like."

"Good gracious, it's your leather jacket [your sandal, your Batman pajama top, your poor Popeye book]." My words usually met with his sad little giggle, the sound of which always troubled me because it seemed to express his brave acceptance of the fact that he was doomed to lose so many battles with inanimate objects and inexplicable happenings. In a tone of aloof disinterest he would say, "Yep, had accident." Thereupon I would offer to take the broken or torn possession away with me so as to mend or look after it for him.

Holding his head to one side as if considering the proposition, he would say with studied casualness, "Yep, he can go." He would put whatever it was in my arms, asking as he did so, "Won't mind, will they?"

At first I wondered if he was referring to the school staff; later I came to think he meant the clothes or toys themselves.

On the days when I found Matthew's bed smooth and without a lump of any kind, I would extend my plumping and patting motions to his body to look for hidden breakage of a more inward kind. As I felt about him I would murmur, "Is there something that needs a bit of repairing here, perhaps here?" Sometimes I would come upon fierce tension in his back or neck, or a strained tautness that used now and again to grip his whole body. Then I would massage him gently as I tried to elicit the cause of his suffering. To the end of his days, Matthew hated to complain; he despised himself if any part of his body was hurting him. Over the years we tried various codes and euphemisms to aid us when

I needed to know, or he wanted me to find, the source of his pains.

Our most used metaphor was the motorcar; Matthew felt its parts related to his own very nicely. He found the engine a useful analogy for his heart and stomach. Matthew's heart had always had faulty valves, and one only had to cup one's hand against his rib cage to feel his heart's awful fibrillation. I had to remind myself again and again not to be alarmed by this, but I was always on the qui vive in case it troubled him more than usual.

IN WINTERTIME particularly, Matthew tired easily. Throughout his life when we were walking together and his pace flagged, I slowed mine so that I could ask him to wait for me. He never seemed to see through my feint of pausing to wipe my nose or retie his or my own shoelaces. To extend a respite I might pick up some article or look into the nearest shop window.

"What does this stone remind you of, Matthew?"

"N' other stone."

"But just a minute, if it were not a stone what would you say it is like?"

"Bit of old bread?" He occasionally prolonged the break with a return question, "If shoe laces wasn't, what they be, Mum?"

"Are they like lazy worms?"

"Brown string, silly."

A couple of years after his arrival at MacIntyre School, his fatigue caught us in front of the window of a chemist's shop in Leighton Buzzard. Matthew suddenly looked so fatigued that he was blue around the mouth. I wanted to sit him down but there was no public bench within sight; we remained where we were and I pulled him against me. "If we absolutely had to buy something from this shop, what would we choose?" In my anxiety I had quite forgotten to be judicious with my words. Matthew perked up and started to scrutinize every object behind the plate glass.

"Have big red 'n blue bottles."

"Oh, no, those are part of the chemist's furnishings. He must keep them for his shop. Pick something else".

"Only want them. *You said.*" A silence ensued, then, "Right, have that." He pointed to an ugly pinkish colored plaster stomach with some kind of medical truss strapped across it.

"Ugh, Matthew, that is ugly."

"Lovely. Want it."

"What could you want it for?"

"Put on me when I fight."

"You never fight."

"Might."

We discussed and bartered in front of that window until I realized that Matthew felt better and our research was no longer theoretical; he absolutely expected me to buy him something from among the pharmaceutical paraphernalia that was on display. I had to settle for a handsome but threatening pair of scissors.

"I think they are terribly dangerous. You are sure to cut yourself."

"Won't."

"Then supposing someone less careful than you borrows them; they might hurt themselves or even harm another person."

"Need nice, sharp, dayjus scissors; a twelve boy now."

"Scissors make me extremely nervous, Matthew."

"Poor Mum."

The purchase of that pair of scissors was of great consequence to Matthew, an important symbol. My refusal to buy them would have amounted to an admission that I dared not trust him with the responsibility of owning them.

We bought the scissors, but not before we had made a contract to which the kindly shopkeeper gave his grave approval. Matthew would keep his new scissors on a high shelf in the art room, and I was to sew a looped name tape through one of the finger holes to remind everybody that they belonged only to Matthew Crosby.

CHAPTER TWENTY-THREE

Gwen and Mark

(Chris)

In his first year at Mount Tabor House, 1975, I made friends with one of the "day carers," a kindly woman named Gwen, who had a warm smile, loud, infectious laughter, and seemed to favor Matthew.

He suffered bout after bout of bronchitis during that first winter, and in order that Gwen might understand his fear of being confined to bed in an empty dormitory, I recounted his experiences at Normansfield Hospital and went on to describe Gladys's alternative method of nursing him; when he lived with her she would wrap Matthew in a shawl and prop him in the seat of his pedal motorcar, which she then parked by a radiator. There he was allowed to doze through the days and answer her offers of food and drink or inquiries as to how he was feeling with the noises of his motorcar.

I didn't tell Gwen that during one of those illnesses we had thought he was not going to recover. How the doctor visited him every day and prescribed penicillin, in stronger and stronger doses, finally saying he must go to hospital. I certainly did not confess my view, which Gladys had shared and voiced more succinctly, "Can't let him go there, it would kill him dead, poor mite, he'd never trust us again."

I spent my days at Gladys's house, we spooned medicines and liquids down Matthew's throat till his body rebelled and he would only accept drips of glucose and water. We lifted him from his car and put him in Dido's old barred cot. There he lay on his stomach, his head hanging over a pillow.

"Seems to like that position best, awful noisy breathing. Sounds like a bus, don't he?"

Gladys appeared almost unperturbed. Every morning I was surprised to find him alive. Gladys and I became extremely close, and I admired her more than ever. Even when she had to sit up most of the night with Matthew, she kept to her usual routine. Her children went to and from their schools, her foster babies arrived in the mornings and she cared for them until evening, meals were put on the table. When Fred got home, he would sit with Matthew, and I would be sent away.

On the last day of this drama, Gladys greeted me with the news she could hardly feel Matthew's pulse. She sounded angry, "Poor little devil, I blame all those fancy medicines for stringing this out. If he's got to go, he might as well pop off now. You won't send him to the hospital, will you? He's better off dying here; I don't mind."

Hardly daring to let the doctor see what Matthew had come to, I explained our shared attitude to him on the telephone. Looking back, I think I was asking for permission to let Matthew die. I cannot recall the doctor's response, but I know he did not come to the house that day. Perhaps it was not by chance that Fred arrived home early. Gladys dismissed me with the words, "Go on back to your Theo, we'll telephone if there's any change." I made her swear she would do so.

I was about to go to bed when the telephone rang. I was expecting Gladys's voice but not her words, "Don't worry, he's all right, near miss though. I didn't dare leave him so Fred cooked egg and chips. Brought me a plateful where I was sitting next to his nibs. You'll never believe, that little monkey raised his head and said, "Ah! Dinner." Bet you can't guess what he's doing now? Only sitting on Fred's knee sucking a chip. Looks a bit peaky, but I reckon we will all sleep better in our beds tonight. See you in the morning."

Gwen and her fellow staff members at Mount Tabor House agreed to let Matthew be nursed back to health in places of his own choosing. These turned out to be either in a big cardboard box, which he placed near the nursery fire, or in a slightly smaller box in the television room. Matthew was allowed to creep into these boxes at any time. No other child attempted to occupy Matthew's temporary bedrooms, but they volunteered or were asked to bring his pillow and blanket from his bedroom. If he was diagnosed as seriously ill, I would be sent for. I used to arrive to find him almost content, his doll tucked in the box beside him, and often as not, his original protector, the girl who had once swept up broken glass for him, hovering by.

Warmer weather brought better health for Matthew, and with it a confidence I had not seen in him before. He wanted to tell me about his school. "John's teacher, tells number lessons. Say words clearly, don't mess 'bout, not be crybaby when hitted by big boys, no hold front of trousers. That lady cooks, eat her stuff. Maureen got wobbly legs, hits with her sticks, she can sing. That boy got no name, 's called Harpo. Feed him sometimes, likes me. His friend wear car racing helmet indoors. Mustn't borrow it for a minute. I take Sharon to toilet, 's my job. She wets like Harpo."

A headmistress was engaged to replace the despotic prison officer and his wife. Everyone called her by her Christian name, Shirley. She was a quick-minded and impulsive woman, her rule unorthodox and amiable. Under her care everyone had to be taken notice of, and even some of the less capable residents were asked to watch over somebody else. The community throve, Matthew among them. Shirley allowed him and one or two other timid souls to remain within the shelter of the junior school long after their age dictated that they should move on. She devised little honorary ranks and responsibilities to insure that everybody believed they were of consequence. When it was feasible, she gave her staff the choice of working within the school or taking one or more of their charges home for a meal, a day, or sometimes a weekend. In this manner Matthew made his way into several many families.

His accounts were revealing. "After supper, Mary [a young teacher] 'n me was out with boyfriend. Had ice cream, he beer. Danced, did my can-can in Mary's house. Very nice."

On one occasion I telephoned to invite him to London for the weekend. He refused, saying, "Calendar says go in Gwen's house. Got a cat there 'n grandpa 'n grandma."

THEN CAME MARK; his very name augured he should become Matthew's closest friend: "Matthew, Mark, Luke, and John, Went to bed with their trousers on."

I cannot recall the rest of this little ditty which we often sang together. Luke was a big black cat who frequented Gladys's garden. And John was Matthew's well-loved teacher.

As soon as a social worker had delivered Mark to Mount Tabor House, this intrepid twelve-year-old boldly pushed open the door from the front hall to the nursery, stood squarely like a little pugilist, and surveyed the large and noisy room. He singled out Matthew from among the other children, then wove and dodged to Matthew's side and gave him a playful punch. Keeping a comradely hand on Matthew's shoulder, Mark turned to confront his new life at MacIntyre School. Matthew's heart was instantly won. A bed was made up beside his and the two were from then on, as his school reports repeatedly told us, "inseparable."

Mark's appearance brought him popularity. His hair and eyelashes were a whitey blond color, his eyes gray green. He was a muscular little boy who made innocent use of his odd little glamour. His breezy caresses were returned casually by the staff and enthusiastically by his playmates. Even before he reached his adolescence, he was sought after by younger and older resident girls.

From the first days of their friendship, it was evident that Mark possessed a surer touch than Matthew; he was offhand in his affection and enjoyed being competitive. There were times when he teased Matthew gladiatorially only to be so abashed by Matthew's forgiveness that he would bounce back to his side to plant a kiss on his cheek. In this, Mark resembled the rubber ball that he carried in his pocket. It was his most treasured possession, his mouthpiece and his messenger, for Mark rarely used real words.

In Matthew's shadowy memory there must have existed an eidolon of an earlier best friend, a fellow inmate at Normansfield Hospital, who for want of a real one tossed an imaginary ball, which Matthew could not fail to catch. Now came another close friend who not merely tossed but flung a very tangible ball in his direction. He would have liked to catch it every time, as he had so easily done long ago, but his eyes were weak and his coordination deplorable. He was never able to see Mark's ball before it hit him.

As much as the ball and the use he made of it were a manifestation of Mark's character, so was Matthew's dexterity with a hypothetical ball a manifestation of his. One morning Matthew was able to "catch" Mark's ball and with a graceful flick of the wrist return it. A young teacher looking on applauded. He told me that Mark was astounded; now it was his turn to search the floor. Matthew went through the action again. After the third confusing round—Mark not even glimpsing the balls as they flew toward him—Matthew put the ball in his hand and Mark caught on. He was more impressed with Matthew's dexterity with the invisible ball than with his own skill with the actual one. From then on he often kept his ball in their bedroom and shared Matthew's imaginary one.

An assessment of Mark's intelligence had accompanied him when he joined the school. It ended with the statement that though his comprehension was reasonably good, Mark was not yet able to form sentences. I believe he made so few efforts to do so simply because he was quite sure that the noises he made were actual talk. Within a few minutes of his fixing upon Matthew, he was sounding like a genteel lady as he put his head close to Matthew's and murmured.

"Sorry, can't understand," responded Matthew.

More convincing little noises were poured into Matthew's ear.

"Be good boy, say slowly."

Matthew's code of manners dictated that he accommodate himself to his friend's ways. He listened and listened to Mark's mimicry till he became addicted to it. They babbled together, at times sounding like newscasters, American tough guys, one or another member of the school staff instructing or cajoling, and all sorts of other people.

When I was told that Matthew's speech was becoming less articulate, I was not surprised. For him language was a fragile commodity, easily distorted by distraction or anxiety. When Matthew was an infant, Dr. Weihs had forecast "an elusive intelligence of a curious sort." If Matthew took up a new interest, it was usually at the expense of an old one. In a school report, we were told he was no longer paying attention to his number lessons. Since numbers had been his abiding interest, this piece of news did surprise me. The next time I saw him, I asked him, "Don't you like numbers any more?"

"Too busy, now I a washer up."

He let me understand he had taken on a new role. He was timing himself as he worked and attempting to keep a chart. He showed me this tattered document, heavily ruled in all directions and sprinkled with tiny hieroglyphics.

"I can't understand it very well, tell me how it reads."

"Shows Matthew's work."

"Why don't you explain it to me?"

He studied his document for a while, then he either pretended to or really read from it, "Says breakfast quickest; tea nicest less plates; lunch horridest sticky; supper tired."

Faster and faster he passed crockery through soapy water and onto the plate rack, till his housemother had to point out that the plates were not properly clean.

"Can't wash 'n get 'em clean; I one thing at a time boy."

The obvious reason for the worsening of his speech was that Mark had become Matthew's prime source. In this respect at least, Matthew somewhat resembled his father. When Theo answered the telephone, Dido and I could soon determine what kind of person he was talking to because his voice sounded like a parody of his caller's. Theo claimed that this was due to "empathy."

ON ONE OF our usual Wednesday outings, I asked Matthew if he wanted to bring Mark along.

"No. Get present."

While we were sitting in Matthew's current *now* six-star restaurant, waiting for our food to be brought to us, Matthew opened his briefcase and handed me a list. "Read, Mum."

The paper was headed "4 Mark." There was a squiggly drawing of a bottle labeled "Clo-cola," a boat of sorts, a coffin shape with "chee-gm" printed across it, and a cutout of a motorcar. Taking up the rest of the page was a carefully crayoned picture of a person: a huge head sprouting yellow curls, supported by a body in a blue dress, green shoes poking forth from under the hem. The figure was enclosed by many fine lines, which appeared to be barbed.

"Who is that, Matthew?"

"You know, silly."

"Do I?"

"Yep, 's you."

"I seem to be in a cage."

"Safe, no Mark."

I pondered this explanation all through our meal. As Matthew sucked up the last dregs of his milkshake I asked him why he thought I needed to be safe from Mark. I had been making myself anxious unnecessarily, since his answer was reassuringly straightforward.

"You my mum, not Mark's."

So we went to buy Coca-Cola and chewing gum for his friend, and we found an object that met his need for the boatlike thing. Mark was yearning for a soap dish; the one we found was shaped like a duck.

On other outings we bought other presents but I was never allowed to invite Mark to accompany us. I dreaded seeing the brave smile he put on as he helped Matthew carry his suitcase to the car when I was about to drive him home.

THEO'S CONVERSION of Mount Tabor's stable buildings into new classrooms was being carried out while Matthew was still trying to adjust to living at Mount Tabor House. On my visiting days, he and I would go to see how the work was progressing so that I could report to Theo when I got home. The sight of that forlorn building being taken apart and put together in an altered form was very unnerving to Matthew.

One Wednesday morning I was told that the job was near completion and some furniture was already installed. I suggested Matthew show me round. It was a cold morning, and the brick path leading from the back door of Mount Tabor House to the outbuildings was iced over. Matthew held my hand tightly. He seemed to be exaggerating his fear of taking a tumble.

"Car puffs [car exhaust] coming out of mouths. Horrid."

When we reached the stable yard, Matthew pulled at me to stop. He looked at the top of the dark Victorian structure and then at the arched doors that were built to receive high-wheeled carriages. I sensed his heart was sinking. "Don't you want to go in?"

"Mustn't go; elephant lives there."

I recounted the incident to his teacher, John, who said, "Well, there's a sign of progress then, Matthew's first fib. He's been a bit backward in that respect, always tells the plain truth, does our Matthew." I was not so sure that telling me an elephant inhabited the new classroom could be classed a fib, since Matthew clearly believed it to be so.

John promised a celebratory feast of cocoa and buns to entice Matthew into the new schoolroom. He asked his pupils to surround Matthew and rush him through the great door.

The day after the feast was a Wednesday. I was told to look for Matthew in the new classroom. I found him sitting on the edge of his chair, wringing his hands. I sat beside him and asked him if he liked his new surroundings. He put his hand over my mouth. "'S all right, Mum, 's not real elephant."

Two days later, without telling me he was doing so, Theo went to make his final inspection of the building. From the window of the classroom Matthew caught a glimpse of his father. He ran up to John and announced, "'S my Dad going on roof."

John told me he did not believe Matthew; he assumed him to be telling another "fib." Matthew lingered by the window all morning. John tried to distract him. When lunchtime came John went to the staff dining room, where he saw Theo. He approached him and said, "I think your son was rather disappointed that you didn't come and greet him."

"Oh, I meant to. Tell him I'll be along when we've examined the clock tower."

Back in the classroom John felt contrite about not having believed Matthew, so after giving him Theo's message he placed his chair by the window. Kneeling there, Matthew saw a foreman, a workman, Theo's young assistant, and finally Theo as they descended a ladder which had been placed only a few feet beyond the glass. He jumped up and waved, but Theo was not looking in his direction. Instead, Theo stood and talked for a long time with the group of men. At last he sent the young assistant to fetch Matthew, who by now had carried his chair back to his desk. "Would Matthew like to come to say hello to his father?"

John turned to Matthew, who refused to move. The young man seemed unsure of what to do next. "Do you want to go and talk with your Dad, Matthew?" Matthew gave an exaggerated sigh, heaved himself from his chair, put on his coat, and wandered to the door. There he appeared to stop and consider, then he straightened his back, opened the door and marched through it.

Theo came home that evening and gave me an account of the scene. "I had to make a final inspection at the Mount Tabor site today."

"I wished you'd told me you were going, I would have given you a little something for Matt."

"Oh, I didn't think of taking him a present. I hardly saw him actually. In fact, though it seems a ridiculous thing to say, he rather hurt my feelings."

"How could Matthew manage that?"

"Well, when the job was finished, I sent my assistant into Matthew's classroom to ask him to come out and see me. Do you know, when he deigned to come, he stamped toward me as if pretending to be a soldier. He stopped yards from me, gave a salute, then turned and marched back."

When we talked again, John told me that after Matthew returned he did not join the other children, but stood holding his coat to his face. John tried to cajole him to join the others, but Matthew could not be persuaded, so he asked one of the big girls to escort Matthew back to the main house, where Matthew pushed himself into a corner of the playroom, his knees against his chin. He remained in this position until his housemother found him and took him into the kitchen to help her prepare tea.

ONE SUMMERY WEDNESDAY afternoon, Matthew and I were lounging in a field from where we could keep an eye on a railway bridge which spanned a high road. He was hoping a train would cross the bridge just as a car passed beneath it. "Gwen 'n them 'n me camping at weekend." (The Whitsun holiday had just passed.) "Sleeped in tent with Granddad, snorted at night. Inside tent, Granddad and me had horrid green faces."

"It was very nice of Gwen to take you with her. I hope you thanked her politely."

"Nope. Don't like camping."

"Why not?"

"Nasty peeing by tree, eated smoke, plates muddy, sitted on grass, no television, both socks wetted all time."

"Wasn't there even one nice thing about camping?"

"Whipping Boy fell in river, Mister Gwen got his legs wet, wasn't cross."

Gwen was a trained nurse. She lived in the village of Wingrave surrounded by a large, jolly family. Matthew loved her dearly and she called him her "little gentleman," a sobriquet he did not like. "Not genile man, still boy."

THE FOLLOWING DECEMBER, Matthew was again often unwell. He and I would sit beside the fire in the playroom at Mount Tabor House. Gwen came and joined us whenever she could. "Well, Matthew, what about spending Christmas with me and the family this year then?"

Matthew shuddered and turned from her. Embarrassed by his response, I began to ask him to answer her politely, but she intervened, "Don't you want to come to us then, Mick"—whom Matthew called Mr. Gwen—"the kids, Granddad and Mum, the cats and all? Don't you want to be at our house?"

Matthew's whole demeanor changed. "Got house 'gain?" A smile of relief crossed his face. "Ah, 's nice, not camping."

"Camping? You didn't think we would all go camping by that old river at Christmastime, did you, Matthew? You silly boy."

"Not silly; camping silly." Then, in a nonchalant tone, "Come if you like."

It seemed that Gwen's family were either very charitable or they did indeed "like," because Matthew celebrated Christmas with Gwen and her family.

"Tea in bed with Granddad an Granmum one morning, Gwen 'n Mr. Gwen morning number two. Cats in my bed all night, big beds in Gwen's house."

CHAPTER TWENTY-FOUR

Good Riddance

Not till four months after Matthew had become a resident at Mount Tabor House did Gladys decide she was ready to let Fred drive her to Buckinghamshire and pay Matthew a visit. A polite letter was sent to Sarah, his housemother, and the date was noted on the school calendar.

"You know, Anne," Gladys told me, "Fred polished that car up for Matthew, and I had me hair done, well, not exactly for him, but I didn't want his school to think he spent that many years of his life living with a nobody. I got a nice boy's beige kind of wool and spent me evenings knitting him a new cardigan.

"His lordship was waiting for us inside that big front door, all togged up and neat as a new pin. I swear he was glad to see us, gave me one of his best kisses. Lucky I'd brought a little something for him. He's grown since he's been down there, and he was properly clean, I'll give 'em that.

"We told him it would be nice to meet his housemother; he told us she wasn't there. He took us through the back to the kitchen. There she was, well, it might as well have been a she; earrings, hair all down his back, silly sandals and a flippery kind of apron tied round his middle. Still, he was friendly enough. Told Matthew to pull out a chair for me, then made him lay us a tea. Said yes, Matthew was being a nice boy and would we mind him getting on with making Sunday supper while we chatted. When our tea things was washed up and put away, he sent us to walk in the garden. Matthew had us sniff all the flipping roses, till it got too nippy and I needed the toilet.

"Show us your bedroom then, Matthew, I said. Hasn't forgotten all his good manners; polite as you please he took us up those grand stairs, then along a passage, past a toilet that was not what you might call hygienic, which didn't put our Fred off. Me and Matthew went in his room. The two beds were made, but talk about untidy. Why did you let him take all that junk to his school, Anne? No more than half of it could have belonged to his friend.

"We sat him on his bed and like you asked, I got his shoes and socks off; a big hole in one of them I might say. They hadn't cut his nails right enough. Had the scissors ready in me handbag so I did that for him, then I set about snipping the hair from over his ears and in front of his eyes. He made a fuss; told him I didn't want him growing up wearing silly sandals and an apron. Fred and Matthew picked up the cuttings because by then I had to use that smelly toilet, since I didn't know the whereabouts of another. When I got back his nibs said it was his turn. Fred and me, we waited in the bedroom, me tidying a drawer or two and putting things a bit straight. Matthew was gone that long I sent Fred to look for him.

"He wasn't nowhere to be seen. We had to find our own way down to the front hall. We looked in the kitchen, hoped to find that fancy fellow, then Fred pushed open another door. It turned out to be a great big playroom. And wouldn't you know, there was your little monkey, cool as you please, playing with his friends; just gave me a little wave and turned his back.

"I was that hurt. 'Oh no you don't,' I said. 'You come and tell your Uncle Fred and Auntie Gladys why you left us all alone in your room. Don't tell me you forgot we was there, because I know you didn't.' Had the grace to look ashamed, didn't he. 'Well?' I said.

"'Had to go and play.' That's what he said. 'Had to,' I ask you.

"'Didn't you want your Auntie Gladys any more then?' 'No,' he said. 'Nor even my Fred who polished the car for you to see?' 'No,' again.

"'Well I've got *no* goodbyes for you, my lad. It's good rid-dance to bad rubbish, if you're going to be like that.'

"Know what he said, Anne? Giving me that smile of his, ever so polite, 'Good riddance, Auntie Gladys,' held up his mug to be kissed. Liked the word, said it again, 'Good riddance, Uncle Fred.' Then he scuttled off.

"Oooh, I was that miserable I cried nearly all the way home. Fred kept saying things like 'He thinks he's a big boy now, and he don't mean it really,' but I know better. Cold-hearted little perisher, he didn't want me no more, I could tell. So don't ask me to have him again. Frederic tells me I've got to be more 'easy come, easy go,' but I ask you, Anne, after all them years. Now I know what they mean when they say he's not all there. They're not so wrong, missing the right feelings, if you don't mind my saying it."

CHAPTER TWENTY-FIVE

Christmastime

Almost every year when the cold and wet weather set in, some member of the staff at Mount Tabor House would declare it about time to begin rehearsals for the Christmas entertainment.

Yearly, Matthew was baffled by being told he was going to be some strange thing.

"Don't you remember other shows, Matthew? You did not stop being yourself, you just pretended to be a snowball, part of a donkey, an angel"—or as he had put it, a man-fairy airplane wings. "I seem to remember you enjoyed being those things."

"Can't remember. Tell Christmas all again."

I would repeat back to him his description of Christmas Day, which went like this: "In bus to big school, huge chicken for dinner, paper hat, horrid pudding. Father Christmas talk like John. Presents, some, love Dad, Mum, Dido. Lots plates to wash."

"Nope. Don't remember, tell it all, Mum." And I, making the best of his version, would do so.

On a Wednesday afternoon in early November 1977, when Matthew was thirteen, he and I were about to indulge in an activity that Matthew called "Mentmore-ing," because that was the name of the vast house (I was told it contained forty-three bedrooms), in the grounds of which we sometimes played a certain game. The elderly owner of the place, with whom I was slightly acquainted, had given us permission to do as we pleased on her estate. She was now dead and her property sold to a mysterious sect, whose cause was served by pale, shaven-headed men, anachronistically uniformed in business suits and, when acting as sentinels, armed in padded jackets and carrying walkie-talkies.

Matthew's reaction to these functionaries was intuitive; he behaved as if they were invisible.

When we arrived at our venue in the tree plantation, I would make Matthew wait for one of these nearly invisible beings to come in a jeep and check us out. We would sit on a rotting wooden bench which encircled a beech tree. Sure enough, within a few minutes, murmuring into his apparatus as he advanced, a clone of the cult would drift into our view. In a voice, at once muted and distinct, he would tell us to enjoy our exercise. Today, instead of getting out of his vehicle, he merely gave us a "thumbs-up." It was hardly possible that our permit to trespass had been granted in perpetuity, but his gesture set me wondering if, in a comradely way, Matthew and I were now credited with being devotees of a fellow cult, perhaps one that was more ancient than that of our hosts, demanding that we practice our ritual in this particular place.

"Going to be dancing lady, learn every day after tea. Like her very much."

"What kind of dancing does your lady do?"

"Stepping on music very fast, kick high, wear three skirts. Watch, Mum." Making gestures that suggested he was flurrying his petticoats, and keeping time to an inner tune, Matthew tripped his dance. In a wild conclusion, he flung first one and then another sneaker-clad heel in the air. How robust he looked.

At that moment I liked him extravagantly, and he appeared delighted with himself, so we were in the right mood to proceed with our exercise cum activity, which required only that we wade along alleys of once-tall grass, now flattened by rain, which divided rows of young spruce trees. We chose separate alleys. To keep in touch with each other we indulged in a great deal of shouting. That was all the game was, a pretext to take exercise while making an assortment of cries.

IN ALL HIS LIFE Matthew never spent a Christmas Day among his family. At first Gladys Strong was asked to make up our deficiency; later he spent Christmases at MacIntyre School. He and I always talked on the telephone on Boxing Day:

"Did you have a good Christmas, Matthew?"

"No more Christmas, thank you, Mum. Have me home 'f you like." He would name a day, usually the following one. Theo expressed the same sentiment, "No more Christmas, thank you," as he gratefully reimmersed himself in his work. Dido would be sent to stay with friends while Matthew came home for a week or so.

During these visits, listless and darkly shadowed beneath his eyes, Matthew let me pamper him and make an invalid of him till he became bored by my excesses. When he wakened in the mornings, he left his bed and came to the top of the stairs to call, "Up now, breakfast 'n your bed, please, cornflakes, two spoiled eggs, butterbread, Dido's mug cocoa. Thank you now, Mum."

I carried everything he ordered up the stairs on a tray, sometimes adding a cup of coffee for myself. I would find Matthew lounging luxuriously against our pillows, his rag doll propped beside him, his squawky little radio placed across the doll's legs. "We got music on."

When he had enough of my company, using his doll as a hand puppet, Matthew turned the knobs of the radio till the loudness of the current pop tunes drove me downstairs. There were occasions when he ordered a second breakfast.

"But you've just eaten, Matthew."

"Hungry. Better have more." Beside being childishly greedy, Matthew was unhealthily thin, so I was inclined to assume that he really was as hungry as he claimed to be, and really tired when he told me he wanted to stay in our bed. I allowed him to remain there as long as he wished; he used to listen to his radio, play with his motorcars, cut out pictures from magazines, or write what seemed to be long, pointless sentences.

I had to launder the rag dolls because they became unwholesomely sticky, and very often I changed the sheets of our bed for the same reason. While I was doing that task one morning, a shower of pebblelike shapes fell to the floor, leaving one of the sheets disfigured by a strange pattern of holes. "What happened to this sheet, Matthew?"

"'S all right now, took all cocoa spills off with scissors. Not do that way 'gain."

For the first day of those after-Christmas holidays, Matthew was tranquil and loving, contented to lead a sluggish, domestic existence. He would wander about the house looking for any changes we had made. "Where's wheely feet chair gone away?" To a new towel, "Don't dry right, do you?" Washing his hands in the downstairs cloakroom before lunch, he found two bars of sandalwood soap, one worn to a mere sliver. I had pressed it to meld with the second bar, after which I overheard Matthew, "'S nice, you got baby at your front. Pretty smell. Mustn't let him fall down plug hole."

He would stand quite still in his sister's bedroom till he was moved to pick up one, then another of her possessions, sometimes holding them to his chest before replacing them. He would open her wardrobe and delicately riffle through the clothes that hung there. He closed the cupboard doors reverently. I tried not to let him become aware that I sometimes watched through the door while he was in Dido's room, or that I could see on his face, as he rejoined me, a look of bleak resignation. After he closed the bedroom door, he always tramped his feet exaggeratedly as he walked down stairs. I supposed he was reinstating the only advantage he believed he had over Dido: his manliness.

CHAPTER TWENTY-SIX

The Lyric Theatre

FROM MY JOURNAL
January 1978

Matthew is in London for his usual post-Christmas holiday. The Lyric Theatre in King Street is offering matinee performances for children. Every time we go shopping, Matthew studies the posters. The entertainer is well known to Matthew, as he is to most children in England. Appearing regularly on television programs, playing his guitar, washboard, didgeridoo, and sundry other musical instruments, he is dearly loved. Parents approve of his gentle manners, ingenuous miming, and his breezy singalongs; children are awed by his picture-making. Matthew too has watched a number of these "creations" come into being. A pianist imitates a drum roll as the camera hones in on Rolf Harris, who stands in front of a large sheet of paper, holding a very long paint brush. With astounding bravura, he sweeps the brush to and fro. His strokes suggest a kangaroo, no, a London bus, but no again, there is the profile of a bearded sailor. Great splashes of color are applied; is it to be a ship? All at once his accompanist brings his trills to a crescendo, and lo! a view of the Australian outback is revealed. Rolf's picture is so dashingly kitsch that perhaps there is something a little miraculous in the way it outglows any landscape imaginable.

It is not only the pictures that impress Matthew, it is also the man who creates them. "Not like you, Mum."

"No, I haven't got a beard."

"Better pictures. Poor Mum."

The date and time of Mr. Harris's final performance are pasted across the theater door. Matthew, who loves calendars and timetables, takes this to be an urgent message specially for him.

"'S right now, Mum, got to go in." He pulls me into the foyer and we buy two matinee tickets for this very day. I select front row balcony seats, foreseeing that, since they are expensive, this might ensure that we will be surrounded by empty seats. I am nervous because Matthew is given to talking to performers while he watches television and film screens. He calls out encouraging remarks to his heroes, telling them to drive faster and not just sit 'n talk. In a crowded cinema he once admonished Superman, loudly telling him to "stop kissing 'n get flying." Luckily this raised a laugh, but at a dramatic moment in a Tarzan film, when the hero has returned to the African jungle with his bride beside him, Matthew shouted to Tarzan, "Tell her t' go home, you take your clothes off, 'n play with monkey friends."

As we take our seats we find the theater is almost empty; we have the entire balcony to ourselves. The curtain goes up and Rolf Harris, accompanied by a sleepy-looking musician, takes us through a few songs which Matthew sturdily beats time to, contributing any words he knows in a loud drawl. Next we watch some simple conjuring, followed by a piece of unconvincing ventriloquism. We are shown how a didgeridoo is played. During this lesson Matthew employs himself tipping our row of empty seats back and forth. When the interval comes, we go to use the lavatories. They are also unoccupied, which means that I can fetch Matthew when I decide he has been washing his hands for long enough. It is a process he is too punctilious about. Sometimes I find he has forgotten where he is and has taken to putting his finger under the taps and squirting water about. Then I have to accost any kindly man who is on his way out of the lavatory and ask him to reenter and ask Matt to dry his hands and join his mother.

This time I bribe him forth with the promise of ice cream, which we take back to our seats. Matthew chooses new places for us to sit. He appears altogether delighted with our outing.

I too feel the afternoon is going very well. Just as the curtain is going up again, the glamorous young lady who assisted with the conjuring approaches us and invites us to go downstairs to the main auditorium. "There are rather few people in the audience today and it would be cozier if everyone sat near the stage. Then we can all really participate in Rolf's performance. He is going to paint the picture now."

"Front seats, Mum?"

"No, not the very front."

But she smiles, "Of course, if he likes, the very middle front seats if you want, dear."

Matthew gives me a triumphant look and steps lightly after her. I collect our coats and follow.

Mr. Harris is adding a few sparkles and highlights to his picture as we take our places below the microphone and much too near the accompanying musician. Matthew calls loudly to the pianist, "Play sunshine noise for picture, sir." The man cannot hear Matthew, but gives him a cheery wave. With a twirl of the paint brush the picture is finished and everyone claps. Matthew stamps his feet. The musician rolls the drums and taps the cymbals. Mr. Harris waves to quieten him and announces that he has a tale to tell, about a little boy who gets lost in the outback. He invites boys and girls from the audience to step up and assist in the telling. He spots Matthew—how could he not, since Matthew is not merely standing but dramatically and obsequiously bowing. Mr. Harris turns away and keeps his gaze firmly on the children behind us. He beckons to trustworthy-looking little children, and the young lady helps them onto the stage. Meanwhile the musician, whom I now suspect of wishing to provoke Mr. Harris, has leaned over and hoisted Matthew up there too. I try to prevent what is about to happen, but the footlights above me make a glaring barrier between the stage and me. The boys are being lined up on one side of the microphone, girls on the other. Matthew blows me a kiss. He has taken the hand of a very little boy, who waves too.

The girls are to make sighing wind noises and the boys whispering grass, to the accompaniment of soft cymbal and piano trills.

"Have all you lovely children understood what to do? Good, later in the story we have to make the noises of a nasty storm."

In a firm voice Matthew says into the microphone, behind which he has now placed himself, "No storm. Make my car noises."

"There are no cars in the outback," says Rolf Harris.

"Now are," Matthew says into the microphone. The musician is leering. I wonder if he is drunk. Mr. Harris has evidently resigned himself. With a strained smile, he is making an effort to keep the atmosphere jolly. "All right, Sonny, you make quiet car noises." He takes up his guitar and in a gentle voice he begins his tale. The performance gathers momentum. Encouraged by the lady assistant, the wind sighs and sighs and the grasses swish and swish. Matthew makes his motorcar engine noises, but quite softly. His friend copies him.

Mr. Harris's voice rises. The children in the audience are asked to sway their bodies as if blown by the wind. The grasses are encouraged with waves of Mr. Harris's hand to blow and swish more loudly. Moving nearer to the microphone, Matthew makes a perfect changing of gear sound as he moves into a guttural second. Some among the audience stop swaying and swishing to clap their hands. The guitar quietens so Matthew seizes the moment to roar into third gear. Some of the boys in the audience make their own car noises. Matthew takes a bow and puts his arm round his now smiling little friend, who bows too.

Just before Mr. Harris removes the microphone, Matthew can be heard saying, "Be airplanes next."

Mr. Harris says in a commanding voice, "We have had enough engine noises, haven't we children? We are going to hear more about the terrible storm." Then turning to Matthew, "What is your name, sonny?"

"I'm Matthew Crosby."

"So, Matthew, if you don't want to be swishing grass in the wild wind you must go back to your seat."

I stand up. Matthew smiles and shakes his head; he does not budge. The musician winks at me. I am mortified.

The attention of the audience is focused on Matthew. As Mr. Harris is beginning to sing his tale, Matthew and the little boy, their arms outstretched, are imitating airplanes landing and taking off. Girls and boys, on stage and in the audience, are joining in. The musician thumps away at his piano, his foot taps a drum.

I know I must put a stop to all this. The young lady assistant is nowhere to be seen, so I go to the side of the stage and brazenly yell to the musician to give me my son back. He at once ceases his mischief and beckons Matthew to his side and persuades him to sit on the piano stool with him. The other little boy joins the chorus of swishing grass and somehow the performance resumes its course.

Matthew interrupts only once more, but again it is devastating. He quits the musician's stool, steps to the footlights, clasping his hands above his head in his well-practiced imitation of a prize fighter, and announces that Mr. Crosby is leaving now. He allows the young lady and the musician to help him descend from the stage.

Even now this awful scene has not come to an entire close because I am unable to persuade Matthew to leave the theater. I am not prepared to struggle with him just beneath those footlights so I give in and we sit down to wait out the remainder of the show. It ends and Matthew claps enthusiastically. As we pass through the foyer we hear little boys saying to one another, "That's hims, that's Matthew." A gratified Matthew nods graciously.

In later years at family gatherings or perhaps when friends are visiting and Matthew feels the occasion requires livening up with a good story, he prompts me, "Tell 'em, Mum, tell about Matthew 'n Mr. Rolf Harris." Then he sits back, head on one side, hoping I will consent to tell this yarn, every word of which he so loves and remembers that if I miss an incident or try to cut it down, he reprimands me, "Tell it right, Mum."

CHAPTER TWENTY-SEVEN

No Weather Today

FROM MY JOURNAL
Wiltshire, Easter 1979

Matthew started the second week of our holiday at our cottage in Wiltshire demonstrating his doleful feelings. Usually I could expect him to be fully dressed before he joined me for breakfast, but on this particular morning he made a dramatic appearance at the top of the stairs wearing only his underpants. He glared ferociously at me, defying me to send him back to finish dressing. Holding the bannister rail with one hand and using the other to clutch to his chest a bundle of his belongings, he began his descent. He stepped slowly and heavily on every tread of the staircase, then walked like a doomed man as he crossed our downstairs room, exaggerating the weight of his burden, which consisted of his clothes wrapped round his shoes, several small motorcars, and his beloved rag doll.

YEARS BEFORE THIS, when we retrieved Matthew from his incarceration in Normansfield Hospital, he brought with him his beloved velvet pig. In its prime it had been a bosomy, ladylike, cream-colored creature about ten inches tall and sewn into a floral dress. Matthew had stood watching while Gladys Strong and I unpacked his suitcase. When the pig surfaced, he seized this now-balding, empty-limbed remnant and clutched it to his chest. To me his pig's forlorn appearance was a symptom of all the misery that he had endured in that institution, and I was glad that it too had survived. But Gladys was made of sterner stuff.

"You don't need that dirty old thing. You get your sister to give you one of her nicer toys."

An American rag doll replaced the beloved pig. The doll had carrot-colored woolen plaits sewn round a flat cotton face, upon which were embroidered large peekaboo eyes, a red triangular nose, and a pursed mouth. Matthew was soon kissing and pressing morsels of food against her prissy lips. He shared his mugs of milk with her till she smelled so sour that I had to launder her clothes and scrub her face.

An American friend who came to stay with us brought at my request a replacement doll for Matthew. She assumed that since Matthew was a boy he would prefer a male doll. Luckily the face resembled its predecessor's. Matthew's new doll wore patched overalls and a red-checked shirt, and its hair was bright yellow. We told Matthew a tale about his dolly's visit to the hairdresser and to shops for new clothes. He appeared not to mind or even notice the change of gender. But over the ensuing weeks I noticed an alteration in his attitude toward his doll. Day by day he grew less tender and more comradely with it. He would chastise the doll when he himself had committed a misdemeanor. Though in those early days his words were often indistinguishable, the vowels and cadences sounded remarkably like Gladys's occasional tirades. It was she who pointed this out to me.

"He shows me up, don't he? Do I really scold that hard?"

"Yes," said her husband.

"No," said I, knowing that Matthew was rarely upset by her excoriations.

Everyone who was close to Matthew became familiar with the character of that doll and its subsequent replacements, which my friend continued to send to us over the years. Theo named him "Whipping Boy." The doll played that and several other roles during his service as Matthew's companion.

On a particular visit home, Whipping Boy was not in Matthew's luggage.

"Where is Boy?" I asked.

Matthew did not answer me at once. He stood for a while, then hunched his shoulders, and with hands pushed into his pockets, he puffed out his cheeks and spun around on one foot. I recognized this little charade as a signal that we must treat this conversation very lightly.

"Fifteen boys don't need dolls."

I was very sorry to hear those words. The Whipping Boy had served my needs too: by observing Matthew's treatment of him, I could determine whether Matthew was being well or poorly treated by fellow residents or even one or two members of the staff at his school. There were times when I was able to gauge the extent of Matthew's persecution simply by observing the rough usage Whipping Boy was receiving.

Once I heard Matthew telling him not to fuss. "Pain go away 'f you don't think bout it." Another time he held the doll high above his head and made it flap its arms. As he swooped it about he told it, "You deaded. You going to heaven. See you soon." Not a close friend but a fellow resident had died recently.

Making sure I had a replacement at hand, I asked if, after tea, we should not go and see if Whipping Boy was hiding in the boot of the motorcar.

"No, Mu-um," he shouted, "not no more," and left the room.

FROM MY JOURNAL (*continued*)

Having dumped his possessions on to it, Matthew dragged the sofa as near as possible to the wood-burning stove, then slumped himself among the cushions to set about portioning the toy cars between Whipping Boy and himself. Today the doll received only broken cars, which I understood to be a genuine, if unconscious, sign of his discontent. On a good day, Whipping Boy might have been told to choose any cars he wanted. After peeping at me over his shoulder to make sure he did not have my attention, Matthew picked up the fire tongs and prized open the doors of the stove. He poked the tongs into the coals till small flames flared, then he fell into conversation with them.

"Not very bright, you got t' grow. You hungry? Nice bits tree for breakfast?" He fed pieces of kindling and twigs between the bars. "Now, you, cheer up 'n keep on burning. 'S your job today." Alternately he fed wood to the stove and put on a piece of clothing, examining each garment, sometimes chastising it, "You wrong, don't look nice today." He struggled into a green-checked blouse with a girlish, rounded collar that he had found in his sister's cupboard; he liked the blouse because it had been part of her junior-school uniform. At last he seemed content with his appearance, so I busied myself making signals. I ran the tap into the kettle, clinked the cups onto their saucers, and jingled cutlery as I laid the table for our breakfast. I wondered out loud how many measures of porridge oats might be needed for two hungry people.

But Matthew was taken up with the fire again. I could hear him saying very softly, "You still hungry? Poor fire, tree all gone. Want paper?"

Before I could quite grasp the significance of this offer, I saw him stand on tiptoe and reach for a pile of my correspondence which lay on the chimney shelf. Putting each envelope into the grasp of the tongs, he fed it to the fire. To tantalize the fire and me, he waved the last letter in the air before consigning it to the flames, saying as he did so, "She don't need it."

This mischievous act cheered Matthew. He cackled with laughter and capered about the room. I did not wish to dampen his high spirits, but at the same time I thought it essential to demonstrate my disapproval, so I resorted to a device that I learned from Matthew himself. I assumed a strict expression and announced that I was going to be cross for a long time. I allowed him to perceive that my proposed anger was a formality, a ceremony to be gone through in the interests of fair play. I sat still and silent in my chair, leaving Matthew to continue the preparations for our breakfast. I tried not to watch too closely while he cooked too much porridge and stirred the pot too rousingly before he poured his lumpy gruel into our bowls, not caring that porridge slopped onto the tablecloth.

I had to break my rule of silence to suggest that the birds would like to eat what we could not, rather than the now nicely burning stove whose flames would die if porridge was poured onto them. I was aware that our heavy china coffee pot intimidated Matthew, but I gave him none of my usual tactful assistance as he timidly lifted it to pour two very shallow cups of watery coffee.

After breakfast I continued to sit as I pondered the problem of maintaining Matthew's renewed amiability.

During this wet Easter holiday, I was discovering that— now that he was nearly fifteen—spending two weeks in the country with me was no longer Matthew's idea of "the best of times." Until recently, mine was the most desirable of all company. He could immerse himself in almost every sort of time we spent together, interpreting the dullest of occupations as enchanting diversions of my devising. A few of our activities were still of some consequence to him. Our daily walks with the dog he now saw as disciplinary missions, undertaken for her benefit. Unnecessarily, he would attach a lead to her collar, then with a serious air and measured steps he walked with me as, in condescending tones, he endlessly admonished the dog. We might take the same path a few hours or a day later, following the perimeter of our property, where ancient and rotting trees protected newly planted saplings. This time the purpose of our walk was to collect firewood, so the dog was allowed to run free. She tore into the underbrush, making little yelping noises as she chased rabbits. Matthew, imitating her cries, loped after her; they were allies now. Together they would emerge from the thicket, Matthew dragging dead branches, which he manfully attempted to snap into manageable length by stamping on them as he had seen his father do.

The activity which Matthew considered of paramount importance was the buying of our supplies. On shopping days he would scan the larder. "Too much wrong things. Silly white yogurt, nasty brown sugar. Nearly none cornflakes, this much milk." Then in a mock despairing voice, "Where's right stuff gone?"

"What right stuff?"

"Ice cream, big bits 'f meat, curranty drink, cocoa dust, proper sugar, proper cheese, plenty 'f jelly, nice white bread. All gone."

I would put together a shopping list, then Matthew would take it away to rewrite it, dictating to himself under his breath, erasing and underlining until at last he was satisfied.

After Matthew washed and I dried the dishes, we stood together at the window, watching rain slide down the panes of glass, distorting the shapes of the box hedges and flattening the great yew tree which stood at our gate. We could see nothing beyond it. The hill that lay across our valley was eclipsed by a solid-looking fog. The expression on Matthew's face conveyed weary disappointment in me and the holiday. "Mum, why you let it rain still?" His certainty that I had the power to supply the things his heart most desired and remedy any mishap was negated by his conviction that I was horribly parsimonious with my omnipotence. It disgusted him when I allowed bad weather to occur.

"Do something, Mum."

"I cannot stop the rain."

"You did it last days."

"It was not I who made the sun shine last week."

"Well. Do it now." Then in a wheedling tone, "Please, Mum."

MATTHEW HAD ALWAYS been on intimate and combative terms with the weather. He gave it his constant attention, particularly when we were at the cottage. He often tried to talk the weather into behaving well. "You be good sky, I be good chap." He would step out of doors before breakfast and scan the sky and call, "'S all right, Mum, no weather today."

He often reentered the house mumbling, "Weather being nice. Now gotta stay that way."

Snow and rain were his enemies, but the wind was his worst foe. "Stop unkind horrid blowing." Strong sunlight hurt Matthew's eyes and gave him headaches. "My glasses very cross, shining back at sun loudly?" "Sun's too near, trying be under my hat." Addressing the sun, "You going in or I have to?" and "Sun trying to get indoors. I shut door."

Changing seasons upset Matthew. He wept the first time he realized that the coming of winter was inevitable. It happened as we walked together in the garden at Mount Tabor House. The day was bright but chilly. This combination annoyed him. "Make up your mind, Mister Weather, summer 'r winter." I started to explain that we were in a time between, called "autumn." Matthew was not listening; he was busy trying to avoid treading on the bright red and yellow leaves that strewed the grass.

"Try walking on them, Matthew, it feels nice."

He gave me a sour look. Just then we saw a rare sight. A Japanese maple tree appeared to give a tiny, decisive shudder, as all of its leaves simultaneously detached from their branches and floated gently to the ground. Matthew was appalled. "Look at lovely tree! 'S gone bare." He ran forward to catch the falling leaves. Unable to do so, he stooped and gathered a few then ran to the trunk of the maple, frantically he tried to plaster them against its trunk. "Come on, Mum, help put 'em back."

He was nearly crying by the time I persuaded him to give up his efforts. I removed his hands from the bark of the tree, "It's all right, Matthew, the tree doesn't mind, it happens every autumn."

"Horrid damn autumn," he stamped his foot.

WE TURNED FROM the window and together contemplated the cottage living room. Dampness darkened the stone walls, making the room somber and humid. The dog, who had been out in the rain earlier, was now dozing by the stove, giving off a pungent smell. Whipping Boy lay on the sofa among Matthew's discarded clothes. During the previous evening Matthew had obsessively sharpened his crayons, each one to a tiny stub. He then had flung them from himself in despair; with all their shavings they now lay scattered across the rush matting. I knew we could not remain cooped in the cottage for another wet day.

"Perhaps we should go to Salisbury."

"That London?"

"No. London is a hundred miles away. Salisbury is a country town, and today is market day."

Matthew brightened, "Aha, market! Can buy things?"

"What do you want to buy, Matthew?"

"Stronger pencils. Let me sharpen properly... See things to need."

"We must be careful with our money, Matthew."

"Why?"

"Your Dad works hard to get money for us all. We must not spend too much of it."

"Not spending Dad's money, get bank money, OK?"

Try as I might I had never been able to explain the mystery of money to Matthew. When he was a little child he had hated to even touch it. I was impressed with his innocent wisdom until I learned from Gladys that he had once put a penny in his mouth and the taste of it had so revolted him that he shied away from all coins. But now he was older, he liked the power of money and loved the magic of banks. He wanted to enter every one we passed.

"Ah, nice bank. Get rich, Mum."

He equated the signs that hung above the doors of banks with those above the doors of public houses; they signified a treat. He was very quick to spot the emblem of our particular bank, "Look, Mum, cross bird, go in there."

"We must not do that, Matthew."

"Why not?"

"We have spent enough money for today."

"Bank won't mind."

"But your Dad and I will."

"Puddin's."

At that time in his life, "pudding" was the most denigrating word in Matthew's vocabulary. Though he might pronounce it twice over in a loud voice, there were times when he could not make it sound scornful enough to express his contempt for my lack of understanding. To augment this most innocent of expletives he would give me a ferocious scowl and add, "Little monkey puddin' you."

I told Matthew that the first thing we must do when we arrived in Salisbury was cash a check. The fact that there was a branch of our bank in almost every town we went to never ceased to amaze him. "Ah, bank. Lots money today." So delighted was he that he acted a little parody for me. "Now, Matthew, put away things like good boy, carry stuff upstairs." And in a gruff voice remarkably like that of his teacher, "Be quick about it, young man." He obeyed himself with smiling civility, making a little bow before placing his foot on the first stair.

His mood was still carefree as I started the motor, though his spirits were somewhat quelled by the time we reached the bottom of our lane and discovered we would have to tunnel through billowing white mists. When we reached the small road that led to the main road, the beams of our headlights hardly pierced the fog. We nosed a passage between guessed-at hedges and farm walls until we left the valley of the Nadder River and came into a plateau of muted sunshine. We could see the shadow of our car bobbing across the layer of mist that filled the dips and valleys on either side of the highroad. To express his relief, Matthew brandished Whipping Boy round his head and sang a triumphant song. "We wonned nasty white, we wonned again, boys, we're the bosses."

In Salisbury we parked the motorcar behind St. Thomas's church. Matthew was "all eager for the fray." We examined the wares of nearly every stall in the marketplace, before, as Matthew put it, "The rain came to get us 'gain." We were driven to take shelter in an eating house. We sat companionably together in a wooden booth, trying to devise a perfect meal for the occasion. After many changes of mind and a request to borrow a pen, Matthew handed the waitress a note requesting, "No.1 pink milkshake. No.2 fish, lot of chips. No.3 yellow milkshake." I ordered bread and butter, smoked ham, and a pot of tea for two.

When we left the restaurant the rain was just as fierce in its attempt to "get us." In Leighton Buzzard, Matthew and I had stratagems for whiling away rainy Wednesday afternoons. If the weather was merely wet and not disagreeably cold, we would visit the local swimming baths. But on days such as this we would turn to other alternatives. Matthew's particular favorite was the town's indoor car park. There he would meander up and down its echoing concrete halls, awarding points to the motorcars. He might pit one level against another to discover which harbored the largest number of his favorite brand of car. We awarded silver stars to the shiniest and most cared-for, but he gave a gold star and sometimes a medal to "the best crashed" vehicle. A scratch or dent did not impress him, he looked for violently bent or broken motorcars. He stood looking at them in awe. In respectful terms he would ask, "Police chase you? Wrong side of road? Never mind, you very brave. You write, Mum, three star crash for poor old number..." He would call out the digits of the number plates. I wrote them in his car notebook.

Of all the places where we took cover from the rain in Leighton Buzzard, our most used shelter was the church. Its doors were never locked, and we rarely met anyone else there. As soon as we pulled the heavy oak doors closed, Matthew and I were in the chill embrace of the church's watery gloom; we would not so much walk as glide up the aisle, Matthew humming the sounds of muted organ music. Then at an appropriate moment, he would turn himself into an obsequious usher and show me to my pew. He handed me a prayer book and a hymnal and reminded me to "be good girl." I was his congregation. In turn he ordered me to kneel, to shut my eyes, pray loud, and sit very still. He liked to kneel at the altar and intone sonorously. As he rose from his knees he often bellowed a rousing "Now, never shall be. A man."

Matthew was familiar with two hymns, "There's a green hill..." and "The sea one..." He would mount the steps of the pulpit and wave his arms as we sang together. His monotone was intrepid, mine insipid. I was nervous in case the sounds we made might be heard by someone else. Now and again I glanced toward the closed door and Matthew would call, "Eyes front, sing up down there." All of a sudden he would tire of our game. Slapping a Bible or hymnal closed, he would bring our service to an end. He scrambled down from the pulpit and sashayed toward me, murmuring, "Collection. Collection. Plenty money, please." I paid up, then after a few more bars of simulated organ music, we would quit the church.

After one such sojourn, I asked Matthew to tell me about God. He put on his idiotic look, which sometimes meant he was thinking. "Not met him."

"Tell me what you know about him."

"God likes money."

BY THE TIME we reached Silver Minster, Matthew could not see through his glasses for the rain, so he took them off and slipped them in my pocket for safekeeping; then he pulled his collar over his ears, took a firm hold on the belt of my raincoat, and crouched behind me. "You lead, Mum." As if we were playing trains I steered him along the narrow pavement of the high street. At the canopy of North Gate, Matthew let go of my belt, stood upright, and opened his eyes. I asked him to put on his glasses so that he could look across the close and take in the vastness of the cathedral. Unless I reminded him to, Matthew had the habit of paying no attention to anything that was not near at hand. When we rode in the motorcar he rarely glanced beyond the dashboard. I tried to tempt him by commenting on other vehicles or reading out enticing number plates, but I was uncertain as to his perception of distance, just as I doubted his comprehension of the third dimension. If he had to descend an unfamiliar staircase, he sometimes took the precaution of sitting on the top step and bumping to the next one till he reached the bottom.

For him, photographs and illustrations had remained unreadable until this holiday, when he came upon a shelf full of his sister's childhood books. He brought one of them to the kitchen table and leafed through it while I was preparing our supper. Suddenly he took fright. I had to wait till his alarm subsided to elicit the cause. "Seed a face sticking out of paper." I believe it was the first time Matthew fully recognized an image on a flat surface. The incident was a revelation to us both.

HERE WE WERE before a great cathedral, a church multiplied and multiplied. Matthew skipped his way into it. He peeled off his wet coat and gave it several vigorous shakes as he marched up the aisle. Then he selected a pew and spread the coat as far as it would stretch. He called loudly to me, "Place for coats, Mum." Fearing he was already making himself too much at home, I put a restraining hand on his arm. I wanted to warn him that this was a very different kind of church from the one in Leighton Buzzard, an altogether more grand and public place where we had to be quiet. "No game playing in this cathedral, Matthew." He had spotted the collection boxes and darted from my grasp shouting, "Need lots of money for slot machine."

Matthew scampered along the south choir aisle, exploring one chapel after another, blowing at the lighted candles and rattling the coins into the "slot machines."

As we came abreast of the main transept we found ourselves the cause of reproachful looks and kindly rebukes. A small congregation was loosely assembled before the sanctuary. As soon as Matthew understood a service was being held he ran and seated himself in an empty choir stall. I had no choice but to go and sit next to him. I whispered that we were not part of the congregation and that we should leave. Ignoring me, he busied himself collecting all the prayer and hymn books he could reach. Now and again he imitated the devotional gestures of the congregation. He hummed loudly as the last hymn was sung. I was most relieved that the service had come to an end.

Some of the congregation remained kneeling, Matthew with them. The organ played softly as worshippers filed towards the open doors of St. Thomas's porch. Unaware that Matthew had left my side, I caught sight of him standing beside the steps of the pulpit looking up at the elderly priest, who was absorbed in his own private prayer. Matthew's stance was reminiscent of a poacher intent upon his prey, all the while mindful of a prowling gamekeeper—me. As swiftly as practicable, I dodged between departing worshippers and idling visitors till I was at Matthew's side. The prelate had gathered the skirts of his robe and was descending from the pulpit. I grabbed Matthew's hand just as he was about to push past the old man and climb the steps. The departing prelate gave us a kindly smile as he hastened toward the sanctuary.

"Matthew, you absolutely must not go up there."

"'S my turn, Mum."

"Please, Matthew." I could hear my voice ringing through the arches of the transept, down the main aisle, and into the chancery. Several heads turned. I realized the pulpit was fitted with amplifiers that must have been left on. I hesitated just long enough for Matthew to elude me. He hopped up the pulpit steps, found a hassock, and placed it so that he could see over the edge. Immediately and with great aplomb he set about making his pseudo-church noises. I couldn't bring myself to follow him up the steps and into the pulpit to wrestle with him. I became paralyzed as I imagined the sound of my pleading voice resounding to the very traceries of the cathedral. I took a certain comfort from observing that almost no one was taking any notice of his antics. I searched among the tourists for a sideman or some kind of cathedral attendant. I spied a black-robed official scurrying from pew to pew collecting prayer sheets. I asked him if he would spare a few minutes to assist me. With fussy dignity he walked away from me till he came to an ecclesiastical looking cupboard. He daintily selected a key from a great bunch that hung from his belt, opened the cupboard door and tucked his papers inside. Only then did he turn to me as I told him I urgently needed him to turn off the pulpit amplifier. He stood still for a moment, then said that if I listened carefully I would hear that the lunch hour service was still "in commencement."

"It is my son who is making those sounds."

"Then you are to be congratulated, madam, he has a fine delivery."

"He should not be up there, and I need you to help me get him down." I tried to make my plea sound flattering. "Your clothes, you know, and air of authority."

I took his elbow and propelled him forward, "Please, you only have to tell me where to find the switch that controls the loudspeaker."

We reached the bottom steps of the pulpit. "This gentleman says that is enough, Matthew, you must be quiet and come down now."

Matthew broke from his sermon and peered down at us. "Hallo, Mum, 's nice up here." He snapped the switches of the lamp that hung over the lectern. As I climbed the steps I tried to overcome my earlier horror of hearing my amplified voice pleading, "That's enough, Matthew."

With relief I heard only an ineffectual noise come from my mouth, inaudible against the other noises of the cathedral. The few curious onlookers who had gathered beneath the pulpit smiled kindly as they turned away. A little girl waved to Matthew. He waved wildly in return, "Don't have to go. 'S Mum's turn next."

I should have guessed that it was Matthew who was still in control of the amplifiers. Those last two words of his came forth in a roar. At the same instant we were both brilliantly illumined. An agile black figure flew past me up the steps into the pulpit. My seemingly ineffectual official swept Matthew's hand from the panel of switches; all became dark and quiet. Only a sibilant whisper could I hear. "Now then, Sonny, down that stair and out of here you go. You have made quite enough mischief for one day. You'd best get on home and make your Mum a nice cup of tea." He shepherded us down the aisle. "Stopped raining, thank goodness." He handed us our coats.

I started to apologize but he cut me short, saying, "It's all right, my dear, don't fret. Sonny boy did no more than cause a few red faces. We're all God's children." Turning to Matthew he added, "And God's children must try to be good children, mustn't they?"

He looked so stern that Matthew could only whisper, "'S right, sir."

CHAPTER TWENTY-EIGHT

Bus Rides

FROM MY JOURNAL
Another Easter (1980)

A cold morning at Eastertime when the sunlight carries no warmth but makes us restless and reveals so much dust in our house that I am able to persuade Matthew to vacuum some of the rooms. His propensity for setting himself interesting targets within what would otherwise be boring jobs applies very well to vacuuming.

He rolls up his sleeves, adopts what he believes is an intrepid "nerly" sixteen-year-old chap's pose, and says in a stern voice, "'M ready, boys, steady 'm always ready."

He assembles the vacuum cleaner and wrestles it into the room, placing it in a strategic position as if he is planning a battle. Next he shunts all the movable pieces of furniture into a corner and tucks smaller objects into places of safety, reassuring them as he does so, "'S not for long, boys." A Noh Theater red-lacquered lion mask is warned, "No biting, please." Oddly enough, Dido used to talk to this mask, too, and from time to time we found morsels of food in its mouth.

Having cleared the floor, Matthew marches over to the vacuum cleaner, grasps the handle and orders it to get started. He vacuums in long lines as if mowing a lawn. Having cleaned from north to south, he sweeps again, east to west. I once interrupted one of Matthew's cleaning games because he was contentedly walking up and down with only the tubular piece in his hand. I pointed out that it was not attached to anything. He waved me aside, "Shhh; hasn't noticed."

I asked him to retrace the work after we reattached it.

"Nope. 'S done."

"But it's still dusty, Matthew."

"Yep, his arm fell off."

Suddenly Matthew switches off the vacuum cleaner and announces that today is not a cleaning day, "More a bus day."

We have heard about a new type of bus ticket; its very name, "Red Rover," is alluring to Matthew. The advertisement says that it will carry a person anywhere in London for the duration of one day only. Matthew puts on his two-toned padded jacket and slips a little red bus and a London taxi into its pockets. He reminds me we must pee before we go. Then he locks up the house for me, and we walk to the bus station. By the time we reach the counter I have coached Matthew as to how to buy our tickets. He is nervous that I will become impatient and say the words for him; he is also nervous that I won't. The only person he trusts in this sort of situation is his sister, who has a quiet way of managing things so that he says the words with her.

With relief I notice that the man serving behind the counter is willing to hear Matthew out. He makes his rehearsed request timidly. I whisper the elusive words and repeat the price the man is asking. Matthew counts out our money, then is rather reluctant to part with it. But he is all smiles when he is handed the tickets. He pokes his hand into the little aperture to shake hands with the clerk, who obligingly offers two fingers in return. The outing is starting very well.

We are both aware that because Matthew carries a special identity card we could have purchased a ticket at a much reduced price, but my wish not to hurt his pride overcomes my parsimony. We decide that we will take the very first bus that arrives at the bus stop. It turns out to be a Number 9, which we know well, and since the bus is near the beginning of its journey all the seats are vacant.

We scramble up the stair to the top deck and settle ourselves before the front window. We watch our local shops and streets go by and in no time we are in Kensington High Street. Today Matthew makes it a point to look out for taxis and cars of English make; he signals and waves his pocket models at them and salutes fellow buses.

He is not tempted to change to another bus till we arrive at Hyde Park. There Matthew sees an irresistible Number 22. We climb off our bus, but he has been slow coming down the stairs so we miss the Number 22 we saw from the window. Matthew is mournful. He cheers up when I convince him that another 22 will appear at any minute. When it arrives, we try for the top front seats again. This time they are occupied, so Matthew applies a maneuver he has pulled off before. Ashamed of the charade that is about to take place, I sit out of earshot. Meanwhile Matthew stands pressed against the front window, obscuring the view of the occupant of the seat he covets. Very soon that person relinquishes it to him. Matthew gives me a triumphant glare as smugly he accepts the seat. He waits for the one beside him to fall empty, then loudly calls me to join him. Having arranged things to his liking, he gives himself entirely to the pleasure of riding on a Number 22.

As we bowl along Piccadilly, I know that at any moment he will catch sight of another bus with a tempting number. Sure enough, we see a 12 heading toward Whitehall. We catch that one only because it is stuck in a traffic jam. To Matthew this seems an act of great cleverness. He is enjoying his outing prodigiously. This time, we seat ourselves in the front downstairs so that Matthew can watch the driver. We cross Westminster Bridge and ride south. The bus picks up and drops passengers less frequently. When the conductor calls out, "Elephant and Castle," Matthew cowers in his seat and slips his hand into mine; he dislikes elephants.

We stay on the bus till we reach Camberwell Green, where we change to a 36. "Three time twelve, Mum."

Our morning's journey finishes in Peckham, only because the conductor shouts, "All change; end of the line." On the pavement we find it windy and cold. As we walk along the dismal shopping street we come upon a public house, "The Three Bells." Matthew tells me he can hear them "very loud." He behaves as if it is our destiny to go inside, as if the whole journey was undertaken so that we could eat our lunch here.

He decrees that we sit by the bar on high stools. I tell him I would prefer we find a table at the back of the room, but he gives me a scornful smile and announces he is going to "love" the nice brown lunch he sees other people eating. I buy him an alcohol-free beer. He holds up his glass and calls, "Cheers," to the depressed-looking regulars who convene on the cushioned benches beneath the large windows. One of them, in drunken affability, shambles toward us. Matthew is pleased at first and very polite. Then after trying to grasp what the man is saying, he gives up and grandly refers him to me. "Wants something, Mum."

The man takes a rather phony stance of being offended and calls to a friend, "What's this chap on about, did I ask for anything?"

His friend heaves himself over to us. Matthew looks anxious and confused. I put my arm around him and tell him to help me carry our plates to a table, but he does not want to relinquish his bar stool. The barman now comes over and admonishes the two drunks. He gives me a reproachful look, indicating we should make ourselves less conspicuous.

I sit there thinking that I certainly would if I could, and I wonder what I should be doing to prevent these outings from turning into this sort of predicament? But I am not cast down for long, simply because it is very touching to see the pleasure it gives Matthew to be allowed to do as other people do in places he can seldom reach without my escort. It is, after all, his day out, and who am I and who are the drunks, or even the bartender, that we should spoil it for him?

We go home following the simple device of reversing the order of the buses. We ride aboard a 36, a 12, a 22, lastly a 9. Matthew is proud of the symmetry. As we go along passing each of them he mutters, "Mustn't get on you, 7, not you, 15, not 19, not 27."

We descend from our last ride to find ourselves just across the street from where we started out. We drop in at the bakery and buy crumpets for tea. Matthew is gingerly toasting them beneath the grill as I write this account. He has made us a pot of tea. I am about to surreptitiously mop up the hot water that is spilled on the table. After tea he will inevitably ask what we are having for supper, and later, what we will do tomorrow, but for the moment buttering crumpets is the only thing that interests him.

CHAPTER TWENTY-NINE

Matthew in Love

By the age of five Matthew had learned to parry the facetious and rather unkind question that Gladys's children liked putting to him, "Who are you going to marry when you grow up?" Love was a much joked-about subject in the Strong household. Matthew probably learned his answer from Gladys herself.

From the day Dido presented it to him, Gladys would comment, "He loves that creature fit to marry." That creature was the velvet pig which had served as Matthew's consort throughout his confinement at Normansfield Hospital, the creature Gladys unceremoniously threw out as soon as he was once more in her care. He must have saved some remembered essence of the pig's identity from its balding and kapok-leaking corpse to reinvest in a more personable lady pig, one Matthew and most of the other children of England watched twice weekly on the television screen.

Gladys's children would tease Matthew, "Go on, tell your mum who you are going to marry."

"Miss Piggy."

"Do you think she's pretty?"

"Don't know."

"Do you want to kiss her?"

"No."

"Why do you want to marry her?"

"Like her."

Now and again Matthew gave a wrong answer.

"Who are you going to marry?"

"Kermit Frog."

"You can't, silly, it's a boy frog."

"Like him."

Year after year, exchanges of this kind never failed to raise laughter, but Matthew's constancy did not waver. He really seemed fond of his cruel-tongued, brassy television idol and of her almost saintly protagonist, in whom he may have perceived something of himself. When he went to board at Macintyre School, I was relieved to discover that this sort of repartee did not take place. Perhaps the staff discouraged discussion of inappropriate and delicate issues, or perhaps those who lived at Mount Tabor House were simply too taken up with the reality of their daily lives.

That is, until the winter of 1979, when Matthew was fifteen years old. At that time there arrived a little person who, Matthew's housemother told me, was sent away from her home because she had become too much of a "handful" for her elderly parents. By all accounts, this handful, whose name was Sarah, fairly shimmied her way into the community of Mount Tabor, swinging her hair about and swishing the pleats of her tartan skirts. She wore pretty blouses with baby-like collars, and she owned a cardigan to match each of her outfits. This picture-book girl possessed not everyday footwear but several pairs of party shoes.

All these attributes registered most deeply among the girl residents, whose admiration and envy of Sarah prompted Gwen and the housemothers to exercise themselves to improve the appearance of all the other girls in their care.

FOR A TIME Sarah remained "a girl's girl." She gathered about herself a little band of the more capable and acceptable-looking female residents, and dragooned them into an obsequious little coterie.

During all the years he lodged with Gladys Strong, Matthew had lived in a womanish environment. Gladys kept him at her side and encouraged him to play the little prince in her all-female court. Until he came to live in Macintyre School, he was taught only by women teachers. I took him to the houses of my female friends. It was not their husbands who gave him the freedom of saucepan cupboards, allowed him to strum on family pianos and pick flowers in their gardens. In those days it was hardly expected of a man that he concern himself with any children other than his own, particularly not ones of Matthew's sort.

Thus, when he was tempted to do so one winter Sunday, Matthew could sense no barrier to keep him from crossing the playroom floor and threading his way through Sarah's little group of sycophants, there to draw up a chair and make himself at home.

He was lying on the floor after tea one Sunday, parking and reparking his toy motorcars between the legs of a chair, when Sarah entered the playroom. He had watched as she bore down upon a group of children who were sitting at the large table in the bay of the window. She indicated that they should clear aside their toys. By the time she was snapping open her flower-patterned suitcase, in which she kept a lipstick she never used, a hairbrush, several ruled notebooks, and her collection of ballpoint pens, Matthew was at her side. He saw that the suitcase also was fairly bulging with tattered women's magazines.

Sarah picked one out and leafed through it. She then snatched someone else's chair, sat herself down, selected a pen, and found a clean page in one of her notebooks. She proceeded to pat her hair and adjust the pleats of her skirt, in doing so allowing her girlfriends time to assemble themselves about her. With a flourish, she proceeded to demonstrate her capacity to copy words from a printed page. Sarah had the neatest and most regular-looking longhand; it flowed from her pen. Matthew was overcome with admiration. His housemother told me he hurried off to find his own pencil case and writing book. When he rejoined Sarah, she had already filled a whole page.

"'S beautiful, c'n I see?"

She graciously held her book out to him. He studied her writing carefully. "You the cleverest. Wha's 't say?"

She indicated that she felt his question to be somewhat stupid. "I don't know. I just copied it."

Matthew's perennial struggle to write clear messages and make readable lists weighed heavily upon him. His scribbly handwriting looked more like tiny contemporary abstract drawings than a cohesive series of sentences. I found his "written work" to be touching and valiant but quite impossible to decipher, so when I next brought him home and he showed me his writing book, I saw what at first seemed to be a miraculous improvement. Words rested on lines and his script was almost neat.

It was my turn to ask, "What does it say?"

"You read it, Mum."

I tried the first sentence. It too had been copied from one of those ladies' magazines. I stumbled through a couple of lines that warned too much permanent waving harmed the scalp. When I saw Matthew's puzzled expression I stopped.

"Try better page, Mum."

I was able to make some sense from the next lines he ordered me to read. They concerned the brake linings of racing cars. For a moment or two I had Matthew's rapt attention. "I write that? Clever chap?"

"Don't you know what you wrote?"

"No. Didn't read. Copied."

"Why would you copy out something you can't read, Matthew?" At once I felt contrite. My question was too sharp. I could see it troubled him, but he found an answer.

"Writing like books, like Dido, like Dad. Sarah does it."

Later he asked me for a "proper man's hand bag for writing things." We found exactly what he meant, one of Theo's discarded briefcases. He took it back to school filled with notebooks, ballpoint pens, pencils, erasers, sharpeners, and a new copy of *Motor Racing Monthly*.

"This stuff quite better 'n Sarah's, you think?"

I escorted Matthew to his schoolroom, where I spoke with his teacher. She told me that at least where writing was concerned, she thought Sarah might prove a good influence. "She seems to encourage him to write clearly." However, she promised she would try to ensure that Matthew understood what he wrote. She added that Matthew was in his own fashion doing quite as well as Sarah, who when asked if she could read, stated the exact case: "Yes, I wead and wite vewy wew but wivout compwehension."

Summer came, and Matthew and Mark rode their bicycles. At fifteen Matthew was taller than Mark. As he outgrew a bicycle, Mark would grow into it. Together they pedaled faster and faster, Mark more proficient, Matthew more stylish. It took a long summer and autumn for Matthew to master the brakes; until he did, he used two devices for coming to a standstill. One, to pedal his bicycle deep into the piles of grass cuttings that were left fermenting on Mount Tabor's compost pile; the second, to steer himself onto the lawn, there to make a cruising fall with his machine. That autumn football games were organized. Mark played any position on the field, whereas Matthew was always a rather stationary goalkeeper.

Within doors Matthew was now happily ensconced among Sarah's gang, the only male permitted. Side by side, he and Sarah did their writing. When the community assembled to watch "after tea television," Sarah would reserve him a place on the sofa, which she now considered her private territory. With a proprietary gesture she would beckon him and pat the cushion invitingly.

I was told by the staff that Matthew bore the honor of her patronage blithely. He continued in his old ways, larking with Mark, being unselfconsciously tender, not with Sarah's chosen few, but with the weaker and less capable girls and boys, some of whom he pointed out to me. The friend with "gone wrong legs got metal bits," another whose head was "too big, voice comes out furry," a little girl wearing "fat glasses with tinsy handles" to keep her eyes open. He could be depended upon to push, without roughness, wavering arms into sleeves and wavering feet into Wellington boots. Despite his distaste, he wiped the littlest girls' and boys' noses.

For one reason or another I sometimes had to bring outsiders to Mount Tabor House. Standing beside them, as if seeing the room through a looking glass, I could for a minute or two catch their impression of the place. A slightly disinfectant-smelling, none too tidy domicile, cackling laughter and inarticulate jabber reverberating down its corridors. Shrinking, shuffling, lunging beings, attended as often as not by raffish-looking, long-haired and bearded, or long-skirted and sandalled, easygoing staff.

I wondered if without Matthew as my intermediary I might have taken in not much more than that view. As it was, I saw the school as a homogeneous community whose staff and residents were touchingly communicative with one another. The more time I spent there, the less constrained I was by the infirmities and afflictions of the residents.

The emotional climate was placid and the pace very slow. Everyone was helped to function as best they could. Lessons were taught and retaught. Unwarranted temperamental behavior, overindulgence, laziness, and other sorts of selfish conduct were amiably discouraged. I realized with profound gratitude that, for Matthew, this sort of institutional life was the best we could hope for. Despite all his fears and failures, he liked it, as well as I did for him.

AFTER HAVING SHOWN so much caution in reconciling himself to boarding-school life, Matthew all of a sudden embraced it. This came about when he discovered that the regulations, which he found daunting at times, and daily rituals were actually the solution to a mystery that had vexed him for a great part of his life. They revealed themselves to be a round-the-clock answer to his great reoccurring question, "What do I do now?" Attuned to his surroundings, Matthew seemed quite as well ensconced as he had been in Gladys Strong's house. Mark's friendship was an invaluable bonus.

His school reports continued to make references to the close-ness between the two boys. Nobody foresaw any harm in either one's dependency upon the other until Sarah's coquettish behavior started to rupture the friendship. Then, with hindsight, it was wondered if Matthew should not have been encouraged to form more than one close friendship.

After years of copying from the pages of her women's magazines, perhaps Sarah had begun to take in some of their messages; or her oncoming adolescence may have brought about the mischief. At teatime one day she announced that she needed a "boy fwend." One of the two members of staff who obliged me by recounting this whole tale verbatim, pointed out to her that she had one already, Matthew; he was a boy, wasn't he, and he had been her companion at the big table and on the sofa for a long time.

"He is not a weal boy. I'm not going to kiss *him*!"

Matthew remained gallant. He answered softly, "Don't have to."

The younger of my two raconteurs did a fine mimicry of Sarah as she pushed her chair from the tea table and got to her feet. He told how she pressed her forefinger to her lips. At once she had the attention of everyone in the dining room. Her finger caressed her mouth as she examined each of the male faces turned in her direction. Her other finger hovered. "I'm go-wing to choose..." She drew a wide arc, then dropped her hand to point at Mark, "Y...you. Mark can be my boy fwend."

That evening, Matthew found himself barred from his habitual place at the work table. He was never again beckoned to sit on the sofa. To prevent his being too aware of these rebuffs, the housemothers would try to distract him. They told him they needed his help in getting the "little ones" prepared for bed, and they asked both Matthew and Mark to help serve the evening cocoa.

After a week or two, Mark's failure to appreciate the honor she did him stirred Sarah to resort to more overt action. One evening she left her place on the sofa and minced across the playroom. She pushed the toe of her shoe between Mark and Matthew where they sat next to each other on the floor, then seized Mark's hand. He laughed as she pulled him to his feet; he was still laughing as she led him back to the sofa. She resumed her seat, repeating the gesture she had so often used for Matthew, she patted the cushion beside her. Mark flopped onto it. Hardly giving him time to settle, Sarah lifted his arm and draped it across her shoulders as if it were a heavy shawl. She wriggled so as to wedge her body next to his, then lifted her head and kissed his lips. She turned to face the room. Making an encompassing gesture, she called out, "You lot have to whistle evewy time I do that—like on telewision."

Mark was an affectionate friend. It was his habit, during television time, to sit against Matthew, holding his hand or encircling his waist. He often tickled or pummeled Matthew. I am sure it did not occur to him to resist Sarah's caresses; instead he called Matthew to join them on the sofa. Matthew gladly rose to his feet. Carrying his cup of cocoa carefully, he stepped across the carpet, then made as if to sit where Mark had cleared a space for him.

Sarah shrieked, "Not you!"

Mark looked bemused but did not object, so Matthew sidled away. Other such scenes began to take place. At first Matthew could not learn from them, nor, for that matter, did Mark. Several members of the staff realized that the kisses were beginning to intrigue Mark and that Sarah was flaunting her power over him. She alternated between withholding or exaggerating her embraces, behaving more outrageously if she thought Matthew was watching.

Both boys were bewildered but as yet not antagonistic toward each other. If Matthew looked dejected, Mark would hug him, though he quickly learned not to do so in front of Sarah. Sarah's coterie felt it incumbent upon them to shun Matthew, some with disdain, others regretfully. Matthew was taken aback by this. He blushed uncontrollably and his eyes filled with tears. Often this made the girls relent.

Mark reacted roughly if he thought Matthew was being a baby. He would pull Matthew back into the room when he saw he was about to sneak away from the amorous scenes Sarah was orchestrating. If he succeeded, he would subject him to a curiously primitive display. He either danced around the downcast Matthew or made threatening boxing gestures till Matthew once again attempted to quit the room. At that point Mark would deftly trip him so that Matthew would tumble to the ground, where he would usually lie passively, forced to be audience to displays of proprietary burlesque. A clownlike Mark would pat Sarah's head, play with her hair, take her hands in his and clap them together, and as a finale, curl himself into her lap and kick his heels in the air while making exaggerated baby noises. If Matthew laughed, then for a while all might be well between the two boys. Decently, this scene was not mimicked for me.

Sarah exhibited signs that she was not entirely flattered by the scenes Mark enacted. When Sarah was displeased, there would be thunder in the air. Mark was pushed aside so that she could ostentatiously rearrange her skirt and pat her hair in place, while contorting her features so as to express disgust for "siwwy" Mark. So as to regain his standing with Sarah, Mark sometimes attacked Matthew all over again.

Having heard all this, I asked myself why would Mark's knocking Matthew to the floor and straddling his chest until his breathing became so labored that those who were watching would run for help bring such exaltation to Sarah? How was Mark able to divine that it would do so? Were all three of them, Sarah, Mark, and poor Matthew, simple though they were, victims of some atavistic and inborn human traits?

CHAPTER THIRTY

Saturday Out

The headmistress Shirley had great respect for Theo; her one caveat was his lack of interest in his son's development. So at this juncture, she decided to send him little month-by-month reports. "Matthew's behavior in the classroom is deteriorating." "Matthew is at times very inattentive." "He now mumbles his words." "Matthew is by no means as responsive to his teachers and friends as he used to be." "Matthew is beginning to isolate himself from us all." In the last note she almost ordered that we both take him out for the day, but cautioned us not to bring him home to London. "We want him to regard this as his home. This is where his problems should be resolved."

I GOT UP early and drove to spend an entire Saturday with Matthew.

"What shall we do with our Saturday, Matthew?'

"Dunno."

"What would please you most?"

"Dunno."

"Are you hungry?"

"'Spect so."

"Do you need any new clothes, is there anything you would like to buy?"

"Motorcar."

"Shall we go to the toy shop?"

"Nope, real one."

"You know I can't buy that for you. You are not old enough to drive on real roads. Only grownups do that."

"Want to do it after I've et lunch."

We talked of motorcars all through the meal. On any other subject, Matthew was monosyllabic. He sat with his head and shoulders hunched. He seemed unable to prevent himself from pulling at the raw and bleeding sides of his fingernails. His clothes matched his mood; he wore odd socks.

While Matthew was small enough, I would sit him on my lap and let him hold the steering wheel of the motorcar as I drove. Sometimes he used to sit beside me and operate the gear lever. He learned the mechanics of driving in no time. I would take him to various estates and parks west of London: Bushey or Richmond Park, Wimbledon Common, sometimes Epsom Down or, nearer to Gladys's house, Osterley Park. The keepers either turned a blind eye upon us or simply did not notice his presence between the steering wheel and me.

In those days he gave me orders as he sat on my knee. "Press foot, Mum, so I do gear. 'S right, now second-third. Like third best." His coordination was good, and he gave all his attention to what he was doing, "Sh, sh, Mum, listening to engine." Since his legs were not long enough to reach the pedals, I was able to keep control of the accelerator and foot brake. "Faster, please, 's good girl."

After Matthew's removal from London to MacIntyre School, we drove the motorcar in this way much less often. I would have been ashamed if his staff heard from him that I encouraged Matthew in a practice they would have rightly considered irresponsible and dangerous. So we indulged in this clandestine pursuit only when it was apparent to me that Matthew was feeling very dejected. Then we would go to the almost empty grounds of Mentmore House.

After being recognized and waved on by the gatekeeper, we were free to drive in the park. For more than an hour Matthew steered the motorcar. I had never before let him drive for so long and never before did he do it so well. As I pressed and released the clutch, he changed gear with great facility; he told me to brake just when it was appropriate to do so. Sitting behind him, his weight upon my knees, I grew cramped and uncomfortable.

"Sit still, Mum, going long far way in motorcar."

I obeyed. Finally to my relief he drew to the side of the road. "Need a pee."

He climbed out of the car and skipped across the grass to a grove of trees. I watched him as he walked back toward me, his whole demeanor changed. Holding his head high, he looked over to me. "Tea time now."

He was charmingly frivolous as we ate tea. He consumed his toast, his buns, and his pink milkshake with a deliberately sloppy gusto. He eyed me from time to time. "Cheer up, Mum, I have your bun?"

As I drove in the dull evening light through the village of Wingrave and we entered the school gates, I tried to explain that I would always be his mum, always love him, but I had to be busy because Dido was ill.

"Knowed all that, don't mind you; mind Mark."

We had not reached the school front door but I stopped the engine. "What is it you mind?"

"Minded ... not more I don't ... Horrid, horrid Mark ... mind horrid stupid Matthew—Matthew can't stop be silly." He leaned forward and banged his head again and again on the dashboard.

I tried to put my arms round him. He pushed me from him. Ugly, wet-sounding groans seemed to belch out of him. I thought he was about to vomit. I gave him my handkerchief. Pushing up his spectacles, he draped the handkerchief over his face. I waited. He was crying, not loudly like a child but softly and piteously, as if defeated. He kept his face veiled, but he allowed me to comfort him, just a little at a time, a pat on the shoulder, a stroke on the back of his hand.

We sat in silence till it was almost dark, then we went into the building. I led him to a bathroom and helped him wash his face and regain some composure. In his room, I found a matching pair of socks and helped him put them on. I accompanied him to the door to the dining room. A boy with irons on his legs held the door open. Matthew took the child's hand. I waved goodbye and went in search of Shirley.

From her I heard the tale of Matthew's love, Sarah's manipulative powers, and Mark's enslavement. Those two had been hastily promoted to the senior school, leaving Matthew to recover his spirits as best he could.

Shirley mused that there were those on the staff, a little conventional but well-meaning, who could not accept that any such incomplete being (I am sure she used a more sensitive or professional term) as Matthew could feel such love, such courtly love, for a friend. But she said there were others who, having day by day witnessed the unfolding of Matthew's drama, gave full credence to his suffering and had done their best to distract him from his melancholy.

A teacher named Penny had recently loved quite as desperately and was now pregnant. She, more than any of the other staff at Mount Tabor House, understood his heartache. She tried to distract him. "Do you know, Matthew, I'm going to have a little baby one day soon."

Matthew had not lived in Gladys Strong's house without gaining some knowledge of that subject. "Very little baby I 'spect, can't see his bump."

Over the weeks he became almost proprietary toward Penny and her pregnancy. He fetched and carried for her, opened doors and bowed as she passed through, offered chairs for her to sit on, went to the kitchen and demanded cups of tea for her. He liked to lean over Penny's stomach and talk confidingly to the fetus. "Come out soon." "Be good boy, all red 'n tiny face."

The next time I paid a visit to Matthew he greeted me with a pictograph he had drawn, little boots, a tin of talcum powder, and sundry parcel shapes. He explained that it was a shopping list. "Things for Penny's baby, Mum."

We looked in the appropriate shops, searching for what Matthew considered essentials for babies. He would not let me choose or pay. "Too big for our baby," he indicated with his fingers, "Penny says 'pocket-sized.'" I divined from this description that she had confided her news to Matthew rather early in her pregnancy, perhaps to distract him from his own woes.

Disregarding Penny's larger and larger stomach, Matthew obstinately clung to the image of the pocket-sized baby. When Penny finally gave birth to a girl of normal weight, he was disappointed.

"Have you seen Penny's new baby?"

"Yep. Girl."

"Is she a nice baby?"

"Yep. Nope. Don't know."

"I'm glad you like her."

"Penny took wrong baby out of bump."

There were no more handwritten notes from Shirley. When she came to London for the next MacIntyre School board meeting, Theo took her out to dinner. He said they did not find time to talk about Matthew till their meal was almost ended. Then she told him that Matthew was enjoying some degree of seniority at Mount Tabor House. Though he did not command much authority, he now had a large following among the less capable children. She said this was a clear indication that his recent setbacks had probably only been due to his amatory troubles.

Theo asked, "His what troubles?"

"Hasn't Anne told you of his recent unhappiness, how he lost his lady love to his best friend?"

Theo invited her to retell the story. When she had finished he asked if one should take "that sort of stuff" seriously. He confessed to her that he found it hard to credit that a boy whose mental age had been assessed as that of a three-and-a-half-year old could feel such emotions. Shirley answered him with a question, "Do you mean to say that you believe that your son is incapable of love?"

When he repeated this conversation to me, he said he had not replied to Shirley's question because he had not wanted to admit that it was impossible for him to imagine any part of what Matthew thought or felt.

CHAPTER THIRTY-ONE

Parting from Theo

Dido's sequence of operations from 1974 onwards robbed her of almost a year's normal life. After that year, more months had to pass before she was free of her wheelchair and crutches. At the end of each agonizing phase, as our tensions eased, Theo and I discovered that our delicately balanced closeness eroded a little further; practices we had assumed integral to our marriage turned out to have no substance. We acted more and more separately until we hardly saw each other, much less touched. I even had the impression that our voices sounded eerie. Through this drawn-out and crucial time—which resembled a perpetual predawn—we depended upon a kind of tender magnanimity in all our dealings with one another.

Through Dido's most harrowing hours, as I sat beside her after she was operated on, as I watched in the nights, then again in daylight, as she dropped in and out of pain-ridden sleeps, a sequence of filmlike scenes would invade my imagination, repeating themselves again and again with minor variations. The story always began with my coming across her as she stood in a river, trying to resist the force of a strong current. The water eddied against her legs, yet she managed to keep her feet planted on the riverbed. She looked cold, but gave a bright smile when she saw me. Not too alarmed, I waded into the river to hold her hand. The water would rise, swirling up to Dido's waist, sometimes to her chest. I moved closer to give her more support. Once or twice the level of the water reached Dido's shoulders, even her neck; then I braced myself firmly behind her and together we pushed to withstand the current.

Next Theo would come into view as he walked along the bank. Despite her struggle to keep her balance, Dido never failed to wave to him, which caused Theo to put down the bundle of papers and the briefcase he was carrying and wave back. Not taking in at first the direness of our predicament, he would keep smiling, till sudden realization made him tear off his spectacles and cast them to the ground.

At that precise moment, the current started to slacken and the level of the water dropped. I wanted to make some reassuring signal to Theo, but I dared not let go of Dido. I never could make out whether Theo had seen the change in the river and so turned and bent down to search for his spectacles, or if in his semi-blindness he stumbled. I know that his momentary piteousness reminded me that I loved him.

While Dido was overcoming her illness and learning to walk again, the most symbolic constituents of that dream underwent a series of mutations which made it easier and easier to bear. In its second-to-last version, Dido and I simply waded out of the cool water to find Theo impatiently searching for his spectacles. As I retrieved them for him, I saw that only one lens was intact. Theo mumbled that he could see well enough with one eye and settled down to read a newspaper while Dido dried herself with a bright mauve towel and I unpacked a picnic basket I seemed to have left ready.

In September of 1976, on the last Sunday before Dido was to start her fourth year at boarding school, and just before we were to pack up and leave our Wiltshire cottage, Theo, Dido, and I carried our lunch across the meadow to eat it on the grass beside the little river, the Nadder, which I already knew was the leitmotif of my dream. Theo's spectacles were being repaired and his temporary ones were making his head ache, so he lay down on the rug we spread, put the spectacles in his pocket and closed his eyes. I sat beside him idly watching Dido, who had taken off her shoes and was knee-deep in the river searching for specimens of water insects.

All at once as if from nowhere a wind came scooping down our valley. It bent the willow trees and riffled the surfaces of the Nadder. Flying cumulonimbus clouds raced across the sun, one after the other. Theo and I had in a desultory way taken up and let drop a rather sour dispute about my growing wish to travel. During the ensuing silence I too lay down so as to watch the clouds as they massed and shredded in the wind.

Though perfectly awake I had the sensation that the three of us were participating in yet another version of my dream. The scenery around us was intimately scaled and our own. I watched Dido as she waded upstream, insinuating first one foot then the other between the hanks of silken water weed. Now and again she would give an irritable shrug of her shoulders. I got the impression that the weight of our presence was oppressive to her.

Though he lay supine, Theo's body was rigid, his eyes not so much closed as squeezed shut, his hands knotted in fists against his chest. I looked at myself; I was no longer idly surveying the scene, but sitting upright, jerkily arranging the objects around me. I was aware that I had a placating expression on my face which was meant to mask my resentful feelings.

In that moment of clarity, I knew that Theo and I had lost perhaps not all our love but our essential liking for each other, and I was appalled. My reflex was to reach out and touch Theo. Although he was nearly asleep I did not catch him unawares. I asked did he think we liked each other enough? His answer came in a cool drawl, a counter question: he asked, "Does it matter"? We exchanged no further words, yet it was as if a terrible quarrel had taken place. I had probed. I had been worse than inept; I had breached our contract.

We went through our prearranged plan, we ate our sandwiches, tidied the cottage, and drove Dido to her school, then he and I took the road to London.

From that time on, our separateness intensified till it became our separation. I suggested to Theo that we seek help from a therapist. When he refused, I half respected him and made visits to a doctor by myself. Theo assumed we were hiding our incompatibility from Dido, but I knew better. I had no anxieties on Matthew's behalf, since he was not aware of the convention that parents came in pairs. Later Dido told me she found a positive relief in our parting, but at the time, perhaps mistakenly, I saw opposite signs and they gave me dreadful guilt.

Later both Theo and I took on other loves, Theo more than one, I one. Not surprisingly, it was that one who caused the final fissure. Theo announced he had found a better place to live where the rooms conformed more perfectly to his notion of "spacious simplicity." Thus in his mocking way he felt able to explain to Dido that it was on account of our less than perfect house, rather than our less than perfect marriage, that he was moving to a penthouse in Whitehall. When Dido was not at boarding school or later at Oxford, she and I stayed in our Hammersmith house, and Matthew spent some of his holidays there, too. During parts of the school terms, when I hoped neither of them required me, I made visits to America to be with the man I now loved.

Inevitably the ice melted between Theo and me. We discovered a new sort of alliance, one we were never able to have before. We dared to talk intimately, to tell our thoughts and examine the years we had spent together. We concluded that our past had been ineluctable. Our old affliction, in which all our best and most affectionate words became, as it were, coated with ice as they left our mouths, disappeared, and a new pattern established itself—though we did not meet frequently, we were close and loyal friends. We advised and depended upon each other. Except for the unsafe territory that surrounded Matthew, the barriers that had existed between us simply fell away.

CHAPTER THIRTY-TWO

Presents

Once Theo and I ceased living in the same house, evenings spent together at Hammersmith when I brought Matthew to London were often constrained. Seeing his father returning to the house as a guest unnerved Matthew; he became agitated and unable to talk. Then he would turn to me and signal that I should take over.

I would try to oblige. "Tell your dad what you did today. Weren't you going to show your dad your writing, your drawing?"

This usually made Theo impatient. He would be abrupt, and Matthew in his confusion would appear sullen. One of these scenes came upon us a month before Christmas 1981, when Matthew was seventeen and had just entered the senior school at Westoning Manor. Having spoken too harshly to Matthew, Theo regretted his words and, in an effort to rekindle some kind of exchange, asked if there were any special Christmas present he would like. Matthew's spirits revived, and his answer was loud and prompt. "Want wife, Dad."

Theo and I were overcome with surprise and laughter. In an effort to reassure Matthew that his request deserved a serious answer, I tried to make a categorical statement that it was impossible to give human beings as presents.

With an imperious wave of his hand Matthew cut me short. "Talking to Dad, 'f you don't mind."

I held my breath as Theo asked what he would do with a wife.

"Can lie on my bed, watch television, stay Saturday 'n breakfast Sunday."

After a few moments of silence, Theo leaned forward and patted Matthew's shoulder. He told him he was not nearly old enough to have a wife. He said he had been thirty-seven when he married me. Even at that age he had wondered if he was quite mature enough for the job. He added that Matthew had better play the field for a few more years.

Matthew looked a little puzzled as he answered, "All right, Dad."

After we said goodbye and Theo left us, Matthew said in a soft voice, "Anyway, 'spect I get old enough have little cat for me to play in field with. Cat can sleep on my bed, all nights and days, can't he?"

IN THE SPRING of 1982, six months after his request for a wife, during one of our now less frequent Wednesday lunches in Leighton Buzzard, Matthew decided we should go for a swim in the public pool. Unusually there were no other swimmers present, and the attendant told Matthew he could accompany me to the "women's side." Matthew and his school friends had visited the pool many times, always entering the water from the "men's side." Disoriented by the change, he dropped from the steps into what he expected to be the shallow end and the water engulfed him. He bobbed to the surface, bursting in alarm and outrage. Because he was smacking the surface of the water ferociously, I had the greatest difficulty towing him back to the steps and heaving him out of the pool.

I sat him on a slatted wooden bench and wrapped him in towels. I offered him my handkerchief and encouraged him to wipe his tears and blow his nose. I promised never, never to betray him that way again. I assured him that even when he was in the water, it had not been dangerous, just frightening.

"You are safe and well now."

"Not well. Never well again." He extended first one then the other of his legs. I was shocked at what I saw. The muscles of his legs, always rather meager, were quite wasted, but his knees had become monstrously swollen and were an angry red color.

"My God, Matthew, how long have your knees been so bad? Why didn't you show me sooner?"

"Not bad knees—poor knees. Don't like people staring."

"You should have told someone about them long before this."

"Why?"

"Because then we could have set about looking for the right doctor to make them better."

Matthew looked at me in amazement. "Better? They deaded in middle." He buried his face in the towels. I put my arms around him.

I had to assume that he was listening as I told him he must learn to *say* when something was wrong. I assured him that there were medicines to help every illness. I said doctors could fix up most parts of the body, but not unless we let them know which part was hurting.

"'S wrong, Mum. Can't fix worse bit of me."

This statement desolated us both. "The most important part of you is perfect, Matthew, very few people have the good character you have."

"Which bit's that, then?"

"It exists in your heart and your head." I tapped his forehead.

"Oh, there, some stuff in there, pictures 'n things."

As I helped him dress, we played a little game of deciding which areas of his body merited "points." He gave his hands "one hundred best," saying they could "hold, press, push, pull, turn, and do tiny things." His arms came next; "look just right like cowboys." He flexed an invisible muscle. He liked his "middle not too fat for jeans." "Feet look OK but don't do what tell 'em to." "Plenty 'f strong hair, right color for man." I forgot the number of points he finally awarded his body, but when we got into the car he found his calculator and they added up to a satisfactory figure.

Before I started the motor, I told Matthew I would like to take him with me back to London, at once, that afternoon. I very much wanted his company.

"Be sensible, Mum. Sausages, mash for Harpo tonight. Birthday jelly. Harpo can't eat jelly proply without me. He wants singing." Matthew had rediscovered his silent friend Harpo and was very pleased.

So I drove him back to school and went in search of his recently appointed "new broom" of a housemother. When I found her I asked if she or any member of staff was aware that Matthew had very sore knees? I told her they must have been giving him pain for some while and for my part I was very contrite that I had not noticed how brave he was having to be.

Not attempting to disguise her impatience, the housemother sighed, "If you lived among them, you would learn to respect these folk. Matthew is in the senior school now. I have to trust him to come to me of his own accord if he thinks he has anything wrong. He knows how much we encourage self-reliance."

As I often did when I got back from visiting Matthew, I dropped in to Theo's office, where as usual he offered me a glass of whiskey and soda. We sat down to talk, and I described the incident at the pool and told of Matthew's stoicism regarding his knees. At that point, Theo's air of kindly disinterest altered to real consternation. I recalled that he often suffered from painful feet and that the pain occasionally extended to his knees.

He promised that he would find an appropriate doctor for Matthew and more or less commanded that meanwhile I should bring him to London and make him rest. I told Theo how Matthew had declined to come that very afternoon. He suggested we bribe him with a promise of a visit to the office followed by a dinner at Roules (how Matthew loved grand restaurants), where we would discuss his choice of birthday present—Matthew was soon to become eighteen. Within a few days I was able to persuade Matthew to let me bring him to London; as arranged, we drove directly to Theo's office.

Theo wanted Matthew to feel he was the guest of honor. He took the trouble to concoct for him what he supposed was an appetizing drink. He poured lemonade and ginger ale into a glass already half filled with ice. He added a dash of bitters, some slices of orange, and flung a cherry into it.

"Medicine, Dad?" Theo answered that it was a cocktail and he should sit down to rest his knees and sip till it was time to go to Roules.

"Yes, Boss. What Roules?"

In much less boss-like words his father told him it was a restaurant where one could eat plenty of meat, which was of course good for knees.

"Silly, Dad, knees never eat."

Just before we left, Theo asked Matthew to roll up his trouser legs; he said he must see for himself just how swollen the knees were. It must have been compassion that drove him to make a second imprudent offer. Over dinner he said Matthew could have whatever he wanted for his birthday.

"Want office, Dad."

After this announcement Matthew put his lips close to Theo's ear. He whispered and whispered till Theo drew away, telling him his ear was hot and he could not hear.

Matthew almost shouted, "Need office stuff like you, Dad. Be a Mr. Crosby."

At this point several expressions crossed Theo's face. First he appeared touched, then exasperated, last of all humorously wary. Matthew, meanwhile, had a happy foolishness about him. "'S right, Dad, get office nearly soon?" He lay back on the banquette and crossed his arms behind his head.

A few mornings later, Matthew and I kept an appointment with a doctor in Welbeck Street. The doctor told us he rarely looked at the legs of people, usually those of race horses. Perhaps this statement was part of the key to his great success with Matthew. At first the doctor's manner seemed remote. He had faraway blue eyes, and he wore a too sharply tailored dark flannel suit; to me, he seemed utterly formidable. Despite his suavity he exuded casualness. He rested a hand against Matthew's back and softly propelled him to a large, tartan-covered sofa. The doctor and Matthew sat down together. The doctor then surprised me by leaning forward to untie the laces of his own highly polished shoes and remove his silken socks.

"Do what I'm doing, old chap." Delicately he began to roll up a trouser leg. "Perhaps we should let your mother help you do this part, if she'd be so good."

I knelt on the Persian carpet, and after rolling Matthew's trousers, I found myself able to observe both pairs of knees: one pair bony and ivory colored, the other swollen and raw-looking.

"Now let us find the hot spots." The doctor began to prod at his own knee. "You try your knees." He watched Matthew's fingers as they touched here and there. Slowly he let his fingers join Matthew's. Matthew lay back against the cushions. "I don't suppose you would care to look between my toes, but if you don't mind I'd like to peep between yours."

The doctor took both of Matthew's feet and put them on his lap. With the tips of his fingers he separated the digital bones of each foot and traced the Achilles tendons from the heels up into the calves. He seemed able to insinuate his fingers between muscles, to dip into the swellings of Matthew's knees. The strain left Matthew's face; he looked almost sleepy.

"Now, my dear boy, I saw by the name tapes you do not own that wretched pair of socks that you happen to be wearing today. I am sure your own are of a superior quality. Always wear fresh, woolen socks, a clean pair every morning."

Again demonstrating upon his own calves, he made Matthew copy his movements as he massaged up and down his own legs, then his own feet.

"I will write to your regular doctor and tell him that the terrible pains in your knees, which I can see you have had for far too long, are due to an infection originally caused by athlete's foot. I will give you a tin of magic powder to help keep it from happening again. Your doctor must give you some injections. I shall give you the first one. Now where would you like it, in your arm or your bottom?"

Matthew knew a lot about injections. "Bottom, please, won't look."

That was the only time the doctor glanced in my direction; he gave me what I can only call a grave wink, which I took to mean: "Have I not handled your son as understandingly as I would a nervous horse? Can I take it my success with him meets with your approval?"

PRIOR TO MATTHEW'S birthday, a Saudi Arabian client commissioned Theo and his partners to furnish a smart new office. This involved designing and having printed all sorts of paper paraphernalia, a certain amount of which had been grandly discarded. Among the pile of rejected items were reams of paper, envelopes, memo pads, account books, and best of all, checkbooks, all embossed with smart logos incorporating ornate crests and emblems. There was hardware, too, plastic in and out trays, paper knives, pens and pencils, all colored green and cream. Theo's secretary gathered and packaged everything together. To make it more convincing as an office, she added a smart but no longer up-to-date typewriter, an adding machine with several rolls of paper, some boxes of carbon paper, and lastly a rather swish-looking swivel chair.

I delivered these vast and bulky packages just before May 26. I went to visit Matthew a day or two after the celebrations. As we drove toward Leighton Buzzard, I asked if he had enjoyed his father's present.

"What's that?"

"Come on, Matthew, you can't have forgotten the office? All that stuff? The typewriter and so forth?"

He was nonchalant. "Not bad. Hugo got no typewriter. Chair goes round 'n round." Then after a silence, "Not proper real office."

"Oh Matthew, we couldn't give you a special room for your office; your bedroom is quite large."

"Yep. Got a room. Need secretary too, like Dad's Celia."

CHAPTER THIRTY-THREE

Honeymoon in Tunisia

FROM MY JOURNAL
Tunisia, January 1984

Here in Hamamet the weather is perfect, quite warm with a slight breeze. Since Matthew dislikes taking off his clothes, he plays on the beach wearing his corduroy trousers, a jersey, socks, and shoes. Unlike the tourists, the Tunisians who use the shore as a high road are just as warmly dressed, so he knows he is à la mode.

Very few people from our hotel come to the beach. They like to remain beside the swimming pool, where it is less windy and there are shops, a bar, restaurant, fountains, loud music, and announcements. Matthew likes all that too, but only for a short while.

We have walked along the sand to a group of derelict thatched umbrellas planted in what seems to be a no-man's-land between two hotel strands. Every morning while I write this journal, draw, or make watercolor paintings, Matthew plays with his newly purchased bucket and spade. He cuts long lines in the sand from one umbrella to the next, and he stops here and there to dig holes. He carves a number beside each one before he draws more roads. Later he lopes along these tracks, talking to himself, checking his territory. When he tires, he sits beside me, turning out immaculate molds of sand from his bucket. They stand in orderly groups, and he puts crisscrosses between them as if his roads have become streets through cities. This great area of sand brings about a conqueror's covetousness in Matthew; each time we come, he claims wider territories. When the wind has erased yesterday's work, he replaces the marks he has lost in the sand before digging new ones.

There are mornings when we find two camels tethered near our umbrellas. I am waiting for Matthew to comment on them; he has not yet done so. Vendors who pass along the beach from one hotel to the next deviate from their path to show us their wares. Matthew looks inquiringly at me. If I shake my head, he does not even glance at the oranges, Arab pastries, toy camels, or leather bags, just continues his digging. If the vendors are too persistent, he signs that they should go away, holding his hand up, palm toward them and making a circular gesture which is oddly final.

There are days when the sky is changeable; from clear sunlight it suddenly blackens, and a threatening wind catches us. Matthew tips his head to look at the sky, then at me. Sometimes we have to pack our traps and return to the hotel. He patiently holds the bag open while I put our things in it. He cleans the paint box for me and washes the brushes in sea water. Yesterday, because I was swimming in the sea, we left it too late. As I came out of the water it began to rain heavily. Matthew stood waiting for me. The owner of the two camels came running down the beach. As he passed us, he called in French, "That is right clever, boy, stand in the nice warm sun." I was angry. I told him not to mock my son and added I preferred Matthew's good manners to his bad ones. He replied, "I am sorry, little mother, in our country we keep such sons within the house."

We are not made despondent by these rainy interludes. We return to our large, white room, which has a pretty tiled floor and a big balcony from where we look across the hotel garden lush with shrubs and bright flowers. Geranium hedges, marigolds, delphiniums, and petunias grow between orange and lemon trees. There are date and banana palms and feathery mimosa trees. The smell of blossoms and rotting dates is rich and pleasant.

Matthew still appears to be unaware of distant things. He does not appreciate this view, but he enjoys the balcony. He likes to spread our wet bathing clothes on the parapet. He lays my watercolor pictures in ranks on the floor. If the weather is bad, we paint on the balcony together; we take it in turns to use the colors. When it is his turn, Matthew mixes the colors of the geraniums or delphiniums that grow directly beneath us. He peeps over and quickly turns back, as if he is spying on the flowers. He hands me the paintbrush, pointing to where I should place a color on the paper. He instructs me to leave a space for the sky, which he puts in himself, because he doesn't think I make it graphic enough. On a particularly stormy day he accused me of "missing out the thunder." Finally, he likes to pour the paint water over the balcony to the ground below. During one of the most violent storms, the rain came down so heavily that the gutters and ditches overflowed; water swilled and eddied beneath our balcony. Matthew became very interested when two men wearing burnooses came hurrying through the rain and with a hooked pole and a long-handled shovel proceeded to remove a metal cover and stir and scrape the drain beneath, releasing as they did so a most powerful stench of sewage. I retreated into our room, but Matthew continued to watch, calling cheerily to me, "'S nice." I was surprised and said I thought the smell was terrible. "No, nose very close smells like honey." He had it exactly. It was one of those horrible contradictory smells.

It was Matthew who did most of our unpacking. A few of his toy cars are parked on his bedside table, and others between hairbrushes in the bathroom. He has arranged our clothes eccentrically, some bundled on shelves, his new karate pajamas spread on a shelf of their own. But the nicest or newest clothes are hung decoratively; a dress of mine and his best jeans festoon the doors of the wardrobe. Our shoes are parked as if they too are motorcars.

I brought with us a little camping stove, which we use on the balcony. After we return from the beach, I make hot cereal for Matthew. His now slightly more faulty heart causes him to be permanently underweight and constantly hungry. On the bottom shelf of our wardrobe we keep little pots of colored desserts, jars of yoghurt, bread, eggs, and oranges. On most mid-afternoons we bring these forth and I scramble eggs for him. We make a ceremony of preparing these little repasts. Matthew cuts dish shapes from the pretty Tunisian wrappings that come with our purchases. I can gauge just how loving he feels toward me by how many plates he cuts out for me. On my worst day, I received a very small saucer-sized piece of paper.

We replenish our stores when Matthew's sore knees allow us to take evening walks inland from the hotel. We have found a little shop nearby where Matthew can choose what to buy. With great care he puts each purchase in our bag, asking the price as he does so. I translate for him. The shopkeeper is patient, and none of the people who are waiting to be served hurry us. When we leave the shop, Matthew will look for a convenient surface where he can spread out the food we have bought. He copies the shopkeeper's tally on his calculator. He is painstaking, but somehow it usually comes out wrong, which means he starts again. Finally, sums right or wrong, he is satisfied. He repacks the bag, and in the violent glow of the setting sun we walk slowly among the villas, every one looking secretive behind its grills and shutters. We peep through railings to admire the lemon and orange trees. We sniff the blossoms, which smell, as Matthew says, "loud." He wants the cats that watch us as we pass to leap down and sit on his knees while he rests on the steps of the entrances he likes best, but the cats are too shy. He calls a polite "Good evening" to shabby, dark-eyed children and the young women who after their day's work pass arm in arm along the rutted, dusty roads.

Not wishing to jar the rhythm Matthew gives to our days, I have made myself slow down. I see how flowing his ways are, how he seems to have a natural tranquillity. Now it comes easily to me to repeatedly show him how to fit the key of the door to our room into its lock, to demonstrate again and again that he must turn the door handle at the same instant that he twists the key. He enjoys the ritual. He opens the door with a flourish, and I walk in first. Sometimes he bows.

Every time we step out to meet the sunshine, Matthew adjusts my sunglasses for me and generally puts my appearance to rights. Then he pokes his own head toward me so that I can arrange the combination of sunhats he believes make him resemble a tough American television hero. He has bought a white peaked cap with "A present from Tunisia" printed across it. Beneath it he wears a tennis visor, which casts a blue gloom over his face. Sometimes he covers these with a cycling cap marked "Peugeot," put on back to front so that its peak shades his neck.

Matthew shows symptoms of a very late and mild adolescence. It would be difficult to guess his age, though he is not accepted as a child any more. This has caused him to lose spontaneity. He cannot gauge the effect he has on people; actually, here in Tunisia, I cannot either. Luckily he still possesses some of his sweet, lopsided charm. I watch his approach to children. He loves them as ardently, but he is willing to sacrifice an encounter with a child if he senses it fears him. He meets its caution with a tenderness that is distressingly humble. If the child turns out to like and trust him, he smiles enchantingly and is at once at ease with it.

Because Matthew is as he is, I believe it would be difficult for me to be, as mothers sometimes are, any sort of threat to his psyche. If I am careful, I shall do no harm by having to be at times very close to him. His present dependency upon me is of an order that is neither healthy nor unhealthy. It is our particular circumstance.

The brochure that advertised this three-week vacation promoted it as a "Tunisian honeymoon." Matthew calls our holiday that. We seem to have come here with a wish to share everything, so he can call this holiday a honeymoon if he wants. I try not to be embarrassed by the word.

It would be hubris to suppose I can get anything like a real sense of how it is to be a nineteen-year-old mentally handicapped boy. I watch that boy as carefully as he does me. We start early in the morning. I see his wakening, see him cautiously touching his feet to the ground as if the distance from the bed to the floor might have altered overnight. He locates his spectacles and presses them firmly on his face. He stands up to pull the curtain back, sometimes pulling it to and fro again and again, because he likes the swishing noises and the changes of light. When he goes into the bathroom, I can hear that he enjoys urinating. "Good lad, no spill." If it is not a silent morning, he will pretend to grumble as the lavatory cistern refills. I hear him asking it to hurry up so that he can pull the handle again. It is far too early to get up. He springs back into his bed and reaches for his little cars, which he runs among the folds of the blanket and round his pillow. He is content making car noises and arranging crashes till I bring the orange juice that I have meanwhile squeezed for him. He hardly moves so as not to disturb the cars that are parked about him. He makes awful drinking noises, smiling over the rim of the glass to tell me it is done to tease.

When he gets out of bed, he skips to the wardrobe to choose the clothes he wants to wear. He acts in rather a dandified manner as he peers in the looking glass, turning back and forth holding his clothes against himself. Until we leave the room to go to breakfast, Matthew has probably communicated only in mime. But once we are in the corridor, he will startle the maids by calling loud good mornings and banging the ribs of the radiators as he hurries toward the stairs.

In the dining room Matthew will sit at several tables before he settles at our regular one. He holds up two fingers, his head cocked, giving me a winning smile. He is hoping to charm me into saying, "Yes, two spoiled legs for breakfast today." If he thinks I have been easily persuaded, he tentatively puts up another finger. Then I am meant to say, "Nobody eats three spoiled legs, Matthew." These repeated jokes are but punctuation, a setting of the scene. On these sorts of days there is no need to look for diversions, they are all about us.

During our stay in this hotel there are times when Matthew feels left out. He watches fellow guests enjoying each other's company and he is envious, sad that he is not included in their activities, not invited to sit at their tables, not even greeted. I have tried to find words to tell him they have their lives, their families, and their fun, and I am his family and we have our own fun. I am aware that I am not managing to sound convincing.

I am not at all able to disguise or account for the behavior of the waiters in the dining room. Having observed that Matthew has a great interest in food, they tease us by keeping us waiting for service. They carry dishes toward us, then ostentatiously deliver them to another table. They will even put a dish in front of Matthew, then whisk it away again. I have asked these waiters to treat him more politely, I have tipped heavily, but I have not overcome their antipathy. Yesterday I arranged to move to another part of the dining room. I chose a table in a corner where at least on two sides we are less vulnerable to such teasing. The elderly maitre d'hotel, while escorting us to our new table, remarked that he regretted seeing me without a husband. "It is sad, Madame, but no self-respecting man can accompany a wife who brings such a son, can he?"

Matthew has found a way to calm our relations with the waiters. He uses a device that he must have employed to placate other bullies in his life. Yesterday he appeared at the table with one of his treasures in his hand, his calculator. Waiters sidled up and asked to borrow it. I forbade any one of them to carry it away to show to their friends for fear we might not get it back. A waiter has offered to buy Matthew's calculator from him; evidently they are as yet unattainable in Tunisian shops. Matthew reveals himself to be surprisingly good at bargaining. He got a waiter to bid twelve dinars to own it right away, nine if he must wait for our departure. Only I am aware that money means nothing to Matthew. He does not intend to part with it at any price. If he did, he would simply give it to the man. He does not make a habit of bringing the calculator to the table. I think he is aware that it must not lose its charm.

We have been here sixteen days. The dull skies and cold winds are gone, but Matthew would not get out of bed this morning. "Look, Matt, the sun is shining. Aren't you going to draw the curtain?" I do it for him, then I prepare his orange juice. He sits hunched in his bed, sipping and looking mournful. He doesn't signal his usual thank you. He hardly nods or shakes his head when I ask, "Are you unwell? Sad? Very sad? Don't you like it here any more? Don't you want to stay a few more days?"

He shakes his head and tears spill onto his cheeks.

"Why don't you get up and come to breakfast? We can go in the pool, dig in the sand, take a taxi into town, write a letter to your Dad, go on a bus ride...two eggs for breakfast?"

Finally a tiny nod, but he is still weeping. I put my arms round him and coerce him from the bed. He dresses slowly, doing everything with his head held down. He is still sniffling as he makes his usual joke of buttoning his shirt wrongly so that I must redo it. This morning I fasten his sandals and brush his hair. He starts to cry all over again. We cannot go to breakfast in this state. I ask him what is wrong, who is he missing.

During the winter, as we planned our holiday, I would ask Matthew, "Where shall we go?"

"Far way."

"For how long?"

"Lot of days, all birthdays."

"Shall we go in an airplane?" Till recently Matthew seemed to view airplanes as flying ornaments; he was rather doubtful that we should get into one.

"Just for bit."

"Who is going on this holiday?"

A shout, "You 'n me, Mum." Then he smugly listed the people who were not to come. Perhaps with some regret as to his teacher and his father, but none for his sister and his best friend Mark, proceeding to positive glee at leaving such "naughty people" as Hugo, his headmaster, and our dog, with whom he had been rather strict lately.

In answering my question, Who are you missing? the same list almost pertains; he misses his sister, Mark, the dog, his father, and several friends and teachers. He cheers up as I mention the names of less agreeable people: "You miss her? Him, even him? Of course Mr. Pocock?" Matthew giggles through his tears.

CHAPTER THIRTY-FOUR

First Weeks in Schoolhouse

Throughout his childhood I saw Matthew as a natural existentialist. All he best understood he derived from direct observations. The present was for him so vast that its dimensions frequently awed him to a point where he felt it necessary to employ devices to reduce its scale. He either applied metaphorical blinkers to his eyes to limit what he took in, or he actually removed his glasses, rendering himself as myopic as he really was. Within the confines of his now reduced field of vision, as if playing patience, he would distract himself from what was going on around him by painstakingly tracing threads or weaves till they reached borders of hems, tablecloths, or bedspreads. With one finger he followed the up and down intricacies of grained wooden surfaces. He liked to sit at a table, again and again swirling the water in his drinking glass, then watching till the water was quite still.

WHEN HE FIRST arrived at Westoning Manor House, the senior part of MacIntyre School, in the late autumn of 1981, he met his uprooting and replanting, as a small child might, with ineffable bewilderment. Despite the fact that we, his parents, had driven him to that place and decreed that he remain there, Matthew neither at first, nor later on, even when he was visited by bouts of sadness, ever attributed blame. In this I used to find myself secretly comparing him to what we call "dumb creatures." I respected Matthew's doglike acceptance of his fate.

Throughout his childhood I watched him accept trustingly every kind of help from any person near. At the senior school he had to learn a new and harsh lesson, to be distrustful.

"There's person sometimes stops me going toilet; why they do that?"

"One big one said, 'Silly to have Whipping Boy when you seventeen.' Is Whipping Boy seventeen?"

"Hugo buried glasses and Dad's wireless in pond. Glasses still work but not wireless."

"I not to walk there: Hugo 'n others say not."

Talking of one of his teachers, "'S not right when Phil says, 'Right.' Phil means cross when he laughs."

Describing the headmaster of the senior school, who was perpetually irritated by Matthew's obstinate refusal to use the prefix "Mister" before his name, "Pocock nearly nice when you gone, Mum."

Normal people hardly remember that as small children they had to make prodigious efforts to learn how to relate to their surroundings. For Matthew this task was a Sisyphean one. Well into his fifteenth year it was his covert practice to caress surfaces and furtively raise objects an inch or two from their places, and give grave attention to their weights and densities. He would contemplate the spaces between them. He made progress in these studies, though heights and depths remained a mystery. Not until he had made himself familiar with a flight of stairs would Matthew dare take for granted that the rise of one step equaled all the others and would continue to do so when his back was turned. Lifts caused him to feel very uneasy. "This horrid room got bad floor, make my legs go shorter. Press stop button now, Mum."

Upon glancing out of a high-storied window he once gasped, "Nasty lift room made us go higher on same place. Better go back. Now."

Matthew had to repeat experiences before he felt confident enough to use the words, "I know..."

When he had mastered some everyday task, such as filling a kettle, cutting slices from a loaf of bread, or merely turning on the correct light switch, he treasured his ability. He loved to be allowed to demonstrate it. "Wait, now, 's Matthew turns it on."

"Follow this leader; ready, steady, go."

And as he grew older, "Hey, presto! The master did it prop'ly."

It troubled Matthew that he had no device, no measure, with which to quantify the past, which revealed itself to him only in fragments (and these were sometimes so vivid that they interfered with the present). The future was even less accessible. If he was at ease with me he might, for a short while, transfer both puzzling dimensions into my care.

"Mum, you tell how's been. Matthew story please." Or, "Tell after now story. Tomorrow stuff please, Mum."

Despite all his ruled lines and underscored dates, Matthew could not make time obey his wishes as he felt it should. On the other hand, there was a sense in which he forgave the past, even the future; no pain or illness spoiled any but the very present.

While still living at Mount Tabor House, most of the dramatic happenings and far-fetched imagery that Matthew watched on the television screen remained safely behind that molded shape of tempered glass. When evening came and the residents congregated in their cavernous, shabbily comfortable playroom for "television time," popular music and sport were the preferred entertainments. Complex ancillary activities took place while the set played. Some children would romp and jostle for favorite seats only to quit them and wander off. Within the span of an evening, friendships were made, lightly broken, and remade, possessions were brought to the room to be displayed or shared. The staff used the time to brush or plait hair, cut fingernails, administer doses, and carry out minor first aid. Cocoa and biscuits were handed round, after which, by turn, the younger and less healthy children would be summoned to bed, so that kisses and calls of "good night" would punctuate the last hour of every evening.

IN 1981 WHEN Matthew really was too old to remain in the junior part of MacIntyre School, he and all his possessions were transferred seven miles away to Westoning Manor in the village of Westoning over the county line in Bedfordshire.

The Manor House was an imitation Tudor mansion with a wide graveled yard flanked on two sides by stables and estate offices, now converted to the school's needs. The ground floor of the house contained large class, recreation, and dining rooms. Subsidiary to them were kitchens, pantries, larders, stillrooms, store- and cloakrooms, all connected to one another by convoluted corridors. The next two floors comprised a maze of staff quarters, dormitories, smaller bedrooms, bathrooms, and lavatories. Beyond the courtyard lay the outbuildings, barns, greenhouses, potting and tool sheds. All this was surrounded by a useful-sized estate, in which small separate "family" dwellings were being built as sufficient funds accrued.

The whole place intimidated Matthew dreadfully. He did his best to conquer his fear by devising a series of little runs, routes that he took pains to fix in his mind. Reminding me of the White Rabbit, he would mutter as he hurried down corridors, "Long here, not big brown door, past coats, ah, here then."

"Out of big front door, round grass and water bit [an ornamental fountain which stood in the middle of the courtyard], one, two, now my three door."

On the days of my visits I encouraged him to cycle beside me as I walked about the place. Together we looked around the old and the new residential quarters. We lingered where a tractor and the two schoolbuses were parked. We stroked sheep—very gingerly—and looked for hens' eggs. Sadly, I was told that for much too long a time Matthew remained too timid to do these things with anyone else.

This carefully prepared-for change of domicile, a move of so few miles from the junior school, the place where he had eaten his Christmas lunches year after year, where he and I had made so many rehearsal visits—why was Matthew so oppressed by the reality of it?

It was clear that he quickly came to trust his new house-parents and was highly pleased to rediscover his well-loved teacher, John. There were also friends who, a few years before, had made the same transfer. Unfortunately, their presence did not at all mitigate his fears; rather it augmented them. This was due to the changes in their appearances. Their new aspects perplexed Matthew. Evidently he was unaware of any alterations that had happened to his own body, and in this he was partially justified. In their absence he had done not much more than grow a little; he remained thin and unrobust, his facial skin pale and smooth. His friends had no difficulty in recognizing him, but to them he was still a junior. Their mild disdain could have been puffed aside by laughter if Matthew had been capable of perhaps jokingly acting on his old conviction that his was a presence to be valued—a conceit that he had often demonstrated when in the junior school by clasping his hands together above his head and announcing, "Here comes the champ," "Our Matthew 'gain, boys," or simply, "Here's me!"

It seemed to me that when Matthew re-encountered those companions from the past—for whom he once felt affection—they were only partially recognizable to him. Familiar gestures and attributes came from wider, more adult bodies. This was particularly dramatic regarding his fellow mongoloids, who had metamorphosed so as now to appear solid and pugnacious, which despite their looks they were not. They filled Matthew with disquiet; he made no greeting, just stood, his hands nervously stroking his own face.

Luckily there was Mark, who had like Matthew undergone little alteration. His likeness to his old self—both the inner and the outer—was reassuringly constitutional. Aware of their past conflict, the staff had lodged Matthew as far from Mark as possible. Their paths did not cross until three days after Matthew's arrival at Schoolhouse, by which time he was truly wretched in his feelings of desolation and bleakness. When they encountered each other, Mark flapped both his arms and skipped toward Matthew. "'S-ss good 's you Matthew here. You g'live here now? 'S nice you Matthew...bike w' Mark...Yes."

In those nearly two years of lost friendship, Mark's manner of talking had remained almost as garbled as ever. It was this absurdly cheerful jabber that Matthew responded to. In a burst of relief he laughed as he always had in Mark's company. It was fortunate that Matthew had not lost the knack of sieving the meanings from Mark's jumbled stream of talk. Delicately and with a new appreciation of each other, they set about rebuilding their friendship.

I had the crassness to ask Matthew if he had remet Sarah. He stood still and looked at me, then blinking his eyes and blowing out his cheeks for comical effect, he held his breath before he exhaled his answer. "Don't know which one she no more."

UNTIL HIS ARRIVAL at Westoning Manor, Matthew had wittingly or otherwise charmed his way through life. In Normansfield Hospital, in Gladys's house, at schools, in streets, on beaches, in restaurants, his blend of innocence, timidity, and effrontery disposed people to like him. His spontaneous gaiety, his impulsive gestures of affection, and his contagious fits of giggles usually ensured that this was so.

Matthew also possessed the gift—or was it a facility he had picked up from Gladys Strong?—of caring for small children. Not only could he give babies their feeds, bring up their wind, and change their napkins, but he liked to coax them to eat and to hold them comfortingly if they were unwell. Their cries disturbed him so much that he wept, too, and he was never known to show impatience toward a child. Six years before, on that first daunting morning when he awoke not in the Strongs' house but in a strange bedroom at Mount Tabor House, Matthew had looked about for a little companion to whom he could devote himself. He found her at the breakfast table, a three-year-old child who was bluish-gray just as Matthew had been for so long. He sat on a chair beside her, took up a spoon, and with practiced hand started to feed her. I was told he held fast to her till I came, and went in search of her directly I left.

Matthew was rewarded for this benevolence, favored by housemothers and depended upon by his frailer companions. He had not known what it was not to be needed by somebody until he arrived at Westoning Manor House. Now he had no idea how to gain acceptance among the residents of Schoolhouse nor the rest of the senior school. He could discern no mode of behavior to conform to, and he did not know how to propitiate those whose own self-doubts led them to ostracize newcomers. Matthew's obvious refuge was to act the simpleton. Coincidentally he had mislaid his spectacles. When I motored up from London to be at his side, I found such a reduced and fearful Matthew as I had rarely seen before.

Not familiar with the erstwhile flamboyant Matthew, the spontaneous boy who had been looked upon as a benign jester at Mount Tabor House, his new houseparents were unperturbed by Matthew's small appetite and his desperate need for sleep. There were other members of the family group who were habitually so. I watched Matthew losing his spirit and his equilibrium, yet despite his sadness, I dared not take him home, knowing that if I did he would only have had to begin his initiation all over again when I brought him back.

AT SCHOOLHOUSE there were certain evening activities, such as "going to scouts," "having film," "a disco." On ordinary indoor evenings, after everyone in the family group had participated in preparing and eating supper, washing the dishes, and tidying up, the television would be switched on.

The television stood in lieu of a fire on the hearth of the communal sitting room. Matthew told me he had to sit on the floor, but he didn't mind because a big girl would come and sit beside him. "Think I knowed her, she says one day I sit high like others."

As the television screen incandesced, so did Matthew. The more trying the day, the more unguarded his behavior. He reverted to the old Mount Tabor notion that the flickering light of the television screen signaled release, congeniality, and sibling-like playfulness.

He began by tiptoeing round the room till he came upon a huddle of friends; with comic miming gestures he would signify his wish that they make room for him. Assuming their refusals to be merely playful, he would gently, almost caressingly, pry a place for himself between them. If they pushed him away, he continued in his error, extending his horseplay, ruffling strangers' hair, patting their cheeks, even untying their shoelaces. After being rebuffed, Matthew would turn his attention to the television screen. If he was not captivated by what was being broadcast, he would with conspiratorial gestures put his fingers to his lips, and belly crawl toward the set and turn the sound down, so that he could substitute his own comic noises.

There were other family members who also did not know how to conform; they were seduced by Matthew's antics. These renegades began to participate in Matthew's playfulness, so that his foolishness was perceived as something of a threat to the leaders of the group. This was why evening after evening he was shoved to the floor and ostentatiously ignored, until he crept to his bed in tears.

CHAPTER THIRTY-FIVE

Jeff Baum and David Niven

T wo new buildings were under construction at Westoning.
Both proved of great consequence to Matthew.

Under the large roof of the first building there came into being a workshop for carpentry and toymaking, a weaving and
sewing room, and a well-lighted area where drawing and painting ("coloring," Matthew called it) were to be taught. Due to the
sweet personality of a young man named Jeff, who, fresh from art
school, had been hired as a teacher, this partitioned-off space
became his refuge. His social problems diminished; here was a
place where Matthew felt entirely at ease. In the art department,
everything he tried to do and say was taken seriously. Jeff encouraged him to come there whenever he wanted. He was allo-
cated a shelf all his own on which to store his materials and un-
finished artworks.

Though drawing and coloring became Matthew's most fulfilling pursuit, it was understood that he must not neglect any of
his other activities or tasks; eventually he found most of them
more or less congenial.

"Work in potted shed some mornings, poke seedles on
brown dirt, horrid cold on baddest days. Do floor polishing in
big house, can't hear no one, lovely noise, swish, pull, swish,
pull. Sometimes mop dirty wet kitchen. Help clean bathroom,
nasty wet wiping. Best's dishing up Monday supper, big spoons,
plop 'n every plate, mustn't lick." He attended classes: "Writing
'n reading words, counting big numbers, try talk proper."

Jeff was quite undidactic in his methods. Anyone could
work in his room for as little or as long a time as they wished or
their timetables allowed; his only requirement was that they "be

serious." He liked to tempt his pupils by putting enticing materials before them. Mostly he encouraged and praised, offering guidance only if he was sure it was wanted. He spent as much time showing his pupils how to prepare their work and how to clean up afterwards as he did teaching them. He cut wide, important-looking mounts to enhance finished pictures and he printed labels to flatter his artists. Then he made a little ceremony of pinning the pictures to the walls.

Jeff showed Matthew how to put onto large sheets of paper the somewhat geometric-looking images that Matthew believed illustrated all the beauties of the motorcar. Using a ruler and well-sharpened pencils, Matthew made artworks that were part picture and part diagram. Though he applied his colors in a haphazard fashion, he tried to be very accurate in his portrayals. When a work was finished he fussed with number plates and naming their makes; they were all English.

Jeff made preparations to help Matthew accomplish his dream project, a portrait of a life-sized ("Car-sized, silly") motorcar. The carpentry shop was co-opted to build screens onto which a great many "elephant" sheets of white paper were stapled.

"Sometimes do it on floor, ruler 'n me down there a bit, then picture 'n me, stand up gain. Scribble, scribble, scribble Jeff's jumbos [pencils] all away, got to make silver all over car. Four wheels, same scribble color, mustn't open doors, windows be closed, going so fast, do it every day. Jeff tells, no hurry."

Though he paid great attention to the styling of motorcars, studied details of their designs, and could instantly recognize British makes and even some years of origin, Matthew's taste in cars was both bourgeois and prosaic. He had a penchant for family saloons, dashboards that were made of imitation wood, puffy seats, and plenty of gadgets. By the age of nineteen he had dismissed from his lists of "bests and favorites" all the more refined makes. In particular he disdained Rolls Royces, Daimlers, and Jaguars. He tolerated Rovers. His absolute anathema was the classic sports or racing car.

Touched by Matthew's love of motorcars and his wish to make art from them, during one of his visits to London, David Sylvester planned an evening's entertainment for him. His neighbor and friend offered to be hostess. She made every kind of preparation to ensure that Matthew understood he was an important guest. As he and I arrived, Sarah and her two daughters were preparing a delicious meal. She kissed Matthew on both cheeks and asked him to pull corks from the wine bottles. She offered him the privilege of deciding where everyone should sit at the dining table.

His enjoyment of the evening had hardly begun when David appeared. He beckoned Matthew from the kitchen. After making a courteous little speech of welcome, David took Matthew's hand and led him to another room, where together they watched David's "piece of the evening"—almost an hour of a flawed and jerky, badly projected 1920s film in black and white, dimly depicting the wobbly achievements of two Bugatti racing cars as time after time they raced round a dusty track. In careful imitation, Matthew took up David's every pose: when David made a move of his head or recrossed his legs Matthew followed suit. They continued to hold hands. When the two reentered the kitchen, Matthew wore the air of one who, having completed a very arduous task, deserved his dinner.

David's look was of true satisfaction. "How well Matthew concentrates. While we watched our film he hardly moved a muscle. I know I am considered somewhat obsessive, but I believe Matthew's capacity for paying attention beats mine."

On the way home I asked Matthew about the film.

"Didn't see film."

"All right, what did you do?"

"Hold David's hand, watched David's game, tiny toy motorcars."

JUST AS JEFF'S gentle character and teaching made the first new building beautiful to Matthew, so the charismatic charm of the cinema actor David Niven suffused the second new building, which contained additional living quarters. Both men raised aspirations in Matthew, emboldened him so that he refashioned himself somewhat.

David Niven was the school's treasured patron and an effective fund-raiser at that time. Though he was very unwell, he visited the school fairly frequently, so of course some of his more lighthearted films were projected there on film nights. Matthew became enamored of him. He had so far remained faithful to his childhood screen idols, Kermit the Frog and Miss Piggy. He also fell briefly in love with Orphan Annie. "She dance beautiful 'n run fast on stairs," and he wanted to join Popeye and Olive Oyl on the screen, mostly because he wished to play with their baby, Sweetpea. All this was nothing compared to Matthew's admiration for Sir David Niven, which was cemented when it was promised that he would be one of the first to move into the newly finished Niven House.

There was an opening ceremony, "Mister Niven did speech. Then after sat down brought him cup of tea, saluted him. Mister Niven saluted back, saluted with both my arms. He kissed me." In his resolve to emulate Sir David Niven, Matthew already possessed some of his attributes—he had lounged and lolled delightfully all his life; he was also by now able to talk in a similar, though terribly flawed, well-bred, telegraphic drawl.

AS PART OF a series which they were to call "What ever happened to . . . ?" the BBC asked my permission to make (years and years after the original) another television film about Matthew. As a consequence of hours of cavorting before their cameras, Matthew felt entitled to view himself as almost on a par with his beloved Mr. Niven. But after the film crew packed up their paraphernalia and said their smiling goodbyes, he was left without any clues as to how to follow his new career. The whole agreeable exposure, however, left him with enough confidence to decide to be "not like you, Mum, a special car-drawer."

A few weeks after David Sylvester's video-watching party, Matthew was again in London. I took him to spend an evening with his father. As we entered Theo's office, instead of hanging his head and fidgeting while I made both our greetings, he strode up to Theo's drawing board where Theo was filling a title block on a sheet of work.

"C'n I see, Dad?"

Agreeably surprised, Theo lifted a large piece of tracing paper to reveal elevations and plans for the Globe Theatre. Matthew was entranced. He peered and peered at the drawings till Theo reached to replace the cover.

"What's paper window for, Dad?"

Theo looked puzzled so I told Matthew it was called tracing paper.

"What's for?"

Theo went to a plan chest and pulled open a drawer. He drew out a folder which he placed on the board in front of Matthew. It contained prints of all the building work that was being done at MacIntyre School. He removed one of the simpler elevations and taped it to the drawing board, then covered it with a blank sheet of tracing paper. He ruled the first few lines.

"I have a go, Dad?"

Theo lifted him onto high stool. Emulating his father Matthew seized the rule and started to trace what he saw through the layer of tracing paper. Wishing to leave them together, I offered to go and fetch some drinks from "the Bosses Trolley." There I lingered a while chatting with one of Theo's partners. By the time I returned Theo had taken the drawing Matthew made and laid it onto a sheet of white paper so as to enable Matthew to see it more clearly. It was a haphazard but readable copy of a side elevation of Niven House. Though Matthew failed to recognize the house, he was extremely pleased with both the drawing and himself. Even Theo looked a little pleased with himself.

We spent an unusually harmonious evening, and Matthew came home carrying a roll of tracing paper and a long T-square, which had his father's initials incised on its head. Forever afterward, Matthew called this precious possession his "Tee Cee" square.

At Matthew's insistence, I undertook to bring back from his school one of his best pictures and deliver it to his Dad's office "for swap." Theo wrote him a thank-you letter. "You are right, Matthew, 'exchange is no robbery,'" an adage which caused Matthew extreme perplexity.

I believe what happened at Theo's office that evening motivated Theo, to some degree, to upgrade his concept of Matthew. Matthew had shown an interest in what his father was doing. He also made Theo conscious of his son's wish to do more than play.

Some time passed before I next went to Niven House to pick up Matthew and take him home. Within minutes of being in his company, I could see he was still enlarging his sense of himself. He had learned that within twenty miles of the school there existed a vast motorcar factory. Vehicles were being manufactured by the hundreds, a vision which made Matthew ecstatic. He managed to explain that he had rearranged his allegiances so that now he was an aficionado of all types of Vauxhall motorcars. As we left the school he persuaded me to make a detour that took us past the factory gates. He ordered me to stop so as to allow him to contemplate an unending vista of parked vehicles. I realized that this was not his first visit when a gatekeeper waved and greeted Matthew by name.

"Got to go inside now, Mum, must tell eleven pictures by me."

"No, Matthew, only people who help to make those cars are allowed through those gates."

"Pudding."

On the day that I delivered him back to the school, Matthew dragged me to the art room to view the "eleven pictures" by him. Jeff was there, and I told him of our drive past the factory gates.

"Oh, yes, Matthew has plans in that direction. His housefather found him trying to make a telephone call to 'the headmaster of Vauxhalls.'"

Later, after a visit to America, I was back in the art room. Jeff recounted Matthew's successes. It appeared that Matthew had somehow achieved a telephone connection with the motorcar factory. He managed to leave his name and telephone number, and somebody at the other end must have understood enough to return the call. His new housefather called on Matthew's behalf to explain that Matthew was desperate to visit the factory. He was politely invited to do so. Matthew insisted Jeff accompany him.

"You tell your Mum what happened when we got there, Matthew."

"We seed all bare engines on wheels, big bits car put down over them, saw spraying 'n polishing."

"What did we do after we left the paint shop?"

"Went to office, showed my pictures to th' man."

Jeff finished the tale. "Would you credit, they fell for Matthew's plan. At his suggestion—well, command really—they agreed to exhibit his drawings in their foyer. I was asked to hang them. They offered to throw a little reception for Matthew. He corrected the fellow, said he should call it 'an opening,' and he reminded him it should be videotaped. They went one further and got in the local press."

"Yep, in paper, Mum, on television 'gain."

Jeff gave me a copy of the local evening paper. There on the front page was a very inky photograph of Matthew shaking the hand of a director. They were standing in front of a row of his Vauxhall pictures. Blurred though the image was, one could see that Matthew had about him the smirk of a successful artist.

CHAPTER THIRTY-SIX

Matthew's Job

For what he called his "twenty-one-man's birthday," Matthew said, "Going to have it nearly night time. Got to have very big presents. 'S important."

Recalling the rash promises of other occasions, I hedged my question. "As long as it's a reasonable request, what sort of presents would you like your Dad and me to find for you?"

With the air of a man wearied by his many possessions, he replied, "Don't know what. You choose a want, Mum." Then in a stagy sotto voce, "Not allowed really want 'n really need."

"I think I know what that is and, no, you cannot have a motorcar."

"*Car,*" he echoed my last word savagely.

I consulted Theo and we decided to provide him with some money. We agreed I should leave an adequate sum with his current housefather, Barry. I asked Barry to help Matthew spend it on things he wanted.

"That will be clothes, I expect."

"But I buy him clothes."

"Not always the right ones, if you don't mind my saying so."

"What are the right ones?"

In his laconic North Country drawl, "We'll see, won't we now?"

When I drove to the school to pick up Matthew, I found him dressed in his usual odd mixture of clothes, but he heaved a garish rucksack into the car. "Gear. Barry gave it."

"I think Barry paid for it with the birthday money your father and I provided."

"'S right, Barry bought presents. Thank you, Barry."

As we drove toward London I asked, "Did you enjoy your party?"

"Not party. Big people's disco, great. Just me allowed put records on. Dancing. Mrs. Pocock best—she wiggly, wobbly, lovely."

I was impressed; she was a woman in her late fifties who was somewhat overweight and quite visibly wore stays. Matthew seemed to be familiar with an aspect of her that parents such as I hardly could have credited. On his behalf I was grateful to her. "Did Mr. Pocock dance at your party?"

"Mum! He's only headmaster, silly.

"Two birthdays. Barry took me 'n Mark 'n best friends out, special, only mens, big twenty-one mens."

"Tell me about it."

"Chinese. Didn't have to eat with little sticks. Took food home for girls in paper white boxes. Got a bit spilled in Barry's car. Said we' puddings."

When we arrived at Hammersmith, Matthew would not allow me to help him unpack the rucksack so I lay on his bed and watched as one after another he took out and displayed to me the new clothes Barry had predicted: a purple and black track suit, a pair of sneakers that resembled bumper cars, a two-toned, green anorak, and two sets of appalling underwear printed with scenes from current American television gun-toting dramas. Smiling broadly he dangled each garment across his front, then shimmied provocatively.

"Horrid, eh? Much horrider 'n Hugo's 'n allbody's. Tra la, tra la."

Matthew did the rest of his unpacking hurriedly. Then he thrust his fingers into one of the rucksack's zippered pouches. With a flourish he drew out a bundle of little manila envelopes held together by rubber bands. He thrust the whole package into my hands. "'S for you, Mum."

"What is it?"

"Wages. Tea time now." He fairly strutted down the stairs and into the kitchen.

While eating his tea Matthew managed to convey to me that despite not having a proper office, a secretary, a wife, or even a motorcar, he was "a nearly proper man." He had a job, and he had just presented me with his first four pay packets.

"You go to work, Matthew?"

"Nope, job." He rose from his chair, carefully rolled up his sleeves, and with a proud smile, said, "Here we go." He at once picked up an imaginary cube shape and patted the air to show me its size. "See, box on bench." He leaned forward and as if using all his concentration carefully picked up from the table a smaller sized cube, which he delicately placed within the imaginary box, murmuring as he did so, "Six this way, six that way."

He repeated his movements. "Now's twelve, now's eighteen, there, twenty-four, two dozen. Cover up, close lid." He went through little fluttering movements of folding and tucking. "Careful and quick, mustn't tear."

He pushed the imaginary box toward me. "There you are, Miss Betty, don't drop. Very break-y."

He reached in the air for another box. I continued to watch as again and again, more deftly each time, he mimed the same ritual. Delighted that he had my rapt attention, he added more touches to his performance. He hummed little snatches of popular tunes, and in a gruff voice he called for more boxes. "Pass 'em along there."

He reminded himself nothing must be "et" till all of a sudden he emitted a high piping sound. "Tea break now. Betty 'n me make tea today."

"Who's Betty?"

Matthew turned from his factory bench, put his arms round a very fat imaginary woman and made the noise of a smacking kiss. "My lovely Betty."

In what was evidently her voice he said, "Sugar everyone. Two biscuits each. Three for Matthew, he's worked so quick."

"But you don't like biscuits."

"Eat biscuits in factory tea time."

When he sat down again I learned that on three afternoons a week, James, Sarah (probably his old love), Dave, and some others would eat an early lunch, then climb into the school bus and be driven to the "chocolate factory." "Do putting in boxes two o'clock t' five, have tea 'n pee 'n wash in middle. Dave 'n James carry things. Sarah does same as me."

I told Matthew he must keep his wage packets.

"Don't want what's inside."

I tried to make him understand that even though going to work was a pleasure, he was doing the job, so the money was truly his.

"Nasty stuff."

"You like getting money from banks, don't you? If you put this money in a bank account, you would be the one to write the checks."

All at once a cloud overcame Matthew. He swallowed the last drops of his tea, then set his cup in the saucer with a bang. He bent over till his nose rested inside its rim. "Don't like checks no more. Don't work, make people very cross."

I was a little puzzled. I gave the subject one more try. "What about putting your money in the care of the post office? They will give you a little account book telling how much you save, the sort of thing you like."

"Don't want to say about money any *more*." He looked so downhearted that I suggested we try pressing the notes in the pay packets with a warm iron to take out their creases. It turned out to be a task that pleased him. Then I put the money in a wallet I had been keeping for him, the only present Matthew ever received from my father—and that by the grace of my stepmother, who saved it for him after my father died. We stowed the wallet in one of the compartments of the rucksack, and we did not refer to the sore subject of money for the rest of his visit.

When we drove back to his school, Matthew invited me into the art room to look at his paintings. There I had a chance to talk to Jeff, who knew all about the visits to the factory. He told me that particularly in Matthew's case, the experiment was proving a success. It had been reported that Matthew was able to assemble chocolate bars into groups of six, eight, or ten and pack them in suitable boxes very swiftly, never making a mistake. He had fallen into the rhythm of this repetitive work easily and had become very popular with the women among whom he worked. Together we considered the manner in which Matthew might be persuaded to save his wages. Jeff thought the whole group should be encouraged to open Post Office accounts, then Matthew would not want to be left out. He was also able to explain Matthew's remark about checks making people cross.

Certain members of the community, Matthew among them, had been granted a new privilege, the right to visit the village shop unaccompanied by a member of staff. Since he disliked sweets and fizzy drinks and had difficulty walking, Matthew did not use the privilege. But on one particular day, with his briefcase under his arm, he accompanied his friends on their shopping spree. As usual, they took a long time choosing what they "needed." Matthew added up all the prices on his calculator. He took his flashy green fountain pen and over-large Arab Emirates checkbook from his briefcase and carefully wrote the sum in the appropriate space, then dated the check, added a few hieroglyphic-like marks here and there, and with a flourish, signed his name, Mr. M. Crosby.

Quite without demur, the young woman who was serving behind the counter accepted the check. ("Don't know why she isn't among our lot," remarked Jeff.) Almost at once, a description of the scene was telephoned to the school secretary by an apologetic fellow customer who said, while she did not wish to imply that Matthew had been knowingly dishonest, she wondered if he actually had an account with some bank in Saudi Arabia.

Matthew's companions licked ice creams and quaffed fizzy drinks as they strolled home. They congratulated him for being the proud possessor of something so magical as a checkbook. In response he invited them all to his room, where a staff member found this happy group waiting patiently while Matthew, seated on the swivel chair at his table, holding a naked razor blade, was very carefully cutting checks from the checkbook, then handing two to every boy, and one to every girl.

DESPITE HIS MANY setbacks, one being the intermittent recurrence of pain in his knees, these were good times for Matthew. His self-confidence flourished with his popularity, and I was able to spend June in America with an easy heart. I wrote biweekly letters or postcards to him. I received very few replies, since his letter-writing depended first upon the good will and a spare twenty minutes of some houseparent, and then upon Matthew's own efforts to get to the post office.

As soon as I was in England again, I telephoned Matthew, but I was told he did not feel like talking. I asked if he was ill. No, though he badly needed a change of scene. I went post haste to find out what was wrong and to bring him home. He was sitting alone in the common room. I went to kiss him but he shook me off. A young staff member whom I had not met before called from the kitchen, "The kettle has boiled, Matthew. Are you going to make your Mum a nice cup of tea after her long drive?"

Matthew got slowly to his feet and walked with small, wandering steps into the kitchen. I followed. "We'll tell her when you've poured the tea."

Matthew went to the counter and taking up a canister blindly groped for tea bags, then lifted the kettle and dribbled boiling water into three mugs. He picked up a teaspoon and jabbed at all three tea bags as they floated in the mugs of hot water. As he pulled each bag out, he waved it to and fro again and again, as if pursuing a ceremony all his own. A little impatient, the young helper got up to join Matthew. He took the bags from him, poured milk into the mugs, and carried them to the table. Meanwhile Matthew was repetitively wiping the counter.

"Are you going to sit down, then?"

Matthew left the sink and came to cringe, rather than sit, as far as possible along the bench from me.

"Now we'll tell your Mum what's gone wrong."

Matthew was silent.

"Do you want me to do it?"

Matthew nodded. The young man gulped down his tea, then told the news briefly, and, I thought, roughly. "Matthew had an accident at work. He caused a lot of trouble, but he is very sorry. Enough said." He got up and put his mug in the sink and started to leave the room.

"Was anybody hurt?" I called after him.

"Not at all."

Having cast himself into the front seat of the motorcar, Matthew did not alter his position till we reached the outskirts of London. His pose was not so much relaxed as inert. As we drove along I discovered that he had an odor about him; his breath, his hair, even his skin smelled strangely toxic.

"Do you want to say any more about what happened?"

"Can't. Mustn't."

"Would you like me to ask you another time?"

"A bit . . . next days."

"I will just say this to you, Matthew. We've been told nobody was hurt, and that is *very* good. If some things got broken, it does not matter too much. Things can't feel anything. Every *thing* can be mended or replaced. Do you understand?"

"Ye-es."

I ordered Matthew into the bath that night and I washed his hair. In doing so I found there were areas of his skin that had the appearance of having worn thin. His knees, feet, and elbows were raw. I dabbed ointment on them before I put him to bed. I heard him murmur and cry in the night, but by early morning he was in a deep sleep from which he wakened very late.

Sitting beside him as he ate his cornflakes, I asked if he would consent to visit a doctor to get an ointment for his sore places. The suggestion alarmed him. He eventually agreed to go with me to consult the nice lady who was to be found behind the counter in "Boots, The Chemist." She was, in fact, the pharmacist from whom many of us sought advice. Acting upon the least of hints from me, she made marvelous recommendations directly to Matthew.

"I am sure you are man enough to swallow a nasty-tasting tonic."

"Yep."

"And I have a special ointment. You must let your mother smother you with it every time you take a bath, then you won't need to use any soap. It is called aqueous cream; that means water cream. I'll give you a big pot of it."

The pharmacist had prescribed just what was required. Masking any sign of affection, I would murmur medical-sounding reassurances each evening as I pasted Matthew's entire body with her cream. "There, that is healing your poor raw feet. This ointment is having a good effect upon those elbows, your knees are beginning to look better." I caressed and smoothed till I feared Matthew would see through my artifice, but his need was such that at each application he gave way a little further to my caresses. After he climbed into the bath the ointment became effective in a different way; he at once succumbed to the sensation it caused.

"I'm all shiny-slimy." He rubbed his hands over his shoulders and down his arms, along his thighs, over his knees down to his toes, then over his face and round his neck. He writhed and squirmed under the water.

"Feel like fish. Lovely."

On the evening of his arrival home, after I had put Matthew to bed, I made a telephone call to the school. I said to whomever answered that I needed to know more about Matthew's so-called accident. The person who talked to me was touchingly protective of Matthew as he described what had taken place. About a week before I returned from America, the foreman in charge of the factory area in which Matthew worked had parked a small, very new, yellow forklift on the factory floor. He announced that not on any account was it to be touched or even approached by anyone. When the tea break came, Matthew went to stand near it. Seeing the keys were left in the ignition, he climbed onto the seat, turned on the engine, put the gear stick into first, and let out the clutch. The machine started to move. Not strong enough to pull it back into neutral or to raise the hand brake, Matthew simply clung to the steering wheel, apparently hoping he could turn the machine toward an open space between the work benches. At that moment several people became aware of what was happening and began to scream. Frightened, he lifted his hands and covered his ears. The machine lumbered forward as everyone scattered from its path. Just as the forklift was tearing into a conveyor belt, the foreman came upon the scene. He leapt toward Matthew, knocked him from the seat, and turned the key of the engine. No one paid attention to Matthew, who picked himself up from the floor and painfully made his way from among the broken boxes and scattered chocolate bars to touch the foreman on the shoulder.

"Sorry. So sorry," he whispered.

In his rage the man seized him, and screamed, "You bloody little moron." Then he dragged a stumbling, weeping Matthew away from the scene, across the factory floor, out of the door and into a yard. He opened one of the rear doors of a van and thrust him into it.

"You can wait there until I am ready to deal with you."

Because the back of the van was divided from the front, Matthew lay in deep darkness. He was there for a full hour before the doors were opened again and the rest of the people from his school were pitched in with him. It was the foreman himself who drove this group of very frightened people back to their school. He stormed and threatened. He swore never to employ imbeciles again. Lawyers were consulted, insurance investigators visited, then apologies were exchanged: the factory owners for the insensitive behavior of their employee and the school on behalf of Matthew.

I suffered great remorse for my part in this drama. It was I who over so many years had encouraged Matthew to believe that he could drive. Matthew was the victim of many people's mistakes. The hour alone in the dark was terrible to him. He emerged in a state of catalepsy. The only thing of which he seemed to be aware was that he had wet himself.

CHAPTER THIRTY-SEVEN

Two Simons

Annual reviews at MacIntyre School always took place on the first Saturday in July. In 1987, Matthew's review was the first on the list. I got up early to drive to the school, where I was welcomed by a nicely spruced-up Matthew. Together we crossed from his house to the main building, where we were ushered into the staff common room to listen to Matthew's end-of-year "assessments." These were put together by his indoor and outdoor teachers and one representative from his house, all of whom were present. Both Matthew and I were meant to participate in the discussions that followed, but at previous meetings both of us had remained silent, he because he could think of nothing to say and I because by Matthew's code it would have been a dreadful breach of honor for me to criticize his school or repeat one of his rare grumbles.

Before the review began I was introduced to a man named Peter Price, who had recently been appointed executive director, in charge of the two existing MacIntyre Schools and more importantly, of the community village that was about to be established in the new town of Milton Keynes.

Peter Price began to address the assembled group, though in effect he was addressing me only, since everyone else in the room must have known the answer to his rhetorical question.

"I suppose you are wondering why Matthew was removed from Niven House and put in Philmead. The answer is that we decided he should take his rightful place among the few who have been chosen to become the first residents of our new community village. You have heard all about that, I am sure."

Of course we had. Laudable and right thinking though the scheme undoubtedly was, it should have been clear to everyone—I had made it so—that Matthew was a most unsuitable candidate for any plan whereby he might be required to look after himself. He simply was not capable of living "a purposeful life in purpose-designed apartments, where residents will *purposefully* learn to cater to their own needs."

Now near completion was a row of houses, a community center, a bakery with a shop attached to it, and a café. Space for a market garden was "in the pipeline." It was intended that this entirely new MacIntyre village would quickly become self-supporting. The more hardy and sophisticated residents in the school were being groomed to acquire the necessary skills. Now it seemed Matthew was to be put among them, and Mark, too. I was horrified.

Mr. Pocock, the headmaster, was now telling us why Theo's son in particular (since it was Theo who was one of the originators of this scheme) should not be left behind in this "great adventure." I glanced at Matthew; he had assumed one of his nonchalant poses, and there was a smirk on his face.

Mr. Pocock continued, "Matthew would not have been comfortable had he been left behind. I think we are all agreed that the training he will receive in Philmead can do nothing but good. I ask you, Mrs. Crosby, to keep in mind that it is by no means a foregone conclusion that Matthew will qualify for the next step."

I stood up. "I want it to be a foregone conclusion that he will not qualify. In fact, I think it would be wise to send him back to Niven House at once."

"I am afraid it is too late for that. We had the go-ahead from your husband. We could not consult you. I understand you were away in the United States."

Since I was in the habit of making telephone calls to the school every week, these last words astonished me. But *et tu,* Theo! I thought of those times in his office when he unrolled before me, one after another, his plans for the village. How I used to forestall him as he speculated as to what role Matthew would play there. Each time I would remind him Matthew must be allowed no role at all. I quoted Dr. Weihs's prediction that we must never expect Matthew to possess capabilities beyond those of a three-year-old. I told what I hoped were endearing anecdotes to illustrate the accuracy of the doctor's prophecy, and every time Theo would ruefully concede that no, Matthew must not be included in the Milton Keynes program.

I paid little attention to the kindly words of the other staff, but I was struck by the report of the Philmead helper who had been elected to assess Matthew's recent domestic progress. It was Petra, a pale young woman in pink-framed spectacles who managed to put me in mind of a hygiene inspector in some Russian film.

She read out an appraisal of Matthew's "lighthearted attitude" toward household "assignments." She told us that she had to "shake her head" at his reluctance to take on any task which he considered "dirty." "A little surprising since I can't help observing that his personal habits are none too clean."

I leaned over and ruffled Matthew's hair.

"He has recently allowed himself to become very sloppy."

As if in a classroom, I raised my hand, "In what way sloppy?"

This young woman's clipped delivery turned acerbic. "Well, if you want me to be more specific, he no longer bothers to wipe his bottom. I am not the only one to have noticed how soiled his underclothes are."

I was aware of a sudden cringing movement in Matthew. I turned, meaning to protect or comfort him, but he had shifted beyond my reach. He had put his spectacles in my handbag and was crouched in myopic concentration, zipping and unzipping the briefcase which a short while before he had carried into the room so authoritatively.

His housefather, Simon, attempted to ease Matthew's and everyone else's embarrassment. With a kindly smile he drawled, "Well, that's not like our Matthew. I know he will take more care in future."

Abandoning my intention of cornering Mr. Pocock and re-iterating my objections to the inclusion of Matthew in the Milton Keynes scheme, I gently replaced Matthew's spectacles across his nose and told him we were off to London to visit his father.

THE SEEDS OF Petra's and my enmity were sewn a few days before the Witsun Holiday which Matthew had wanted to spend in London. I telephoned her to ask when I should collect him.

"We can't help thinking that it's about time Matthew learned to make the journey to London by train. We feel he needs the exposure."

"But trains frighten him; he doesn't think they are designed for people to get into."

"If you don't mind my saying so, Mrs. Crosby, you should be discouraging those silly fancies of his. It could be your overprotective attitude that is holding Matthew back."

We reached a compromise. Two of Matthew's oldest allies, James and Michael, had grown quite used to taking the train to London together. They too were spending the holiday in London. It was arranged that they escort Matthew. Needless to say, I got to St. Pancras Station too early, so I settled myself on a bench to watch the arrivals board. As the minutes passed and no notice of the train from Flitwick came up, I became increasingly nervous. I held out until five minutes before the time Petra had told me the train would be due, then I hurried to the enquiry office; there I was told that no train from Flitwick was expected.

"How can that be? I am to meet three very particular boys who absolutely must not get lost."

The clerk suggested I consult someone in the stationmaster's office. I rushed across the station. My agitation must have been very evident; the stationmaster himself came to the counter. He took me to his desk and offered me a chair. He asked me to describe my "lost children." I realized he was about to make a station announcement.

"Would it do to call them three very special young lads?"

Without a change of expression he switched on his machine, slowly and clearly he announced the loss of three very special young lads. He put his hand over the microphone, "Their names, Madam?"

I gave them. "If you are on the station James, Michael, and Matthew, please come to the stationmaster's office."

As he switched off the device, his telephone rang. He exchanged only one or two words, then glanced in my direction. "The train you wished to meet drew into Kings Cross a few minutes ago, Madam. I suggest you go there. I will arrange for someone to escort you." He beckoned to a less grand official who stepped from behind a desk, put on his uniform cap, and ushered me through the door. Just as we reached the concourse I saw the three: James, short and stout, was leading the way; his tall and shambly friend, Michael, was shepherding Matthew who had a beseeching smile on his face, an expression with which I was sadly familiar.

James broke into a run, "Hallo Mrs. Crosby; we've brought Matthew for you, Sorry, sorry it took so long time; we comed from Kings Cross you know."

I moved toward Matthew meaning to put my arms round him, but James was already doing so. "It's all right, I knowed what was happened. Petra told everyone wrong station. Me and Michael sometime comed to this station, so we knowed."

I marveled at James's power of deduction. "How intelligent of you."

"Yes, intelligence us. First me then Michael."

Matthew said nothing. I took his hand. "Where are your suitcases?"

"They all together waiting under the clock in Kings Cross."

"Shouldn't we take a taxi there at once?"

"We can walk; it's tiny way."

The station official smiled, the self-possessed James insisted on shaking his hand. "Thank you sir."

The four of us did walk, it calmed both Matthew and me to do so. The others were in no need of calm; they were delighted with themselves, as well they should have been. Sure enough, their luggage was stacked under the clock in an absurd pile; three rucksacks, a briefcase, a roll of drawings tied round with pink wool, a piece of amorphous carpentry in a transparent bag, and to top it all, a furled umbrella.

"'S Michael's," the first words Matthew had spoken.

Michael's were more flowery, "Nice to have seen you again, Mrs. Crosby." Pointing his umbrella at Matthew, "Have a nice Witsun with him." James embraced me again, kissing me wetly, then said, "Goodbye all Crosbys. Mustn't worry any more. Petra forgot. I'll tell my Dad. 'Spect he'll tell her off very fierce."

LEAVING THE WRETCHED assessment behind us, Matthew and I got into our car. The other cars on the road glittered in the sunshine, but on that day they were of no interest to Matthew. "Does the light tire your eyes? You could move into the back seat."

He put his fingers to his lips and shook his head.

"We are not to talk?"

He cocked his thumb to indicate I'd guessed correctly.

IN 1987, THEO had bought a vast glass-roofed studio and work space in Whitechapel. Attached to it was a suite of rooms which he converted into a second studio and living quarters; these he planned to share with his new girlfriend. Hoping to maintain some part of his bachelor status, he divided his week between these new premises and his old Whitehall flat. In the White-chapel studio he had room to work in clay and plaster, do his stone- and woodcarving, and practice any new activities that interested him. Whenever his girlfriend was absent for more than a day or two, he would invite me to bring Matthew there.

Now Theo welcomed us by serving coffee and a plateful of doughnuts in a pretty sitting room. Matthew shook Theo's hand and started to wander to and fro. Theo ordered him to come and sit down. Matthew pointed toward the bathroom and left us. While he was gone, I recounted the part Petra had played in Matthew's review. Because I did not want to spoil what I hoped was going to be a "treat weekend" for Matthew, I did not broach the subject of Theo's "go-ahead."

Matthew was absent for so long I felt I should check on him. I knocked on the bathroom door. Silence. "Matthew, I know it's not a talking day, but I need to know if you are all right . . . If you are, give one knock, if not, two."

Immediately there came two knocks.

"Can I come in?"

Two knocks.

"Will you come out?"

Two more knocks.

I thought for a minute or so. "Can your Dad come in?"

After what seemed a long time there was one timid knock.

"You know, Matthew, your Dad doesn't care for this no talking business; perhaps you'd better talk to him. Shall I go and fetch him?"

One more knock.

Theo was visibly upset when he and Matthew returned from the bathroom. In a gentle voice he asked Matthew to go and fetch his luggage from the car. Moving as if his limbs were freed from some invisible bonds, Matthew answered, "Aye, aye, sir," and loped off. Hurriedly Theo told me Matthew's underpants were soaking in the hand basin. They were stained with feces and blood. He said he thought it was possible he had piles—but he added there was a worse possibility. At that moment Matthew returned.

"I'll help you sort out some clean clothes, Matthew."

"Thank you, Mum."

I gave him a kiss. Then we both carried his rucksack to the bathroom. He put on a clean pair of underpants while I washed out the soiled pair. We wrung them out together and he spread them to dry on a windowsill.

I left Theo and Matthew to prepare lunch while I went to buy some kind of helpful ointment from a chemist's shop. When I got back Theo was opening a bottle of sherry. He told us we needed fortifying. His face still looked white and pinched, and I felt like vomiting.

The day was spent quietly. Theo showed Matthew how to make drawings of buildings. He allowed Matthew to use any amount of tracing paper. Wearing a peaked cap and a pencil behind his ear, Matthew shared Theo's drawing board. He asked his father if we could go out for dinner; it seemed even under stress Matthew recognized an opportunity.

While in the chemist's shop I had discovered a red inflatable rubber cushion. It had a hole in the middle. Matthew was intrigued and blew it up at once. He carried his new possession to the restaurant.

"My wound's better on here, sitting nice 'n high." He ate ravenously.

That night we stayed with Theo. After Matthew had gone to sleep Theo and I talked. He told me he was quite certain Matthew had been "interfered with." He said that in the bathroom he had asked Matthew what had happened to his bottom. Matthew pressed his finger, first to his own, then to Theo's lips. Theo suggested I try to find this out before taking him back to the school.

All of us passed an uneasy night. I had to waken Matthew from dreams in which he whimpered and swore, "Bad monkey ...pee-er...hell-er...worst pudding," and I noticed the light in Theo's room was on till very late.

As soon as the Hammersmith surgery opened I took Matthew to see a local doctor. He cautiously verified Theo's guess, but added that if I was considering making an issue of it, he would probably back down and deny that he had said anything so definite. He told me it was essential to get Matthew to his own doctor before making that kind of accusation.

I told him I was not considering any such action; I just wanted Matthew healed. When Matthew saw that the ointment the doctor was about to apply came with a white plastic applicator he became alarmed and refused to let him use it.

I kept Matthew in London long after the summer holiday was over. Dido came home and we looked after him together. Friends of hers who visited us were very sympathetic. He allowed them to try his cushion and they took him on little outings. Despite the fact that he was seldom without pain, he managed to enjoy himself, at least until Dido left to go back to Oxford. Then life at home seemed dull; even so he was loath to return to the school.

The time came when it was possible for us to talk about what had happened to him; we did it in parts.

"When will you want to go back to school, Matthew?"

"Dunno. Some days, p'r'aps."

"Don't you want to go?"

"No—o."

"Tell me why not."

"Can't."

On the next occasion, "Was there something that happened at school that you didn't like?"

"Yep."

"When did the horrid thing happen?"

"Nights."

"More than one night?"

"Lots."

Horrified, I turned from Matthew to hide my expression. "That is worse than bestial. It must have hurt you very much."

"Course 't did."

I questioned him again. "Did the bad thing happen in your bedroom?"

"Yep, when we done teeth."

"We? I thought you had a room of your own."

"Did. Petra said someone else's turn."

"Matthew, when I take you back I will make quite sure that you sleep alone again. Is the person you share with the one who hurt you?"

"Can't say. Mustn't say nothing t' nobody. 'S a secret. Mustn't, mustn't tell."

A few minutes later I asked, "Whose secret must we never tell?"

"Simon's."

I was aghast. "Your house father did that to you?"

"*No*, Mum! Not nice Simon; other Simon."

"I don't think I know him."

"The bedroom share Simon."

"Well, my darling, I have an important thing to say. That horrid thing will not be done to you ever again. I will make quite sure of that, too."

"Thank you, Mum."

"Now do you feel you can go back to school?"

"Soon."

Soon turned out to be the next day. Upon going to waken Matthew, I found him stuffing all his possessions into his rucksack—"School today."

I telephoned to say Matthew felt well enough to return and I had something important to discuss. Could Matthew's housefather, Simon Hardcastle, be there for me to talk to?

Matthew perched himself on his cushion for the drive. On the way I tried talking. "Did you tell that beastly Simon how much he was hurting you?"

"Yep. Can't tell his trick to no one, Simon Beastly said."

"Poor Matthew. What a disgusting trick. Does Simon do his trick with anybody else? Some of your friends, perhaps?"

"Don't know."

By the time I reached the school, I was breathless with anger and agitation. I left Matthew in the art room and carried his rucksack over to his house. I had imagined being able to talk to Simon Hardcastle alone, but he and Petra were busy in the kitchen.

"Is it possible to talk to you alone, Simon?" I looked at Petra.

"I should be present," she said. "I suppose you want to discuss the remarks I made at Matthew's review."

"I don't. Oh, well, in a way I suppose I do, but I would find it easier to talk to Simon."

Simon answered, "I think, Mrs. Crosby, it would be better if both of us were to hear what you have to say. Let's sit down." He and I sat on the bench. Petra stood with her back to the sink.

I started by asking how it had come about that Matthew was in a double room when it had been long ago agreed his health dictated he have a room to himself.

"I explained to Matthew exactly why he was being asked to give up his bedroom and he made no objection at all," answered Petra. "He has been in with Simon for about six weeks now, and there was never a word of complaint. I don't know why as soon as his mother discovers he no longer sleeps alone..."

Interrupting Petra I turned to Simon, "Something terrible has been happening in that bedroom. After the review I took Matthew to visit his father. We discovered Matthew was having pain sitting. He allowed his father to go into the bathroom and look at his bottom. Theo found Matthew's anus bleeding and he saw bruises. Later our doctor discovered Matthew's back passage to be torn."

Simon Hardcastle put his elbows on the table and covered his face with his hands. It was Petra who spoke. "I can't help feeling your doctor is jumping to conclusions. I have my suspicions that Matthew is suffering from hemorrhoids. Of course now you have made this plain we will fix an appointment with our own doctor. Meanwhile I don't think we should continue this meeting. From right now, Simon and I must refuse to discuss this with you."

"I think someone should go and find Mr. Pocock."

"There is absolutely no need for that and anyway Mr. Pocock is away. When he comes back he will of course be informed of your fears." Petra's voice was wintry.

"I must take Matthew home again unless he is put into a room of his own. We should sort that out at once. He cannot go back to sleep with that boy."

"Mrs. Crosby," Petra continued, "you are making a most serious accusation against an innocent lad who you haven't even met, one who is years younger than your son. If you don't mind me saying so, you yourself could be in very serious trouble. Matthew is perfectly safe in our hands. Why don't you go home and think this over. We will be in touch with you as soon as we get a proper doctor's report."

As Petra finished, Matthew came into the room; he slid his cushion along the bench till it pressed against Simon, then he sat on it.

"Matthew, I am trying to fix it that you have your room back again."

"Thank you, Mum."

Petra folded her arms tightly across her bosom, let out a great sigh, and closed her eyes. The inertness she achieved was unpleasant and forceful. We were all silent.

"Matthew, rather than leave you here to sleep in the same room as before, shall we go home?"

Simon had removed his hands from his face; now he said, "We can probably make sure Matthew won't have to sleep in that room, but we can't promise he'll have a room to himself again."

"*Probably?*"

"All right, I will make quite sure."

"Do you want to stay Matthew, if you can't sleep alone?"

"'S my place, Mum."

I FELT DEFEATED. I drove from the school knowing I had not kept faith with Matthew. Over the next few days I made telephone calls to both Matthew and the school office; the latter were answered by staff members who contrived to be both placating and evasive. Mr. Pocock was out or could not be found; it was Simon Hardcastle's "time off." When I managed to talk to Matthew he sounded almost content.

"Nurse says Brave Matthew put stuff 'n my bottom, liked it, did morning too. Now 's me has to do it."

I asked him where he was sleeping.

"'N bed, silly."

"Well of course, but do you have a room to yourself?"

"Nope."

"Who else is in the bedroom?"

"People."

"Is Simon 'Beastly' one of them?"

"Not saying his name no more."

Finally, one morning, without forewarning them, I drove to the school. I went to the art room, the obvious place to look for Matthew.

"May I come in, Jeff?"

"'S all right Jeff, 's my Mum." Matthew blew me a kiss.

"As Matthew says, it's all right." Jeff seemed embarrassed.

"I'm not here to talk about what happened to Matthew. I just want to see how he is doing."

"Doing coloring, Mum."

"Young Matthew, why don't you find your folder and lay out your best pictures. Perhaps we can let your Mum choose some to take home." Matthew wiggled his fingers in the air and went to look for the folder.

"We've all of us been told we are not to discuss the subject of Matthew's . . . well his health. But I must say there has been a lot of feeling about the subject. Simon Hardcastle was very distressed that he might lose his job."

"For what reason?"

"He believed what you told him. So he questioned your Matthew, then let them know you were right. They sent him on leave."

"I'm so sorry."

"Don't worry, he is getting over it."

Leaving Jeff and Matthew to roll up the pictures I had chosen, I went to Mr. Pocock's office. Though I thought I had glimpsed him through a window, I was assured he was absent from the school. I walked across to Philmead House. There, evidently back from leave, I found Simon Hardcastle.

"Well, Mrs. Crosby, I should not be seen talking to you, but so as to feel right with myself, I'd like to let you know Matthew told me how it was between him and Simon."

"I'm very grateful that you took the trouble to question Matthew and had the decency to believe what he managed to tell you. What I want to know is, has he been examined by the school doctor?"

"I think that is part of what Mr. Pocock calls his strategy, probably waiting for him to heal up a bit first."

"Is Matthew sleeping in the same room as the other Simon, whom Matthew now seems to be calling Simon Beastly?"

"He is in with several lads now. Petra's strategy, safety in numbers."

"I wonder what the strategy is concerning Simon Beastly. How do they plan to deal with his sexual propensities?"

"Mr. Pocock and some others wonder if it wasn't only Simon, perhaps Matthew was doing it back, so as to say."

I was angry. "What Matthew told makes it quite plain, I thought that's what you believed."

"They think he might have had feelings of that sort."

"Please let 'them' know I am taking Matthew out for lunch."

MATTHEW AND I drove to Leighton Buzzard and ate in our old favorite restaurant, The Star of India. I set up a conversation:

"Dear Matt, are you managing to do your bottom balm properly?"

"Sort of, Mum"

"Does anyone help you?"

"'S rude."

"Not nearly as rude as what Simon Beastly did to you."

"Nope."

"What would you like to happen to him?"

"Nothing."

"Don't you ever wish he might have pain and trouble like you do?"

"Don' know."

"I think you are a kind man, Matthew. If Simon were to have hurt me the way he hurt you, I would..."

"'S very rude, Mum, don't tell."

"Oh, so you don't want to hear what I would do to Simon Beastly?"

"Do."

"I would fill his mouth with sand every morning and every evening, just at the time when you have to apply your bum balm."

Matthew nodded.

"Make him put his foot in lav'try, make him eat sick new girl did 'n her plate." He was giggling now. "Eat sick wi' knife 'n fork"—he was hooting with laughter, so much so that he had to take off his glasses—"put him in cold sea, no clothes on."

Matthew turned from the table and smacked his knees as tears ran down his cheeks.

"He be frightened then."

"I don't think any of what we have said is bad enough for that wretched Simon Beastly."

Matthew stopped laughing.

"What I say, Mum, make Simon be *nothing*."

CHAPTER THIRTY-EIGHT

Before Milton Keynes

After the annual review, Matthew and the others chosen for Milton Keynes lived amicably together in Philmead House. Twice in that time I made visits to America. In my absence Dido watched over Matthew. She telephoned him and wrote him letters, but most importantly, she carried him off to London to spend weekends with their father and his girlfriend, whom Theo introduced to Matthew as his "live-in partner."

When I got home Matthew reported to me, "Livin lady there. Dad 'n me did work 'n studio . . . Livie Lady and parrot too shouty. Dog licked my face, didn' mind. Cat bit handicapped. No tail."

After Dido brought him to London a second time, he told me, "'Nother handicap person there, nice Granny, stayed in her bed. I got in too. Had walking sticks, let me try 'em." After both visits he was so exhausted that he fell asleep as soon as he got into Dido's car and did not waken until he arrived at the school.

It was clear from subsequent anecdotes that Dido had not flinched from letting Theo know that Matthew must not be patronized. She was right. He needed us all to recognize how grownup he was trying to be. He had developed the idea that his "bad bottom wound" (which is how he referred to the unhealed lesion in his rectum) had been some sort of mandatory process of initiation, and he was trying to convince himself he was now "more tough."

Rather than toughened, Matthew was in fact debilitated by his "wound"; he nonetheless persevered in his hope that he was man enough to spend the next chapter of his life "living 'pendently"—he had been well indoctrinated. Mainly he yearned for the magic of adulthood. "When I'm growed up . . ." "Soon be proper man..." "After big twenty-six day can call me Mr. Crosby."

Matthew still conveyed his ideas telegraphically, but anyone who was an intimate of his could construe his usages and elicit evidence that he did plenty of pondering, and was at times able to draw surprisingly original conclusions.

The school was both right and wrong in their prediction that Matthew would benefit from being placed among the aspirants for the Milton Keynes project. Right, simply because they had already placed him there, so that with the defilement (by now more or less acknowledged) and injury he had suffered from the repeated sodomy, it would have been too cruel a blow to withdraw him and thereby crush him all over again. Wrong, because apart from his being an improper candidate, it was now noticeable to me, though apparently not to those looking after him, that Matthew was becoming frail.

During his eleven months of so-called "training" for life at Milton Keynes, Matthew spent many hours alone in his room. Each time I went to visit him or to bring him home, he allowed me to understand a little more of what he was doing there. He was not preparing himself for "living 'pendently" so much as appraising himself. He began by sifting through his possessions. Acting the parts of both shopkeeper and customer, he spread about his room an array of his things. "Don't need all."

I guessed that I was to sanction the casting out of childish belongings and justify the keeping of others, "Do you want me to take some of this stuff away?"

"Yep, far way." He lay on the floor to reach beneath his bed for his carefully filled copy books.

"Am I to take those home?"

"Thank you, Mum. Put carefully."

A row of little cars was parked on the windowsill; he sighed as he picked one up.

"You can't live entirely without cars, Matthew. Everybody must have something to play with, no matter how old they are."

"What Dad have?"

"All those African masks and little statues."

"What Dido have?"

"Her dog, all that junk in her work room—she has lots of stuff."

He looked relieved. "All right." He began to sort the cars over, humming his old engine noises as he did so. Eventually I was given two-thirds of their number to look after. "You going to London car park, boys."

The next time I arrived to drive Matthew back to London, I found he had emptied his wardrobe and piled all his clothes on his bed. "Need all new clothes, Mum."

Thinking of the cost, I said, "Don't you like any of these? You look nice in your corduroys, your new windbreaker, the leather jacket your Dad bought you, the sneakers Dido helped you choose, all those checked shirts you made me buy, the woolen socks recommended by the horse doctor..." We put about half of his clothes back on the hangers and shelves. From then on, his way of measuring how much he should own was both practical and symbolic, though it struck me as melancholy. When I came to his bedroom, he would drag out from under the bed his red canvas suitcase, take his rucksack from the top of his wardrobe, and unfold a plastic bag with "Bus stop" printed on it. Then wearing his leather jacket and his favorite cap, he went through the motions of packing. He put his clothes in the case, his shoes in the rucksack, and his papers and cars in the carrier bag or his briefcase. What was left he commanded I bring home. The shelf I kept for him in the store cupboard of our London house became filled.

Matthew carried out the last stage of his winnowing process in our London kitchen, directly he arrived for his spring holiday in April of 1988. He tumbled the contents of his briefcase onto the table, saying as he did so, "Brought some big work to do. Need two writing books, three pens, sticky stars."

I supposed these purchases were intended for yet another round of grading and star-awarding activities, but as I watched Matthew writing his full name in capital letters on each side of the first few pages of one of the new copybooks, I was not so sure. Next to his name, which he underscored several times, he wrote with a blue pen the word "Is," then on the following pages, with a red pen the word "Not." He ruled boxes round these words, and said to me, "Ready?"

"Is it a game, Matthew?"

"Cert'ly not, Mum, serious." He offered me the writing book. "You write."

"I don't want to spoil your new book. Shouldn't we practice on some of my paper first?"

"Good girl." He picked up a pencil and ruler and in no time had made a rather careless version of what he had just done on the paper I offered him. He handed me his pencil and eraser. "Might make mistake, you write."

"What do you want me to write, Matthew?"

"It says, silly. 'Matthew Is.'"

"You mean Matthew is the son of Theo and Anne Crosby, the brother of Dido . . . ?"

"Not that stuff."

"Matthew is going to be twenty-five?"

"Wrong 'gain."

"Give me a hint."

"Nope, have a guess, Mum."

"Matthew is . . . able to count to very high numbers? Is able to adjust digital watches?"

"All right."

"Is able to . . ."

Matthew was suddenly impatient, "Saying wrong, not 'able to.'" He snatched the paper from under my hand. "Do it 'gain, write some 'Cans.'" He busied himself all evening ruling lines on pages of his exercise books and my writing paper. We resumed our work the next day. He showed me the new layout. With the green pen he had printed the word "Can" in big letters on several pages. "Made 't easy 'f you, Mum."

"Matthew Can . . . ride a bike very nimbly?"

"Write it."

"Shall I write 'wash dishes, do suction cleaning, rake leaves, iron certain things'?"

"Silly, everyone do that stuff, have 'nother think."

"Can look after little babies?"

"'S better. More please."

". . . and baby animals?"

"Not tigers, Mum. Now do Nots a bit."

"You do them, it's your turn."

"You, Mum, don't be lazy."

"Matthew is not lazy . . . not unkind . . . not ugly . . . not cross. Will those fit?"

"Doing it wrong, Mum, not that kind Nots."

"You'd better give me an example of the right 'Nots.'"

After a painful silence he mumbled, "Not good as Dido."

"Oh, Matthew, you are so good."

He continued, "Not clever at skates . . . Not to reading 'n writing . . . 'n talking . . . lots of Nots for biggest things."

"Do we have to put these kinds of Nots on paper?"

"Must."

"Why must we?"

"Counting."

"Counting what?"

"To know." He looked desperately serious.

Pencil in hand I waited, but as he sat hunched over his writing he became less and less able to pronounce any of his "Nots." Whispering to himself, he twice took off his spectacles and put them on again; he gave a deep sigh and stood up. He gathered his books, the ruler, his set square, pens and pencils. "Things. Every things. Stupid pudding." He left the kitchen and tramped up the stairs.

I took a piece of the discarded paper and jotted a few lines. Next I loaded a tray with glasses, some ice (remembering that Matthew felt the presence of ice to be very chic), and two bottles of alcohol-free beer, which was his current "manly" beverage. I called, "Can I come up?"

"If you wants."

"Look, we forgot to mark spaces for the things Matthew has Done in his life. Why don't we think of some of those?" I put the tray on the floor, as near as possible to where he had squeezed himself between the bed and the wall. "Will you open the bottle while I read to you the Dones I thought of?"

"P'raps."

"We ought to write there was a television program about you. All England saw it on their screens. You had an exhibition at the car factory where you sold some of your pictures. You flew in an airplane to Tunisia. While you were there you stayed in a grand hotel." By this time Matthew had started to creep from his refuge. "Have you still got your penknife bottle opener?"

"Yep."

"Be a dear and pour us some beer." I looked at my notes. "We have not said how well you used to drive the car, how you often visited your Dad's great big office, and you have eaten in many posh London restaurants. What about all the activities, outings, and holidays the school arranged for you? You have had experiences that a great many people long for. You have done things others never get a chance to do. I have made a list of some of the Dones. You could copy out the ones you think would be right for your book."

"Might."

"By the way, I can think of a part of you that is better than Dido."

"So can me. You tell first."

"You, Matthew, are far more patient than she is with old or handicapped people."

"Like 'em."

"Well, that counts as a big Good, doesn't it? Now you tell."

"She a girl."

Perhaps Matthew did manage to determine his own worth and discover assets enough to reconcile himself to himself. Maybe the act of writing his own record was cathartic to him. Certainly by the end of 1988 when he came to London, I was aware of a change. He seemed to be willing himself into maturity. That word is defined in the dictionary as "the emergence of personal characteristics and behavioral phenomena through growth processes"—a rather here-and-there growth in his case.

DURING MATTHEW'S WEEKS with me the weather was bitterly cold. Though his breathing was labored and the skin was dark beneath his eyes, he had about him a lightness. He had brought home a Christmas present given him by a member of the school staff, a pink, padded photograph album that he intended to fill. "Need best pictures go in this." I got out a cardboard box of family photographs, and there followed several invalidish days when, other than devouring appetizing meals, Matthew needed little entertainment. He spread the photographs over our large glass-surfaced coffee table. He threw back into the box every photograph he considered unsuitable to his purpose; the rest he laid out in order of "very niceness." Taking inordinate amounts of time and using his own scissors, which he had brought from school, he cut round and round the photographs, destroying several as he went along. "Little Matthews first; bigger 'n bigger, bit of Dido too. Need twenty." He took great pleasure in gluing his final selection into the album, but he found labeling them very taxing.

THE "TRAINEES"—as they were now being called—were expected to commit to memory their future address—Haddon, Great Holm, Milton Keynes—a sequence of sounds neither Matthew nor Mark could get their tongues around; they settled for "Had-a-Home, Meltin' Key, ha ha." I wondered what a friendly policeman would make of this sad sobriquet should either of them ever stray from the village.

On several occasions the select few were taken on instructional visits to Great Holm. Dido asked Matthew what it was like there.

"'S muddy."

Parents who could afford to do so were asked to provide furniture for their children's bedrooms. Beside his television set, Matthew already owned a chair and a desk. "Your Dad has given you some money to buy a really good bed, and you will need curtains for your window and a table lamp."

"Don't want curtains."

"A rug for the floor."

"Stop it, Mum. Want nice empty in my room."

When Matthew had been so violently unhappy earlier in the year, Theo designed and had made a present he was sure Matthew would like: a cabinet that was part chest, part dressing table.

"Not having Dad's thing in Had-a-Home, Meltin' Key. 'S for you now, Mum." He asked Mark to help us carry it to the car. I realized Matthew really did mean to disencumber himself.

On one of our Wednesdays, I think it was in March, Matthew and I drove to "Had-a-Home in Meltin' Key" to meet his future co-worker—a title that made no sense to me—Brenda. "Color on nails, shiny hair, smells all nice." Brenda sent Matthew to the kitchen to ask for a snack, then escorted me to her nowhere-near-completed office. From a stack of files coated with cement dust, she drew out one labelled, "M Crosby, d.o.b. 26.5.64."

"I have Matthew's details here. I believe he is twenty-four." From where I sat the file appeared to contain only one sheet of paper. "Have you any information you feel should be added to the file, Mrs. Crosby?"

"I suppose you know Matthew has a bad heart."

"I'll make a note of it."

"His knees give him trouble."

"Oh, I have not had any notification of that."

"Does your file contain a reference to Matthew's recent trouble?"

"Trouble? Something I should be aware of?"

"Probably."

"You may confide in me, Mrs. Crosby, that is what this meeting is for. Together we must build a picture of Matthew, his background, his strengths and weaknesses, even his little foibles."

I drew a deep breath and, attempting to use clinical and dispassionate words, gave Brenda a brief account of what Simon Beastly had done to Matthew. With nervous fingers this time, Brenda scrabbled through her stack of files. She picked one out, sat upright in her chair, and turned to me, her face pink. I liked her for being so upset. "But Simon is coming here; he is part of our first intake. I already have his notes." The folder she was holding appeared as empty as Matthew's. "I wonder why they didn't give me any of this information."

"I suppose whoever provided it didn't want you to know. When you inquire you will be told it was consensual sex. You will probably have to accept that, but it wasn't."

Brenda looked ill at ease. "I've never had to deal with things of this sort. Perhaps when he comes here I should make an appointment for Matthew to see the doctor so that we can establish... I think it would be best if you came too, Mrs. Crosby. Matthew might not like to go with me, he might feel shy. I simply do not know what attitude I am going to take toward this Simon creature. Oh dear, of course, that is not your concern." She slapped both files closed and in an attempt to sound professional said she was glad I had been so frank, though it was clear she was not.

CHAPTER THIRTY-NINE

At Milton Keynes

COMMENTS FROM STAFF

September 1988

"... Matthew and his three flatmates are settling in very nicely. There is just one thing, he says his mum uses a gas cooker, and she would like him to have one too. Did you tell him that?"

"... Over these first difficult weeks Matthew's sense of fun has been a godsend..."

"... Some of us find Matthew's polite manners quite quaint, sort of old world..."

"... There are occasions when Matthew's bursts of high spirits infect everyone. His friends start behaving as he does, irresponsibly..."

October 1988

"... We are wondering how to impress on Matthew the importance of checking the weather before he gets dressed in the morning..."

"... I can assure you, Mrs. Crosby, the burn on Matthew's hand wasn't serious. There is no reason for him to be scared of using the electric stove..."

November 1988

"... Matthew seems a little out of breath. We had hoped that the walks to and from his flat were going to pull him into shape..."

"...We are a little disappointed to find Matthew so reluctant when it comes to outside work."

"If anyone is feeling poorly or homesick we send Matthew to comfort them..."

December 1988

"...I can assure you, Mrs. Crosby, a member of staff checks on every flat just about every day. His little group are managing very well..."

January 1989

"...Matthew seems pleased to be among us again."

"...Matthew should not be frightened of Claire. He must learn to stand up for himself. He could teach Claire a thing or two, manners for a start..."

"...I can tell you confidentially Claire has been given a little scolding. I don't think she will scratch Matthew's face again..."

"...Matthew is twenty-four years old; one would think that by now he might have taken in the fact that cold weather means warm clothes..."

February 1989

"...We have had a little bother over door keys. Matthew has locked himself out several times..."

"...We're beginning to think your husband has a point, perhaps Matthew does experience some difficulty with the stairs. As you know, we have no ground floor flats; we'll try to put him on a first floor..."

"...Does Matthew have bronchitis every winter?..."

"...Matthew has been helping Brenda in her office this week. It is nice and warm there and she is keeping an eye on him until his cough gets better..."

"...Don't keep Matthew away for longer than need be, he is just getting the hang of having a real job. He is to do three mornings and one afternoon in the bakery from now on..."

April 1989

"...While he is in London could you help Matthew buy an attractive key ring of some sort? We are hoping it will encourage him to carry his key with him at all times..."

"...We find it gratifying that Matthew enjoys working in the bakery so much. He is particularly good at the till; rarely gives the wrong change..."

May 1989

"...I think you're right, Mrs. Crosby, Matthew could do with a nice long time at home, but we must have him with us when we go on holiday. He is such good company..."

MATTHEW'S COMMENTS

September 1988

"...Got no little ones at Had-a-Home..."

"...Don't have art room Jeff, no pictures to do..."

October 1988

"...Everyone buyed ticket book for town bus, ten rides. Did four on Saturday. Bus man says better I be conductor, ride all day..."

March 1989

"...Learn some piano playing, they promised, please say them again..."

April 1989

"...Mark says Brenda's Mark's 'n my pinup. What she pin up, Mum?..."

June 1989

"...Brenda says me 'n Mark next rooms soon. Tra la la..."

I SAW MATTHEW only once between the beginning of September, when he moved into Had-a-Home, and the beginning of October. I then heard that Roger Reith, my friend in Washington, was to undergo a course of chemotherapy, and it was necessary that I be there. Because telephones had not yet been installed in the residents' flats, I extracted a promise from Brenda that should she have even the mildest anxiety about Matthew's well-being she would call me in Washington. I tried to say something of the sort to Matthew during a brief visit to Had-a-Home. "Don't need Mum 'n stuff, got my Joan. Goodbye." He offered me a hearty handshake in lieu of a kiss.

"Give me a proper kiss."

"When you here again. *Good*bye."

Joan Purchase was the welfare officer who had looked after Matthew's interests during the years he lodged with Gladys Strong in the borough of Hounslow. She still visited him so regularly that he quite rightly had come to regard her as his forever, private friend not connected with me. However, since the "Simon Beastly episode," as she now called it, I regarded her as my friend too. Matthew liked to gently taunt me. "You not got dog no more, my Joan has, take me 'n him to lunch in pub, let me pay her money." Mrs. Purchase told me she was "thrilled by, approved of, and was most interested in" the Milton Keynes project. She didn't share my misgivings regarding Matthew's fitness to be there.

From Washington I telephoned Matthew only during the hours when he was likely to be in the principal building known as the Center.

"Hallo, Matt."

"Ah, Mum. You 'n Washington? I 'n Had-a-Home."

"I expect it's cold by now. Are you keeping warm?"

"Can't, got no anorak. Lost."

"Please find it, Matthew, you'll catch an awful cold."

"Got two."

"How can you have two colds?"

"One inside, one outside."

"Who is looking after you?"

"Me 'n Brenda."

Again Dido brought Matthew to spend a weekend with their father, who in a letter described Matthew as lethargic. Later Dido told me Matthew was merely trying to appear grownup. When I got back to England I put aside my jet lag and rushed to see Matthew. He looked quite exhausted; I at once suggested that we wrap him warmly and I bring him back to London. We struck a bargain. He would come with me provided I take him back to Had-a-Home in time for his first Christmas there. I agreed to this, so I was granted my long delayed kiss.

Late on Christmas afternoon I received a telephone call. "'S Matthew Crosby."

"I know it is, my darling, Happy Christmas."

"Can bring me home *now* 'f you like."

"It's a bit late to make the drive now. It's getting dark. What about tomorrow, that will be Boxing Day morning?"

"Be 'nuff early, not late."

During our ride to London he let me know he had found the Had-a-Home version of Christmas a pretty dull affair. He murmured grim criticisms to himself.

"I am sorry, Matthew."

"No more Christmases for Mr. M. Crosby, thank you."

He at once settled down to enjoy yet another of his post-Christmas recuperative holidays. This one turned out to be sweeter and more tranquil than any before. Dido, often accompanied by friends, came to see us, and Theo found "several spare moments" between finishing work and going elsewhere. One evening he arrived carrying a bunch of flowers, which he handed to Matthew.

"Must be f' Mum, Dad."

For some reason what Matthew said embarrassed me. "Your father brought those for you. You love flowers."

"Yep, down on ground."

The next time Theo came he gave Matthew a roll of paper and some felt pens. "No good, Dad. Not playing no more."

Theo was sharp with him, telling him he was old enough to understand that art was work. This caused Matthew to hang his head. I tried to lighten the moment by reminding him that no one, not even his dad, was too old to play. Matthew instantly brightened. "Play cards, Dad?"

Theo agreed to a game of Snap. It didn't occur to him to make allowances for Matthew as I so weakly did. Quite ruthlessly Theo set out to win, so that Matthew was cast down all over again. I offered Theo a glass of whiskey on condition we play a second round. "Tactfully this time."

As Matthew shouted his final "Snap" and gathered the whole pack of cards to his chest, he extended a hand to Theo. "Good tact, Dad. Glad let me win."

Dido's visits were more fulfilling. She came unencumbered and had the knack of articulating what Matthew wished to say without upsetting him, and his elliptical speech never fazed her. In fact, she and her friends would improvise with Matthew until they achieved an absurdly mangled language that reduced him to giggles. He was noticeably quicker and funnier when Dido was about.

At times I now saw Matthew as a weary soldier on leave from his own front line. One morning he asked me to help him retrieve his toy cars and Superman books from the shelf in the store cupboard. He did not name him, but I included Whipping Boy in my search. He was not to be found. I wondered if Matthew had disposed of the doll during some previous visit.

His only other requests were to visit my friends' houses, to be again allowed into their kitchens, to help lay their tables or cut slices of bread. He wanted to sit and stroke any dog or cat they had. These friends whom he had known since he was a small child were not in the least disconcerted by his childish wish to hold their hands and kiss them goodbye.

Sometimes he seemed sad. "Busy lying down, Mum. You go play."

"What sort of play do you think I ought to do?"

"Usual."

"What is my usual?"

"Painting."

"Would you like to come upstairs and paint, or perhaps draw something?"

"Can't."

"Why not?"

"Not got Jeff no more."

Our idyll came to an abrupt end. "Not be here, Mum. Work 'n stuff to do in Had-a-Home." It was the soldier who spoke, proud that he was rejoining his regiment, but dreading his next tour of duty. "Got to be there *bit* more."

"I don't see it that way. I think it would do you good to be here with me a *bit* more. I bet your friends can manage to do the jobs you left behind for a few more days." I had said the wrong thing.

Matthew sounded alarmed, "Go tomorrow."

"Do you think you are going to want to stay there for a long time?"

"Want a cat."

"Would you be allowed to have one at Had-a-Home?"

"Nope."

"Where would you like to be with your cat?"

"You 'n me. Do cooking. Me feeding cat. You sweep. I clean windows . . . not yet, Mum."

"Do you have good friends at Had-a-Home?"

"Got best, Mark. I say, 'Good man, Mark,' he says, 'Same you mate.' They says, 'Buck up, Matthew,' I say, 'Cut t' out.' They says, 'Get on with 't, Matthew,' I say 'Give t' a rest.'"

"That sounds somewhat quarrelsome."

"Yep."

"You never used to talk like that."

"'S what to do Had-a-Home."

"What a pity."

"Yep."

CHAPTER FORTY

End at Milton Keynes

By the end of the first week of May 1989, Roger Reith had arrived in England, and the two of us went straight to the Wiltshire cottage. A few days later I set out to collect Matthew from Had-a-Home. Parking the car in front of the Center, I went into the building to look for him. The first person I came upon was Mary, a wistful-looking young woman who, despite her fluttering limbs, was attempting to vacuum the corridor. Recognizing me, she smiled, turned off her machine, and said, "P-oo-r Ma-tth-ew s-upp-osed t-o b-e clea-ni-ng hi-s r-oom."

Although it evidently required a great concentration of her entire body, she insisted upon accompanying me a little of the way toward Matthew's flat. "Why did you call him 'poor Matthew' when you told me he was cleaning his room?"

She lifted her face toward mine and, in a truly aristocratic accent, she said, "He-e i-s s-oo ti-r-ed yo-u se-ee."

It was clear she knew all about tiredness. I patted her shoulder as she turned to weave her way back to the Center. As I walked on, I imagined with each step what it surely cost Matthew, Mary, and probably others to make this sort of journey at least twice a day. I arrived at Matthew's front door with a heavy heart. The entrance of the three-storied building was open. Fulminating on Matthew's behalf, I climbed the stairs to the first floor. No one was about so I continued up the next flight. Fixed to Matthew's bedroom door I found a typed notice: "Please nok 2 X quitly thank you MC." I knocked.

Barely a month had gone by since I last was told to come in "f I liked." In that time, Matthew and his room had undergone distressing changes. He was sitting hunched on a chair beside his bed.

"Didn't come down; can't do up trouser."

As I hugged him, I felt a new boniness in his arms and chest, even though his stomach was visibly swollen.

"Too fat for all trousers."

"Then it's time we bought you some new pairs; we can do that in Salisbury, can't we?"

The amount of trouble Matthew had once taken to transform his bedroom, starting with the "champion's den," then "headquarters room for car drivers," "Matthew 'n Mark's workshop," till it was finally and permanently an "office for proper man," always afforded me insight into Matthew's interests and level of energy. From the day he ceased living with the Strong family and was thrust into permanent boarding-school life, he expressed an offhand gratitude every time I offered to help "do some arranging." We used to employ this euphemism not simply to allow me to assist in the changes he wished his room to undergo, but to account for my removal of discardable objects, my washing away of accidental stains and sticky surfaces, and my establishing over and over again a logical order among his miscellaneous possessions. As we grew wiser, both Matthew and I came to realize that I was trying to impose upon the room—and thereby upon him—a scheme of neatness that made no sense to him.

Matthew derived his concept of order from his belief that the things he owned affected his actual being. Rather in the manner of some rich people who assume that their wealth will cloak them with characteristics they don't possess, so Matthew felt that his possessions could augment him, lend him some part of themselves, not so much to alter his outward appearance—though nowadays he minded about that—but more significantly, to change his inner appearance, his self-image. This osmotic action depended upon a hierarchical system of arranging his belongings so as to keep to the fore those objects that had this power. As he so succinctly put it, "Always gotta have best stuff 'n front, Mum." To Matthew this was the only satisfactory way in which to classify objects and create order. A scheme evolved whereby front hanging spaces, the most accessible shelves and drawers, would display the "best stuff." As time passed, out-of-date favorites could be pushed behind or aside, into less and less conspicuous spaces, till they ended in eccentric bundles that he secreted on less reachable shelves or on the floor of his wardrobe, from where it was my task to retrieve them and sort out which were to be carried home and which thrown away.

Before Matthew's move to Had-a-Home, arranging his room had been an important aspect of his life. Outsiders, less sensitive members of staff, and, on his rare visits, his father shook their heads at the sight of Matthew's most fancied, often grubby clothes being treated as art works, clumsily taped to the walls or festooning the furniture. Theo would sigh at his array of a Superman tooth mug next to a green sun visor, a few toy cars, a hammer, a tin of talcum powder, his pop-up book, Dido's obsolete camera, a broken alarm clock, and his own defective watches; but none of it, whatever his critics assumed, was randomly ranked.

When Matthew started putting himself and all he possessed through his private review, each of his rooms (there had been three moves since his arrival at Had-a-Home) reflected a new aesthetic. He now required all visible surfaces to look exquisitely empty; only the newest and glossiest essentials were to be glimpsed. What he called his "office stuff" he placed—often crammed—into yellow envelopes, which he stacked neatly on top of one another here and there about the floor. All the rest of his "gear"—there was much less of it after the appraisals—he stored well out of sight. That is, till today. Never before had I seen Matthew's accoutrements, his clothes, shoes, bed linens, and medicines spread in such disarray. I was very disturbed.

"Are you feeling unwell, Matthew?"

"Feeling cross down here." He gave his diaphragm an angry little punch.

"I expect that will get better when we get you to the cottage."

He did not stir from his chair as I reached under his bed to find his suitcase. He watched as I picked up from the floor a few clothes, some shoes, and his ointments, all of which I packed into the case. Hoping somebody would be nice enough to send them through the washing machine, I carried the bed linen and dirty clothes that had been lying on the floor to the laundry room. "Shall I put all the rest of your stuff in the wardrobe?"

"P'raps." Matthew seemed dully uninterested while I set his room to rights as best I could. I discovered his briefcase and held it out to him; he gave me a sudden smile and grabbed it.

I told him I was going down to the Center to fetch the motorcar and that I would be back soon. I was hardly out of the door before he reached forward and switched on his little television set. I left him slumped in his chair, seemingly intent upon a puppet show that catered to the tastes of very young children. At the Center, I knocked on the door of an office and was told to enter. I asked a rather distracted-looking woman if she could give me any information regarding my son's recent health. No, she said, she did not deal with "that side of things." She sent me to look for "whoever was on duty." I found a young man supervising an unwieldy group of people who were attempting to hoe and weed a newly dug patch of earth. I asked if I could talk to him for a minute or so.

"Break," he yelled. Everyone smiled and waved, then all at once melted from sight. "I'll have a devil of a job rounding that lot up again."

"Are you familiar with Matthew Crosby?"

"Of course, who isn't?"

"Have you been told or have you noticed any recent reverse in his health or spirits?"

"Matthew's been fine. Actually putting on a little weight at last. His cooking must have improved or is he a bit piggy when he works in the bakery, I wonder?"

I told him I needed to talk to Brenda. He said she was not around. I suggested I telephone her.

"I shouldn't bother. She's on holiday."

WE SPENT A NIGHT in London to rest Matthew before I drove him back to the cottage. The day after we arrived I took him to the local surgery, where we encountered a young doctor who was solicitous and thorough. He told me that "first and foremost" Matthew was tired and undernourished. He prescribed an antibiotic to deal with what he suspected was a lingering infection of the lungs. He said Matthew's swollen stomach might be due to a secondary infection. He questioned me about the condition of Matthew's heart. I answered that though I knew it to be "chronic," the valves having been faulty when he was born, miraculously they had not deteriorated much since. I acknowledged the enlargement of the heart was plain to see, and its beat was so irregular that there seemed no synchronism with the pulse. The doctor warned me of what I already knew, that this was worsening with age. He advised me to keep Matthew by me for a while, feed him properly, and persuade him to rest, then sometime soon to arrange with his own practitioner that he have a thorough checkup. I knew this was excellent advice and I telephoned MacIntyre Schools to ask that their doctor arrange the relevant hospital appointments for Matthew. They promised to call me back.

MATTHEW AND ROGER had so far spent almost no time in each other's company. After some initial shyness, a delicately balanced comradeliness set in between them. Matthew appreciated Roger's maleness. He liked to sit as near as possible to him, stand at his elbow, walk in his steps. Roger's bouts of fatigue, due to the chemotherapy, gave Matthew cover for his own, as he saw it, shameful weakness. When Roger crept upstairs to take a rest, like a shadow Matthew slipped after him. As Matthew entered his room, Roger would obligingly heave himself to one side of his bed and pat the space he had vacated, giving Matthew permission to stretch out beside him. There were times when Roger propped himself against the pillows to read the newspapers; then Matthew, in an effort to disguise his need for fatherly comfort, would lean rather oppressively against Roger's shoulder and pretend to read, too. After a while Matthew would tenderly lift Roger's arm and wrap it round himself. No words were ever exchanged. When I came into the room, I would discover the two of them loosely clasped in a somnolent embrace.

Roger grew healthier day by day, and Matthew improved in color and was able to fasten his trousers once more. As the days passed I saw that the antibiotics, food, and rest were taking effect. Roger went down to the barn to overhaul the mowing machine, and Matthew accompanied him. The next day Roger invited Matthew to help him cut the grass. This made me anxious, till spying through a window, I saw that as Roger pushed the machine Matthew walked encircled by his arms, his hands resting beside Roger's as they proceeded back and forth across the grass in easy unison.

At the end of ten peacefully dull days, Dido and her friend Robert appeared, bringing with them Dido's little terrier, Millie. The presence of all three added sparkle to Matthew's holiday; he began to look altogether more robust. It was as if he simply decided to feel well again. Mindful that he must not be allowed to lose face, and that any but the most circumspect reference to his being less hearty than the rest of us was tantamount to accusing him of being a "stinky weed," I caught him at a moment when he was alone.

"I'm sorry you don't go and rest with Roger any more."

"Don't need, thank you."

"Well, I wish you'd loll around now and then."

"Don't like lolling now."

"Haven't you noticed how much everyone else likes being lazy?"

"Don't want wasting time."

After a few days Dido and Robert waved goodbye and drove down the hill past the village and on to the London road. Matthew stood looking over the hedge for a long time. I was grateful that Dido left her dog in our care, but her company proved a great disappointment to Matthew. She did not have the good manners of our erstwhile dog. Every time he attached a lead to her collar she pulled him over. When he set her free she raced in circles and barked at him. If the three of us took her for a short stroll—all Matthew or Roger could manage—the dog followed, but at some distance.

"Now your mum not here you naughty, not your friend any more, pudding." He turned from her and muttered to himself, "Not kind play without me."

I devised tasks to distract Matthew from his ennui, but he would not cooperate as he used to do. "Shall we write down what we must buy in Shaftsbury market?"

"Not do that stuff any more, Mum."

"Won't you even ride in the motorcar with me?"

"Stay with Roger."

"What have you been doing while I was out?"

"Done same nothing's same 's Roger."

MATTHEW'S BIRTHDAY loomed before us. I tried approaching the subject on several occasions.

"What shall we do on the twenty-sixth of May, Matthew?"

"Be twenty-five."

"Other than your perennial wish for a car, is there any particular present you need for your birthday, Matthew?"

"Don't need no car more."

"Can you name something you'd like instead?"

"Nope."

"Shall we spend your birthday at the seaside?"

"Who?"

"You, Roger, Milly, and me."

"Oh, them."

"Can't you think of any outing or any present that would please a man who is celebrating his twenty-fifth birthday?"

"Doesn't matter, Mum."

"Why doesn't it matter?"

"Not having birthday this time. No friends."

"Oh, Matthew, shall we telephone Had-a-Home and say you are coming back to celebrate your birthday there?"

"Nope. Got to get very better."

"Can you tell me which part of you isn't very better yet?"

"Don't know."

ALTHOUGH HE PUT ON a show of being completely bored by the outing, I took Matthew shopping on the morning of his birthday. From a vast display I selected a pair of jeans I thought would fit him comfortably. He sighed with vexation, but obligingly followed an elderly and very correct shop assistant who guided him to a cubicle to try them on. They returned to the counter sooner than I expected.

"Madam, your son is very knowledgeable regarding the styles and intricacies of jeans. I am afraid we don't stock the brands he fancies. Perhaps you should take him somewhere more, how shall I say, 'with it.'"

I thanked the gentleman for his advice. Matthew smirked, and I was rather impressed. We went and ate some ice cream. I gave him a promissory note. "You may buy two pairs of any make of jeans you want. I shall foot the bill [by now he understood this Theo-ism]. Love, Mum."

That evening we took Matthew to his favorite pub, The Compasses, an ancient, barnlike building. There, after a round of darts and several goes at skittles, we were shown to a table in a low-beamed and shadowy recess. A waitress put before us a menu, a box of matches, and a candle. I was a little nervous about Matthew's interest in the candle. I cannot recall what we ate, only that throughout the meal Matthew made a great show of blowing out the candle and relighting it.

When we stepped out of the pub Matthew was startled by the dark of the night. He clung to Roger's arm. "Look carefully, sir, 's not morning yet."

Our drive home took us along familiar narrow lanes, which on this moonless night seemed to Matthew incapable of piercing the formidable blackness of the trees. Every time we emerged to pass between meadows, Matthew sighed, "Ah, bit better."

I did not dare ask him if he had enjoyed his birthday; I was pretty sure he had not.

"Only one candle. Had to light twenty-five goes."

THE NEXT DAY as I watched Matthew ostentatiously lounging at the breakfast table, I understood I was being invited to notice his new air. Gone was the young fellow who was bored by the tedium of country life and dull company; in his place we had a man utterly wearied by the crassness of his mother. It was obvious I had forgotten something of consequence.

"Has the time come for you to go back to Had-a-Home?"

"Not Had-a-Home, Mum, guess more."

"Are you thinking of a visit to London? We could go to see Dido and take the dog back."

"Too late for London."

"Why?"

"Come on, Mum, soon holiday date."

"What holiday?"

"Mn . . . nm. Don't know nothing."

"You mean you want to go on the MacIntyre holiday after all? I thought you said no."

"Got to go."

"No, you don't. It might be very strenuous. Lots of walking, and some camping even."

"'S right stuff for champions. Mister M. Crosby, twenty-five."

"Shall we telephone Had-a-Home?"

I was glad of the excuse, since there had been no word concerning Matthew's hospital appointments. I telephoned Had-a-

Home and was told they were fully expecting Matthew to rejoin them in time for their holiday on the Norfolk broads, but as yet they had not got round to asking the school doctor if Matthew needed any hospital tests.

"It is not a matter of *if* he needs certain tests; it is obvious he does." I repeated what I had told the person who had answered the telephone the last time I had called—that Matthew's swollen stomach was not due to overeating; in fact the doctor here had found him undernourished.

"Well, there is a whole fortnight before his holiday starts. I am sure we can fix something."

"I don't think he should go on holiday until he is passed as fit."

"We'll telephone the doctor again."

We packed up Matthew's belongings. Matthew helped Roger lock the barn doors and fasten the yard gate. Then he climbed into the motorcar, lay back and clasping his hands, stretched his arms as he called out, "Goodbye, country. 'Bout time, too."

After we had driven to London, the three of us spent the evening at Dido's house and got home to Hammersmith rather late. Matthew woke the next morning looking pale. I asked if he wanted to wait a day or two before we drove to Milton Keynes.

"Don't want no more driving."

"So you'll stay here."

"Might go 'n train."

I said I could not see why not. I called Had-a-Home to tell them we were coming. Brenda told me which was the most convenient train, and we arranged that I would deliver Matthew into the hands of whoever was coming to meet him at Milton Keynes station, which would allow me to catch the next train back to London. "Are you sure I'm not imposing on you?"

"No, we do it all the time; glad to be having Matthew in time for the holiday."

"I am not sure that he is really fit enough. Have arrangements been made for him to be properly examined?"

"Don't worry, Mrs. Crosby, we'll get the doctor to look at him."

"But I asked some weeks ago for a hospital visit."

"I've been on vacation."

"Please, Brenda, do sort it out. The doctor here said he needs proper hospital check-ups. He put Matthew on a course of antibiotics; he said he might need the prescriptions renewed."

"I am sure his time with you has put him in good shape."

"Well, I'm not at all sure."

"The holiday will do him good. You worry too much."

"Try to arrange it, Brenda."

Matthew was pleased with the plan. He said goodbye to Roger, adding, "Got be brave walking in train."

"We don't have to walk in it."

"Yep, going have coffee in special bit 'f train."

The movement of the train did disturb him as he made his way to the refreshment car.

"Careful, Mum, train too excited."

But once we were seated at a table he started to enjoy himself. "Nice 'n wobbly."

The cups rattled in their saucers. I had difficulty pouring our coffee. The sugar bowl slid toward the edge of the table, which had a lip on it. Out of the corner of my eye I watched Matthew nudging it; I put out my hand just in time.

"That's a rotten thing to do, Matthew."

"Didn't do it, train did, wanted to go over edge helping him."

The same young man who had been in charge of the digging party greeted Matthew at the station. "Hallo! You all right then? Glad to be back among us, eh? How was your birthday?"

"Didn't have birthday."

"Well, we must get going. Say goodbye to your Mum."

I tried the subject of Matthew's health once again. "By the way, last time I saw you, you suggested Matthew might have been eating too much. It turned out he had not been eating enough. Please remember he is becoming more fragile as he gets older. I'd be grateful if you'd remind everyone else, too. I'd like to hear what the doctors discover."

The young man's expression told me I was one of those "nuisance mothers."

I sat on the train pondering the question of how I should convey my concerns without provoking hostility or being dismissed by various levels of MacIntyre School staff. I had seen quite overbearing sets of parents being treated with respect, timid parents being reassured, angry parents gently placated— even parents who continually grumbled seemed to get a hearing. I appeared to fall into a category of my own—a parent who, though she had had a strong hand in forming MacIntyre Schools, was now of small consequence, perhaps because she was no longer joined with her husband, who was chairman of the board. I dismissed that version of myself and decided to get Theo to telephone the school. I worried as to why I was such a threat both to him and to the collective psyche of MacIntyre Schools.

CHAPTER FORTY-ONE

The Camel

"Hallo, Matt. I know you are off to Norfolk early tomorrow morning—I am telephoning to say that even now it is not too late to change your mind if you don't want to go."

"Not *off*, Mum, *on*. Got t' say '*On* holiday,' '*On* N'awful Broad.'"

"Well, let me remind you that if something, *anything*, does not suit you or makes you want to be brought home, you can ask one of the staff to help you make a telephone call to me. The words you might say are, 'I want to talk to my mum on the telephone.'"

"Only postcard on holidays."

"Perhaps I should have a word with someone who is going with you. I want to be sure you can make a telephone call to me if you want to."

"'S alright, Mum."

I managed to contact a young man who said he was Matthew's "key worker." I was unable to prevent myself from sounding apologetic as I explained that while he was in Norfolk, Matthew must be allowed to telephone me should he wish to do so. The young man cut across my words, assuring me that Matthew had been passed as perfectly fit and was "raring to go" on this "adventure holiday."

"Oh then, have you heard the results of his hospital checkup?"

"That's about the size of it, Mrs. Crosby, cheerio."

I came to the painful conclusion that it was unlikely any checkup had taken place and I would not be hearing from Matthew within the next ten days. Every morning I listened to the BBC weather forecasts. For the most part they told of blustery winds and rain showers. On the last two days before Matthew was due to return to Milton Keynes, I felt a positive physical relief simply because the weather had improved.

I resisted making my welcome-back telephone call to Matthew till the morning after his return. From some very tangled sentences I gathered from "another person who lives here" that though it was "so so late" Matthew was not awake yet. I rang Brenda's office. She reassured me that Matthew, along with all his friends, had had a marvelous time, but unfortunately some of them—Matthew included—had returned with "slight head colds." The plan was to keep all these people cozily tucked up in their beds for most of the day so that they could "sleep off their chills." She was sure Matthew would be answering the telephone by that evening.

However, he did not answer the telephone then nor the next morning, so I telephoned Brenda's office again. I was told that Brenda was on another line. Within half an hour she called me back. She was all apologies; she had been out of the office because she had been visiting Matthew. She had found him looking plump and rosy. He had made his own breakfast and was lazing in front of his television set.

"The doctor suggests we give him one more day."

"One more day till what?"

"One more day to rest before you come to see him."

"What else did the doctor say?"

"Other than the cold there doesn't seem much wrong."

"Doesn't Matthew want to see me?"

"He doesn't seem too bothered, if you know what I mean."

I supposed I did. I rang his flat again that evening and this time Matthew answered my call.

"Hallo, Mum."

"Oh Matthew, I am so glad to hear your voice. How are you feeling?"

"All right. Had cold inside."

"Is the cold gone now?"

"Better tomorrow."

"Do you want me to bring you home for a while?"

"Not yet, Mum."

"I've bought another motorcar. When would you like me to come and show it to you?"

"You say, Mum."

I was mildly—far too mildly—surprised that the news about the change of motorcars elicited such a lackluster response.

"I'll come as soon as it is working properly."

"All right." He put down the receiver.

After Matthew's departure for Norfolk, a feeling of unease had prompted me to find a replacement for our old unreliable car. I bought a somewhat newer and sturdier one, and took it to the village garage, where it failed its Ministry of Transport test.

I now believe that my acceptance of Brenda's reassurances that Matthew had returned to Had-a-Home with only a cold, then eight hours later my unwillingness to catch Matthew's meaning when he said "better tomorrow," were partly due to dread. I also believe that my rationale that I could not set out till the new motorcar had been passed as roadworthy was an evasion. I must have come to my senses as I slept, because I woke up at dawn the next morning with the clear knowledge that Matthew had told me he was ill—"Better tomorrow."

It was far too early to contact the mechanic, but I nonetheless bolted out of bed. To use up the hours, I set about tidying the cottage as if I might not return to it for a long while. I packed a bag for myself and put the kettle on to boil. Though it was not yet seven o'clock, I decided to telephone Mr. Kent, the mechanic. Without my having to utter more than a few words he assured me that he would immediately set to work on the car and come fetch me as soon as it was ready.

I took my tea and toast out to the garden. It was an uncomfortably hot day, the first of July. I was in a painful state of impatience. To while away time till it was late enough to talk to Brenda,

I dialed Dido's number. I wakened her with the news that I was off to visit Matthew. I told her I thought he might be very unwell, and would let her know how much so when I had seen for myself. I gained a certain calm from hearing her reasonable responses. When I got through to Brenda, I did not wait to let her complete her description of Matthew's relaxed and contented state. I almost shouted that I meant to be there as soon as my car was fit to drive. Meanwhile she must ask the doctor to come at once. She said she would.

I detected in Brenda's voice, first, a tone of relief—"I'm sure Matthew will be happy to have his mum at his side"—then of embarrassment. "When I dropped by to check on him before I went home yesterday, his flatmate confessed that it was he who had eaten up all the little snacks I was leaving to be warmed up for Matthew. He said Matthew told him to. He also mentioned that Matthew has not been making breakfast for himself. I wonder where I got the idea that he had. Do you think some instinct told him not to eat too much?"

"Who is looking after him now?"

"He is fast asleep."

"Go and wake him up, tell him his mum is coming. Tell him she will soon be there to look after him, and she won't leave him again till he feels quite better."

"I know he will be pleased to hear that."

"Then go and say it at once. Please, Brenda, don't leave Matthew alone all day. If you can't be there yourself, get someone else to sit beside him. Someone he likes. Ask them to keep making him sip water."

I did not start my journey till after midday. Though the brightness of the sunshine was distracting, the first part of the drive was easy, since I was able to take the highway that led toward London. After Andover I had to turn northeast and make my way across the county of Berkshire and most of Buckinghamshire. My route took me through villages and small towns, where I was again and again caught behind lines of cars and lorries.

By the time I reached Matthew's front door it was after five o'clock. Brenda was waiting for me. Though her appearance was as neat and groomed as ever, it was evident that she was sorely agitated. She at once started to explain to me that she had sent Matthew's flatmates down to the Center so as to allow him some peace and quiet. There was something more she wanted to tell me before I climbed the stairs to Matthew's bedroom, but I was too impatient to listen. I stood for a moment to take a slow breath and be calm before I gave a soft knock on his door.

It was my expectation that I was going to find Matthew in a wretched state, but what I was confronted by as I approached his bed was more dreadful than I had ever seen. Dressed in his daytime clothes, Matthew half sat and half lay on top of the bed covers, his head supported by a pile of pillows. His damp hair was childishly peaked, his face looked swollen and inflamed. Both of his hands were clenched round the unbuttoned waistband of his trousers as if he meant to rip away their restraint. Far from being "plump and rosy," as Brenda, presumably the doctor, too, and sundry members of the staff had perceived him to be, Matthew was bloated and clearly in mortal pain.

As I came near him he very slowly turned his head and looked at me. His eyes were beseeching. I was aware of a putrid odor coming from his mouth. I pulled up a chair and sat beside him. I stroked his hands and said as gently as I could, "I am here, Matt. I am here now. I've come to help you."

He fluttered his eyelids at me and tried to smile. I asked Brenda, who was hovering just inside the door, "Has Matthew been drinking water?"

"We haven't been able to get him to."

"Did you try giving him a straw?"

"Oh, that is a good idea. Shall I go to the Center to see if we have any?"

WHEN SHE LEFT US I crossed the room and opened a window. Telling Matthew I'd be back in a trice, I ran down the corridor to the bathroom, where I chose the cleanest-looking towel and wetted it under the cold tap. Having squeezed away some of the water, I brought it to Matthew. I dabbed his forehead, his cheeks and neck, at first softly, then with the full weight of the watery towel. He sighed and nodded, so I lifted his tee shirt and spread the cool wetness of it down his chest. He dropped one hand against his heart, then lay back calmly. One end of the towel slipped further down his body to touch his diaphragm, causing him to wince. I at once lifted it away. Despite the fact that the towel was still laden with water, it felt warm to my touch, so I went to fetch another. Not caring at all about soaking his tee shirt and bedclothes, I covered Matthew from beneath his chin downward, encasing both arms and wrapping his hands. His body relaxed and his face, now less flushed, took on a look of immense fatigue. He rested quietly till Brenda reappeared, then he surprised me by sitting upright, casting the towel to the floor as he did so. I reached for the tumbler of water which had been placed on his bedside table.

"You must try to drink, Matthew."

He swallowed tentatively two or three times, then murmured, "No room inside."

"Why hasn't Matthew been sent to hospital?"

"The doctor didn't seem to think it necessary. We've been taking his temperature; it has never been far above normal, and you know . . . we thought he was eating." Brenda sounded miserably contrite. "The doctor was here this afternoon. He left medicine but Matthew says he can't swallow it."

"The man is an idiot."

"To do him justice, Matthew seems to have got a lot worse in the last hour or two." I believed her.

"We must send for an ambulance right away."

"I don't think we can without a word from the doctor. It might be hard to get hold of him. He doesn't have surgery this evening."

I turned to Matthew. "I shall have to drive you to the hospital, Matthew. Are you brave enough to let me help you down all those stairs to the motorcar?"

"An' Brenda?"

I heard us answer in unison, "Of course."

"I couldn't let the two of you drive to the hospital alone," Brenda said. "Anyway, you'll need me to show you the way." She was already putting together tee shirts, underclothes and a sponge bag for Matthew.

"Let's see if Matthew can stand." I slipped his bedroom slippers onto his feet and very gently lifted his legs over the side of the bed, then slowly pulled him to his feet.

Matthew looked surprised and rather gratified. "Need a pee."

While Brenda went off to make arrangements, Matthew and I made our way to the lavatory. I left him propped against a wall, urinating only somewhat in the direction of the lavatory bowl. While I was searching for his spectacles, I heard Matthew apologizing, "Sorry, old floor, wet you."

The three of us made a slow and cautious descent to the motorcar. I reached to open the passenger door for Matthew.

"Rest a bit. Mustn't spill any my insides."

Saying she had one more thing to see to, Brenda hurried down the hill toward the Center. We drove slowly after her. Just as we pulled up, Mark burst from the main door. He moved like the scrum half that he often played. I quickly climbed out of the car and ran to restrain him from wrenching the motorcar door open. He was shouting in his anguish.

"N't take him...way. Mustn't g' t'osple...Not go, Matthew, don't go-o-o."

I tried to put my arms round Mark. First he hit me, then he locked his arms round my neck. I had to wrench my face away from his to say, "We've got to take him, Mark, he has to be made better. I'll bring him back." I found my handkerchief and wiped Mark's eyes, then his nose. He made a loud blowing noise. This childish reflex seemed to calm him. By now, Brenda was standing beside us. She took his hand; sorrowfully he turned from me and trudged behind Brenda to the Center.

I looked toward Matthew. He appeared to be gazing through the windscreen with concentrated intensity. It was not till Brenda climbed into the back of the motorcar and I took my place beside him that I was able to properly examine his expression. He had taken off his spectacles and was clasping them between his knees. Never before had I seen him sit so gravely and seem so adult.

Despite all the care I took in my driving, Matthew had to admonish me, "Drive smooth, Mum. No bumps for middle bit."

When we arrived at the emergency entrance to the hospital, Brenda jumped out to fetch a wheelchair. A porter came back with her and deftly lifted Matthew into it. Brenda walked beside Matthew as he was wheeled away.

After parking the car, I entered a large and deserted casualty reception room to find that the porter had managed to lift Matthew onto a high examination table. Matthew was turning his head this way and that to avoid the glare from the strips of fluorescent light that poured from above. I found a battery of switches and darkened the cubicle, then went to search for a couple of chairs. Brenda told me that a sister had greeted them, asked a few questions, then hurried off to "contact a doctor." It came to me that I ought to send Brenda home. At first she was reluctant to go, but then admitted that she had arranged for her husband to wait in the car park.

I had not thought of her as married. I found I was pleased she had someone to comfort her. She kissed Matthew good night and left us. After feeling desperately impatient with her, it was now as if a comrade had gone off duty.

BECAUSE I WAS UNABLE to crank the backrest of the examination table to an angle at which Matthew could recline without slipping down, I resorted to taking off my shoes and joining him there. I propped myself behind him so that he could rest his head and back against my chest and be bolstered on each side by my outstretched legs. The air had turned chilly; I wrapped us in blankets which I had already purloined from other cubicles.

Matthew seemed not so much asleep as in a torpor, a torpor that was disturbed by bouts of sweatiness or shivering. We had been closeted in our isolation for so long that I was plagued with the notion that we were forgotten and was dreading the moment when I would have to abandon him to go in search of help.

At last the sister returned and explained that rather than put Matthew in the charge of a young house doctor, who was already loaded with too many cases, she had decided she must try to contact his boss—who unfortunately had left for home minutes before our arrival. She said he was the best person to deal with the severe condition that Matthew was in; he was in fact the director of the hospital.

I wondered that a nurse, expert enough to have made such an instant and decisive assessment of Matthew, could then leave that same patient unchecked for nearly two hours. As if subscribing to my unsaid censure, she sighed, "You see, we are desperately understaffed."

It was midnight when the doctor-cum-director flipped the curtain open. Before I could make a move toward climbing down from the table, he said, "Stay where you are; we want to disturb him as little as possible." He rubbed his hands together briskly, perhaps to warm them. Indicating that I should pull up Matthew's tee shirt, he began to lightly press his fingers up and down his torso. His dour-looking face loomed over Matthew's suffering one, indicating nothing save the all-important guarantee that I would hear the unambiguous truth.

"We must find him a bed at once."

"May I stay with him?"

"It is essential that you do. I'll see you on the ward." He was gone, the sister with him.

The old porter was with us again. On a stretcher Matthew was wheeled as I walked down a surreally elliptical corridor and into a ward which reverberated with snoring, murmuring, and irritable stirrings of wakeful patients.

"Who've we got here, then, a little king riding in his carriage?"

"You all right, darlin'? Want a bed by me?"

We reached a tiny side ward, where a nurse came to help me undress Matthew. A few minutes later the doctor walked into the room. We stood contemplating Matthew, who by this time was buttressed upright by a careful arrangement of pillows piled against a backrest. I could see that this contraption and the bars fixed to the side of his bed made him believe that he had been placed in a cage. He was very frightened.

"Can't we let those railings down?"

"He may fall out."

Matthew opened his eyes and croaked, "Won't."

Smiling, the doctor let one set of bars down. "Only on your mother's side. You can fall on her. She'll be next to you on a camp bed."

"Good girl." Matthew closed his eyes again.

It was as if nothing but short, abrupt sentences could cut through the stupor of all our fatigues. The doctor announced his, "Beyond prescribing something that probably won't alleviate his pain to any real degree, there is precious little I can do for him just now . . . I shall be thinking about what action I must take . . . We'll go over that tomorrow morning . . . As a matter of interest, why didn't you get him here before he got into this state?"

"I didn't pay proper attention when they told me he had a cold."

"So you weren't there; I thought not. By the way, that's the one thing he hasn't got—a cold."

"I know."

The nurse said, "We won't bother giving your boy much in the way of a wash. There's no clean towels to be had till morning." She slipped injections into first one then the other of Matthew's buttocks, intoning as she did so, "Who's the brave boy-o, then; who's the little hero?"

"Me. Got to."

Instructing him to ask his "mam" to press the bell when he felt his trouble coming on too strong, she stroked Matthew's forehead, lowered the lights and left us.

Matthew spent most of those dark hours sitting bolt upright, at times letting out anguished sighs against his "Big Hell Pain," then almost sensuously submitting to his back being gently rubbed or to accepting sips of water. When summoned, the nurse tried to relieve his distress with "just one more injection, my boy, this should do it"; she gave him three.

As the dull light of dawn began to be visible through the great plate glass window, Matthew whispered, "Nasty camel, staring like honeymoon," and promptly fell into a peaceful sleep. Not till that moment did I discover I had only one torn sheet to cover the camp bed, which, as the nurse put it, was "anyway as lame as a three-legged donkey." After dismantling the bed to make space enough to fling the sheet and pillow onto the floor, I lay down and slept.

CHAPTER FORTY-TWO

Minor Miracle

I was wakened by the same Irish nurse, urging me to sit up and take some tea. She had managed to "wash the boy all he needed without his opening an eyelid," and if I wanted a peaceful go in the bathroom I'd better take it before she went off duty.

Later Matthew was wakened by what sounded like a bacchic babble; a flustered nurse looked in to make sure Matthew was not too disturbed. She told us the mixed ward was quarreling again. "We have a loony troublemaker, and last night you took her room. We will have to give it back after breakfast."

'Breakfast"—this last word caused Matthew to raise his eyebrows twice, and murmur, "Bit hungry for cornflakes."

I went to look for the breakfast trolley. I had just placed a tray in front of Matthew when a smiling West Indian orderly, who had been rhythmically sweeping his way through the door to Matthew's bedside, put aside his broom and produced a pocket knife. He mimed a slitting gesture, pointing toward Matthew's milk carton and cereal packet. Matthew nodded, so he stepped forward and, with a flourish, executed both packets, chanting as he did so, "Heads off, they knew you were coming, son, see, your name is printed all over them." Matthew smiled and smiled again.

A foolish insouciance came over me as I watched Matthew and this new acquaintance slop milk, then shower cornflakes into the bowl. After eating two mouthfuls Matthew shook his head. The orderly surprised me—evidently not Matthew—by deftly spooning the spilled flakes back into the bowl, then eating the remainder of the breakfast.

Watching him do so made me aware that I too was dreadfully hungry. The orderly offered to stay by Matthew while I once more went to look for the trolley. I found the flurried nurse and asked her if I could help myself to some breakfast.

"The trolley is only there for the patients, you know."

"Don't listen to her," a voice growled. A self-sufficient looking gentleman, wrapped in a heavy brown dressing gown, was sitting on a neatly made bed reading a newspaper. "Yesterday's. Can't get a paper here—the wife brings it. She's never afraid to help herself from the trolley—no one has objected so far. You do the same, argue with them afterward. It's bedlam here, women on either side of me, powdered and packaged meals, even the building goes in circles. Have you seen the camel yet? All that money spent on a piece of sculpture, then they skimp on food and clean linen. Crazy."

I left him to his grumbles and went to steal my breakfast, a carton of milk, cornflakes, and powdered coffee in tepid water. As I picked up my tray I saw that, true to the nurse's threat, the West Indian and another orderly were indeed trundling Matthew's bed out of our room. I could see that the jolts were upsetting him.

Matthew's bed was positioned between those of two talkative women. I seated myself beside him and hurriedly swallowed my breakfast; having disposed of the tray, I drew the curtains about us. A nurse came over to pull them apart again, saying, "We only close those when privacy is required."

I laid my arm behind Matthew's shoulders, hoping that the gesture might suggest shelter from all the bustle and chatter that swirled round us. I was fervently wishing that the doctor would appear when, like a genie from a bottle, he manifested himself at the foot of the bed.

"Good God," were the only words he uttered before vanishing again. A few minutes later Matthew was being moved back to the room, far more carefully this time.

The doctor held a folder with Matthew's name scribbled across its cover. After examining him, he asked if I had been in touch with the boy's father. The suggestion agitated me; I realized that I ought to have done so and that I'd forgotten to telephone Dido as I had promised.

"Not yet."

"Is there any difficulty in getting hold of him? Are you divorced?"

"Not exactly."

"Then come to my office and use my telephone." He beckoned to the West Indian orderly. "You sit with this young man till his mother returns."

As we walked down a corridor, the doctor explained that Matthew should by now have been transferred to a hospital where there was a heart unit, but so far he had been unable to locate one with a bed to spare. He said he was very worried; he dared not let much more time pass. It could become, "well, too dangerous to move—Matthew. Oh dear, once I use a patient's name I find myself overinvolved. Well, in this case I probably was already part of the story."

He told me there was a measure he was tempted to take. "With his father's and your consent I could bring Matthew instant relief. You can use this telephone to talk to your husband— do it right away."

He left the room and I dialed Theo's number. His friend, "Livie," answered. When I explained that I was calling from a hospital in Milton Keynes and I needed to talk to Theo she went to get him. Theo's response to all I had to say was that he was very sorry—he felt awful—but he was busy; he had an engagement he could not postpone. He asked me for the hospital telephone number so that he could call for further news that evening. I read off the number pasted on the telephone. Then I went back to sit beside Matthew, who by this time looked quite miserably ill again. The doctor came and asked how I had got on.

"He said he was not free."

"On a Saturday while his son is in danger of dying?" He swept from the room.

Half an hour later he was with us again, tapping Matthew's chest and abdomen. "I received a call from your husband— apparently you gave him my office number. I took the opportunity to thoroughly explain the circumstances, very thoroughly. He has changed his plans. He finds he can break his journey to fit in a visit here. Did I hear him correctly? He and his fiancée are driving to Buxton. They are to attend a service in the abbey where an altar cloth his fiancée has sewn is going to be consecrated. What sort of people are they, professional embroiderers? Fiancée? I thought you said you weren't divorced."

Matthew and I dozed intermittently till a nurse wakened us. "Your husband is here." Theo and Livie approached, she looking almost fluorescent with health, in contrast to Theo, who resembled a night creature. His hair sprang from his pale forehead as if in alarm, and behind his spectacles his eyes blinked repeatedly. I offered him my chair, then pressed myself against the wall of the very confined room. Wearing that sculptured smile I knew so well to be his armor against his special foe—strong feeling— Theo leaned forward to greet Matthew.

Matthew was as yet unaware of his father's presence. I took his spectacles from my pocket, and Theo helped me hook them over his ears. The replacing of the spectacles had by now become a signal for Matthew to open his eyes. With a look of solemn surprise, he whispered, "'S my Dad."

Theo kissed him.

Livie reminded Theo that they could only spare an hour and they must "liaise with that doctor" before they left. Just then a nurse came into the room to announce that the doctor was in his office and had a few minutes to spare; he could see Mr. Crosby if he would come at once. Theo kissed Matthew again, saying he would be back soon. Followed by Livie, he left the room. I returned to the chair, whereupon Matthew dropped his spectacles into my hand and we both closed our eyes. I was touched on the shoulder by the same nurse. "The doctor wants you there, too, Mrs. Crosby. I will tend Matthew. Do you think he might manage to eat something?"

"Pink yog' please."

I gave her the spectacles.

Evidently the doctor had already explained how hazardous it might be to move Matthew to another hospital, supposing one was to be found. He beckoned me to sit down and began to describe the procedure he would be willing to perform if he had both Theo's and my cooperation.

"I can drain the edema and relieve the ascites which is causing such terrible pressure round your son's heart and abdomen. If I can rely on you two to soothe and restrain him, hold him quite still for one very important minute, I can do what has to be done quickly and easily."

"When will all this take place?" It was Livie who asked.

"Probably later this afternoon, when my houseman comes on ward duty. He can help us."

"I'm very sorry, but we just can't stay that long. You see, we are en route to Yorkshire where we have a very important engagement. We..."

Theo interrupted her, "Doctor, could you give us a few minutes to discuss this?"

"Of course. Go back to your son. I shall be along to take another look at him in a few minutes. You can let me know what you mean to do then."

Theo and Livie lingered in the corridor while I returned to Matthew's bedside. When they joined us, what Theo did reminded me of my maneuver of the evening before. He pushed aside some of the pillows that supported Matthew's back and positioned himself more or less in their place. He lifted Matthew very gently and lay him against his shoulder, then he began to lightly massage Matthew's upper back. I recognized and almost felt each stroke; he used long ago to make them for me when my asthma was bad. Matthew's face took on a look of serene acquiescence. For the first time since his arrival, Theo talked to me. His voice unexpectedly tender, he suggested this might be my only opportunity to take a breath of fresh air and find something to eat; he and Livie would stay for a while.

I looked at Matthew, who was now basking in his father's presence. I blew him a kiss and left.

Someone directed me to a battery of vending machines from which I extracted a package of sandwiches and a Styrofoam beaker of tea. I carried my lunch out of the main door and found my way to the grassy bank that bounded one side of the car park. Upon it I spread myself and ate my picnic. Just as I was beginning to feel properly alone, Livie's shadow fell on my face. She smiled and sat down beside me.

"I am very sorry we couldn't reorganize our weekend appointment. What a decent little hospital this is. So nice and convenient for Matthew's chums when they come to see him. He looks much fitter than we'd been led to expect."

I lay on my back, staring into the limitless blue sky. Seeing beyond the seeming disingenuousness of her words, I felt a certain sympathy coming from her. In a rare act of accord we both rose to our feet and made our way back to "our men"—Livie's unthinking expression.

Everything was altered. Matthew lay against his pillows once more, his pale face expressing stoical indifference to all things. The expression on Theo's and the doctor's faces were alike in their stoniness.

"Ah, Mrs. Crosby, I understand it has all been discussed. We are to cope without your husband. I shall have a lot to arrange, so I'll say good day." He made another of his swift exits.

I could hear myself saying too loudly, "Couldn't Livie go to Yorkshire by herself? Why won't you stay and help us? Only till tonight."

Theo took my arm and propelled me from the room. Livie strode past us. He pressed of all things his phonecard into my hand. "You can phone me anytime, call Dido, too, whoever you want." He gave me a light kiss and hurried down the corridor in pursuit of Livie.

How was I to telephone him? He had left me no number.

The doctor was there again. "Perhaps it has turned out for the best. Throughout the day, my houseman and I have been taking turns contacting hospitals up and down the country. My houseman thinks he has located a bed; he is trying to confirm it at this minute. I persuaded my two very best nurses to stay on duty, so they are ready to accompany your son during his ride in the ambulance. We have a very experienced driver. It is going to be a slow journey, but as far as possible a smooth one. The nurses and the ambulance will be equipped with any and everything that might be needed. What else can I say? To be frank, I am relieved; far safer to send him to a large hospital that has the proper facilities. The only thing is that damned journey. Oh, well."

"Where is this hospital?"

"Oh, didn't I say? We are sending Matthew down to London to Hammersmith Hospital."

I was silent, reveling in our good fortune, until I started to imagine the suffering the journey might cause him.

"Faith and expert nursing will get him there. It has one of the very best heart units, you know."

"Yes, yes, I do know, I live in Hammersmith. Matthew was a patient at that hospital throughout his childhood. We live nearby."

"You were under the care of the marvelous Miss Chater-Jack then? Well, well, it appears my houseman worked a minor miracle on your behalf."

He told me I would not be needed on the ambulance ride. "We have to keep it as professional as possible—easier for the nurses and your son, not to mention yourself. They have promised me that a doctor will be there to meet our ambulance, and you should be there, too. Give us three hours or so."

It took me much less than three hours to get to London. I drove excessively fast, not quite knowing what I meant by the words "catching up with myself" as they echoed in my head. I felt I was driving with a particular virtuosity; whether I was or not, I arrived in Hammersmith with a great deal of time to spare. I went to our house, where I had a cold bath and changed all my clothes. I ate and drank what came to hand. I was ready and waiting at the ambulance entrance of Hammersmith Hospital by seven o'clock, much too early. A uniformed attendant said Matthew was not expected for another hour. At exactly that time, a sturdily built blond woman with a silver necklace and a stethoscope swishing against her white coat joined me.

"You have to be the mother of Matthew Crosby. I was told you were coming."

The doctor and I continued waiting together. Two more hours passed. I was surprised at her patience. "It is essential that I am here when he arrives." She told me she had gone over Matthew's case very thoroughly with the Milton Keynes physician on the telephone, and she had studied all of the old files on Matthew. She gave me an account of the procedure she and a colleague would follow to relieve the accumulation of lymph that must by now be badly hindering Matthew's heartbeat. Then she described the role I was to play. "The physician said you were quite up to it. I expect he's right."

A little later she murmured, "Don't worry, if he had died on the way they would have driven here in double-quick time; no need to drive slowly once that happens."

When at last the ambulance pulled up, she forbade me to leave the porch. It was a while before Matthew's stretcher was wheeled past me. The doctor called, "He has made it."

I caught up with her and bent over Matthew.

"'S all right, Mum."

"Tell your mum how nicely the ladies who rode with you said goodbye."

"Big kisses," Matthew whispered.

"They had to stop and let him lie quietly a few times, then they lost their way a little; not used to London, especially at night. We dared not move him from the ambulance till he caught his breath. I offered them supper, but they were in a hurry to get home, so I said your goodbyes for you."

The doctor was telling me all this as we hurried along corridors and into a lift, which when its doors ground open debouched us directly into an operating theater.

Beneath an intense cone of white light stood an operating table, and beside it a trolley shining with surgical instruments. From an invisible high ceiling, constellations of palely glinting lamps punctured the orange tinted gloom. Green-overalled human figures padded about in the peripheral darkness. We had reached the goal everyone had been aiming Matthew toward, an ominously silent place that I had desperately hoped would be our theater of miracles. Yet as if that cone of light illumined too much, I now found myself wishing him a quick death.

Matthew could hardly have sensed my sudden loss of conviction, but maybe he had become aware of these formidable surroundings, because a terrible fear overtook him. Gasping for breath, he pushed himself upright. I caught hold of him and pressed him against my chest. He pulled at my sleeves. Crooning as I did so, I wrapped my cardigan round his head and shoulders.

"It's all right, Matt, we are here together, we won't be staying longer than a few minutes—then we'll go and find you a nice bed to sleep in. Try to be your champion old self for a little while longer. Everyone here wants to help you. Come on now." I had talked myself back into order. Matthew poked his head from under my arm and looked about him.

He whispered, "Want my specs." I had no idea where they were.

A voice answered, "Not just yet." Two pairs of green-clad arms reached out from the gloom, lifted Matthew, and seated him on the table. He closed his eyes against the blinding light. Gloved hands stroked and held him.

Somebody tossed me a green smock. "Matt won't recognize me if I put this on."

"Then forget it. Put on the other."

I recognized the doctor's voice. I was handed an orange-colored metal apron, somewhat reminiscent of the ones Gladys used to wear. I struggled into it, moving close to Matthew. The apron felt like armor between us, and he recoiled.

"Mum..."

I looked round. The doctor was not wearing hers. "Don't worry, I'll take it off." No one objected.

My task was to distract Matthew from what was about to be done to his chest. The doctor's voice warned she was now going to inject local anesthetics into three places. "The first will freeze his skin." Matthew sat quite still. I grasped his hands and in whispers relayed what was being said, trusting that without his spectacles Matthew could not properly see the horrible preparations being made. I told him he had to be as still as a stone. He took a deep breath and in a firm, clear voice said, "Don't let murder me, Mum. She not t' kill me. Don't want t' die."

His words electrified us all. Everybody paused in what they were doing. The doctor seemed the most startled. I heard the intake of her breath as she stepped back from Matthew. Though I knew she had heard and understood his words, she asked, "What did he say?"

I avoided answering her by addressing him. "Don't worry, the doctor is doing something good. It will be better if we don't watch, so look at me, Matt, and we will be as brave as brave can be."

He let out a deep breath, and as he did so, the doctor thrust the trocar between his ribs.

Matthew cried, "Hurts 'n hurts, Mum."

"I know it does, I know it is awful. Go on being brave."

We both looked down. Bloody liquid was pouring from the incision. The doctor was making another.

"'S bad 'n better," Matthew said wonderingly. Two people pulled down their masks. We all smiled, even Matthew.

The doctor's voice was confident. I could hear relief in it. "That's what we meant to happen."

She inserted the trocar one final time. Kidney dishes were being held against Matthew's chest to catch the fluid, and still it flowed. A man's voice remarked, "I've never seen such a quantity."

I tried to prevent Matthew from watching, but he removed my hand from his eyes. He did not flinch as the cuts were stitched together, but he became almost hysterical as two nurses attempted to tape the electrocardiogram disks to his torso. I tried saying they were like medals for bravery. He looked at me with disdain. Then I added they were what spacemen wore—get-well messages came through them. He turned his horribly white face to each nurse in turn. They both nodded. He lay back reluctantly, and they completed the task.

It was a triumphal ride in and out of the lift, along one corridor, then another, and into the ward where a bed was waiting. Friendly nurses welcomed him, helped me persuade him to pee, then washed him and seated him in his newly warmed bed. A young nurse leaned over Matthew and asked if there was anything he wanted.

"Television, please."

Smiles all round. She dashed off. Matthew's was the middle of three beds, those on either side empty. Wearing a flowered nightgown and crouched against the usual pile of snow-white pillows, he looked unbearably diminished. His head was lowered so that his chin rested on his chest. His right hand clutched his glasses, which had turned up from nowhere, while his left hand repeatedly wandered from one to another of the EKG plugs that were fixed to his chest.

I sat down on a chair beside him. "We must leave those just where they are, Matthew."

"Maybe this will help distract you." The young nurse was heaving a small television onto a bedside trolley, which she then wheeled into position astride Matthew's bed.

She switched the set on. "We mustn't have the sound on, because we don't want to disturb the other gentlemen."

Matthew nodded, his gaze already fixed on a silently gyrating drag queen. Though I doubt she was aware of the fact, this pretty nurse was probably five or so years Matthew's junior; she was certainly young enough not to be surprised that he craved the distraction of television.

"Now 'e 'as 'ees telly, what to eat?" An utterly unexpected figure stood before us, clad in a nightgown which excelled Matthew's in its inappropriate pattern beneath which I spied the tiniest pair of mauve underpants. He was a small, wiry man with receding black hair, half-closed dark eyes, and a drawn expression. "You are 'ungry?"

"Ye-ep," Matthew whispered.

"Jelly what you want?"

"'S right."

The man turned, signaling me to follow. He led me to a small kitchen just outside the main doors of the ward. He padded over to a vast refrigerator and opened its doors. Bottles of colored drinks, little packages, and covered dishes filled the shelves. "Private food, jellies enough for your boy. Choose."

"Don't they belong to the patients?"

"They sleep or dead, not 'ungry, not like your poor boy. Explain them in the morning. 'E like yellow or orange?" He thrust two little frilled cardboard dishes into my hands. Then he pulled open a cupboard and rummaged. He found a red plastic spoon and a large, Christmassy paper napkin. Everything looked absurdly festive.

"'E need to drink?" He seized a bottle of lemonade.

Together we returned to where Matthew's little television set flickered in the darkness. The man tucked the napkin under Matthew's chin and put the spoon in his hand. Matthew gave him a brief smile, and taking one of the dishes I was offering, began to eat very delicately. His shoulders went down, and after a mouthful or two he rested his head against the pillows. Our new friend seemed as relieved as I by this spectacle. He drew up a chair next to mine and put out his hand. "Giovanni," he said.

"I am Anne."

"And 'e is Matthew, eh?"

He told me he was a chef at Claridges. "I come 'ere often." He might have been talking about a favorite park bench. "I 'ave bad 'eart. I stay a bit, they fix me a bit, they say don't, but I go back to my work." He explained that Matthew would remain in this six-bed section of the ward, close beside the nursing station, "till 'e is safe." Then they might move him to the second section, four bays of three beds. Then if he was getting better he'd be moved into the end section. "Lots of beds there. I never there, go off 'ome then. Maybe 'e and me, we go to the next room together tomorrow." He explained he was now in the first room because he had just admitted himself again. "I feel pain so I return, am better 'ere among friends. Some still 'ere, some gone. Now I sleep like 'im."

We shook hands and off he went. The young nurse came over, turned off the television and wheeled it aside. She read the graph made by the dreaded electrocardiogram plugs, then lowered Matthew's backrest so that for the first time in many days, perhaps weeks, he was lying almost flat.

"Go home, Mrs. Crosby, there are plenty of people to take care of him. You can leave your telephone number at the desk. Of course, you may call us if you are worried, but you don't need to be. He'll be fine. We'll see you sometime tomorrow morning."

CHAPTER FORTY-THREE

The Heart Unit   *M S*

A t eight o'clock the following morning, the horrid sensation that in abandoning myself to sleep I had welshed on some promise I might have given Matthew made me leap out of bed and telephone the Heart Unit. A friendly voice said, yes, of course she knew who Matthew Crosby was—he was sitting up in a bed right opposite the nursing station, eating scrambled eggs and listening to the radio on earphones. She told me it was more than likely he would be transferred to the next bay as soon as the doctors had made their rounds, and perhaps I should come and settle him into his new surroundings around eleven o'clock.

I arrived to find the move already accomplished; Matthew's bed had been placed near a corner, its foot just short of a large bay window. Two elderly gentlemen occupied the beds which stood between Matthew's and the wide arch that led back to the nursing station. Evidently these two were friends, for an uncompleted game of chess lay on a trolley between them.

Matthew's hair had been washed. The skin of his face and throat was now a calm, pale color, and he was wearing another flower-patterned hospital gown which made him look comically beguiling.

"Got medicine for bottom. No more 'lectricity stuck on front." The difference in him was wonderful. After I had kissed him and on his insistence exchanged the gown for a pair of underpants and an old tee shirt of Dido's which I had the foresight to bring, I sat down on his bedside chair and looked around.

Across the room from Matthew's bed, a man lay, eyes closed, with all the stillness of a carved crusader on his stone grave. He was long-bodied and pale-haired with an extraordinarily handsome face. In the bed next to his, partially obscured from us by a newspaper, was our friend, Giovanni. He called me over to introduce me to his "bee-uutiful" neighbor.

"'E is Peter. 'E waits 'ere for a spare 'eart."

Without appearing to have taken in my presence, the Crusader smiled and whispered, "Been waiting for weeks." He held out a thin hand for me to shake. The instant I put mine in his a most distressing pity overtook me. "Oh, God, I am so sorry."

He lifted his other hand so that both of his clasped my one. Tears appeared between his eyelashes; I watched them drop down the sides of his long nose. As if of their own volition, the fingers of my free hand reached to his night table and plucked a tissue from a cardboard box, then dabbed the tears away. I was immediately embarrassed by the liberty I had taken. The Crusader opened a pair of startlingly blue eyes and in a soft Somerset accent said, "I'm afraid I give way too easily."

"No, no, it's better, my friend, nice to 'ave this lady to cry with." Giovanni patted a place on his blanket beside his knees. "Now you come sit 'ere; I tell you something. The gentleman in the bed next to your son is not easy, not easy at all; 'e don't understand the kind o' boy yours is. You must talk to 'im."

I thanked him for the warning and said I had better return to Matthew, but I would pay another visit.

By the following morning Matthew was anxious to place his television set so that his two nearest neighbors might see the screen. He was making efforts to catch the eye of the gentleman in the bed next to him. "Mister, 's cricket time soon."

"Is he talking to me? What's he saying?"

"My son wants to know if you would like to watch the test match."

"Well, yes, I wouldn't mind at all." He turned to his chess partner. "What about you, Abrams?"

A nurse came to help position the set. She cranked the bedside trolley as high as possible, positioned it before the window, and drew the curtain. She then switched the set on.

"Now Matthew, Mr. Abrams and Mr. Cohen may watch the test matches with you, but if either one says he is tired you must turn the set off. I hope that is understood."

She handed back the remote control.

Matthew nodded. After a few minutes he leaned toward Mr. Cohen. "Better no-noise cricket today?"

Mr. Cohen turned to me. "What's he saying now?"

Mr. Abrams interceded. "Nice boy, your son. He's right, more restful that way." The silent watching of the silently played cricket match induced a languid harmony between the two gentlemen and Matthew.

By the afternoon visiting hour of Matthew's third day in the heart unit, Mr. Abrams had decided the time was ripe to introduce Matthew to his wife. He whispered to her to go over and make herself known to his "quiet little friend"—"Seems to have been brought up old-fashioned; only speaks when he's spoken to, wish there were more like him in this world."

Matthew sniffed appreciatively as she approached his bed. She was all smiles and smelled strongly of cologne. "I've heard about your son's thoughtfulness, pressing his bell in the nights if he thinks anyone needs the nurse." She was addressing her words to me but gazing—if not staring a little—at Matthew, who smiled back with some of his old smugness.

Wearing a hospital blanket as a toga, Giovanni strolled over "to 'ave a chat with the ladies." He kissed Mrs. Abrams on both cheeks, then patted Matthew's hand. "'E 'asn't yet got the 'abit of sitting up an' sleeping, so 'e stays awake an' provides a fine service. 'E's a good boy; likes to be 'elpful," he added slyly. "'Is mother 'elps 'ere and there. She 'olds 'andsome Peter's 'and when 'is wife don't manage to come. I myself go to kitchen, cook into wonderful omelettes 'is fine eggs from Somerset. Matthew 'elps eat 'em, eh?"

After confiding to me in loud whispers that he no longer felt too "put off" by having such a different kind of "kid" in the bed next to him, Mr. Cohen also found himself willing to allow his wife to say hello to Matthew. She usually arrived during the evening visiting hour because she had to "mind the business" during the day. A little breathless and laden with carrier bags of food and other small comforts, she almost waltzed up to her husband's bedside. She kissed him, disencumbered herself of the bags, then flourished a change of silk pajamas. Mr. Cohen thanked her gravely.

"This is our television monitor. Giovanni tells me he is partial to your jellies. He devoured two of them the moment he got here in the middle of the night." He smiled at Matthew. "You say some sweet nothings to Mrs. Cohen and she might make you two more."

With a comical expression of earnestness Matthew carefully enunciated the words "sweet nothings" three times. "That 'nough?"

Everyone laughed. Glancing at Matthew, I was not at all sure he hadn't meant them to.

So it came about that Matthew was adopted into this doughty little community. I was told I need not stay late into the evenings. "He looks out for us in the night, we see him right at other times, it's only fair." And Giovanni assured me, "You 'aven't to be 'ere. 'E never noisy or naughty boy, an' always I understand 'ees little ways. Nurses make a pet of 'im; I wish I 'ave as many kisses as 'e gets."

So for a few days, while both his neighbors and his health remained quiescent and while steeplechasing or cricket matches were being relayed on the television screen—by courtesy of "Mr. M. Crosby, television monitor"—I was able to leave the hospital at about seven each evening and not return till nine o'clock the next morning. Now and again I tried quitting Matthew's bedside for a couple of hours in the afternoon, but I soon discovered that if I went back to the house I was quite unable to distract myself. And because it was high summer, nearly everyone I would have liked to spend a little time with was gone on holiday.

As the days passed, certain ceremonies and observances grew into being. Some of them concerned cricket and steeplechasing. Mr. Abrams kept note of the cricket scores and instructed Matthew to do likewise. He or Mr. Cohen would go over Matthew's lists of names and numbers and make him copy out the corrections. This activity gave Matthew the feeling that he had important work to do each day and that he was part of a very grownup and rarefied triumvirate, which indeed he was.

Mr. Cohen kept a steeplechase book. At first I was not aware of the fact, for he feared I might disapprove. The company took it in turns to stake Matthew, mostly in pennies. They would read to him from the sports page of the *Evening Standard,* then help him choose which horses to back.

There was the pleasurable business of filling out the menu sheets. Each morning, the following day's menus would be handed out with the breakfast trays. For the first few mornings either Giovanni (he proved too critical: "Better only 'ave bread than eat that") or Mr. Cohen would help Matthew put ticks in appropriate boxes, until one morning they decided that he was capable of choosing his own fare. After long cogitation he put a tick in every box, leaving out only prunes for breakfast, turnips for lunch, and mulligatawny soup—the only word he could not read—for supper. Then he added a codicil, "Bit mor ice cream, chips orlways please love M Crosby." This was curious of him because by this time his appetite was, as Giovanni put it, "dainty."

The kitchen took Matthew's menu sheet to be a piece of mischief, so they inflicted their usual penalty: For a whole day Matthew's trays were delivered to him labeled "fatless and reduced diet." He managed to remain unperturbed by his breakfast, but when confronted with a morsel of boiled fish, half a steamed potato, and a water biscuit for lunch, he broke down. "Wrong stuff on this tray, please."

"The only time I seen 'im cry. 'Ow right 'e 'ees to take 'is meals so seriously."

Supplements and tidbits were donated from all sides. The green-uniformed girl who delivered the trays was made to feel she ought to apologize on behalf of the kitchen. Never again was

Matthew left unsupervised when the time came to put ticks in boxes.

On the more painful side of ward life, certain "observances" were applied. When a patient was seen to be "resting," a nurse would be asked to pull his curtains round his bed, but not so fully that fellow patients could not "look in on him" now and then.

If someone gave signs of being upset, no one appeared to notice. This was explained to Matthew, who in his turn cautioned me, "Mustn't notice, Mum." If a loved one visited and there was an obvious need for privacy, as long as they were well enough to do so, the patients on either side of the pair would put on their dressing gowns and slippers and "go for a chat with a friend," or take a newspaper and stroll down the corridor to sit for a while on one of the benches.

OBLIVIOUS OF THE official visiting hours—the limits were never enforced—Dido might float into our field of vision at any moment of the day. I do not know why I was always so astonished to see her; possibly her presence reminded me that there were other ways of existing, other ways of loving, and other people to think about.

I was able to use Matthew's manner of greeting his sister as a yardstick by which to measure the encroachment of the dysfunctions that I now knew were slowly detaching him from us. The first time Dido skirred to a standstill beside his bed, Matthew was capable of turning his whole torso toward her and saying in a loud and cheerful voice, "'S Dido here, Mum." His welcomes became more and more muted as the days went by, till he greeted her with only a smile and a soft wave of his fingers.

After she had settled herself beside his bed, Dido sometimes sent me away. I was never able to imagine the kind of conversations she and her brother had when they were alone. The mystery lay in how contented Matthew seemed after she was gone.

"Did you have a nice talk with Dido?"

"Yep."

"What did you talk about?"

"She told and I told back."

"What sort of things did you tell each other?"

"Telled her, not you, Mum."

Sometimes Dido brought Robert with her. His presence gratified Matthew, and was perhaps a protection to Dido, whose gallant blitheness no longer masked her horror of her brother's illness and his hospital surroundings, She looked a little more dismayed and frozen every time she had made the journey across London to sit with us. The day came when it was necessary to persuade her that Matthew was in the safest of hands and that he and I had got the hang of hospital life and were in no way discontented. I told her that she should use her precious summer holiday to finish the piece of sculpture she was working on in the barn in Wiltshire. I promised to send for her when it became necessary. I was relieved that she consented to go. In a placid and resigned way, Matthew missed his sister, but I found the task of minding him simpler when I did not have to witness Dido's acute distress.

Since Matthew was now so well adapted to ward life, I wondered if my constant presence might be an embarrassment or even a burden to the fragile male patients surrounding him. The presence of the "Lady Doctor"—her usual title—and of the female staff was, of course, crucial. Even though I discerned in one or two of the patients a wariness, which I suspected was caused not only by Matthew's being "mentally deficient," but also by my presence, any response from me would have been part of the constraint I dreaded imposing.

I questioned the ward sister. Her attitude was that at all costs Matthew must be kept secure and calm. She assured me I fitted in remarkably well and was regarded as humorous and useful. She suggested I should take time off when I judged it to be all right, but to always let a nurse know when I was leaving the building.

The next morning the same sister let me know that my presence might be helpful to others beside Matthew. She asked me to be a little more bold; I was grateful.

So every time Matthew took a nap, which he did more and more frequently throughout the days—and, I was told, the nights —I would crank his backrest down a few notches, put the rubber bulb of the bell in his hand, and slip across to ask the Crusader if there was anything I could do for him. I read the newspaper, cooked bowls of porridge, and, when he requested me to, rather self-consciously bathed his face and hands. As the days passed, his most urgent need was that I sit with my ear close to his pillow and listen to his tales of home, his farm, his children, but mostly of his young (second) wife, how horrible it was to be far away from her. He used to fall asleep talking. These were times when Giovanni would put a hand on my shoulder and whisper, "Thank you, thank you. Eet is not easy, that job of comforting."

Early one evening, just before the doctors decided the Crusader must be removed to the front section so as to be nearer to the nursing station, I was crouching over him, holding both his hands. He had talked himself almost to sleep when he mumbled that he was frightened. His wife appeared at his bedside. Distractedly she whispered, "I am glad we have someone else." She looked terribly tired. I was touched by her air of utter helplessness. When I crossed the room to rejoin Matthew I found him near tears. "Mister Peter's heart's broke, Giovanni says."

If the Crusader was asleep or simply did not feel like talking, I was sometimes asked to sit by some other patient. When I offered to read aloud, I was usually handed a newspaper and asked to turn to the sports or sometimes the financial page. Only once was I asked to read something less prosaic, Rudyard Kipling's "Barrack Room Ballads." I would write letters, and there were endless requests for cups of tea. Whenever I carried out these tasks, I was unable to quell the feeling that I was spying on people at their most vulnerable time.

I was not so much frightened of Matthew's death, nor of the manner in which it might happen, but of all the pain I could not protect him from. Our doctor was not so much inexplicit as evasive about Matthew's condition. She disliked my asking questions. When I did so more and more pressingly as the days wore on, she replied using such phrases as "We must be patient," or "We'll have to see how he gets on, won't we?" I felt these to be most unhelpful answers, and I believe she did too, for she would sigh and add almost pleadingly, "Meanwhile he doesn't seem too uncomfortable, does he? He is doing all right for the present, don't you think?"

I wanted to blurt out, "I don't know how to think on this subject; no one seems to want to guide me." The doctor had an expressive face, which told me she was not yet properly inured to some aspects of her work, so I connived with her, saying to myself, "Matthew is content here. This is the best of all possible alternatives; we are safe in this place. I must be thankful." And I was.

When Matthew and I talked, we kept our exchanges safely within our well-established bounds.

"Are you comfortable, Matt?"

"'F you are, Mum."

"Would you like medicine for your pain?"

"You have't, Mum."

And on another occasion, "You all right, Mum?"

"Yes, if you are, I am."

"We all right, then."

"Shall I try to make you more comfortable?"

"Yep, you be more comfortable."

On another occasion, "I shut eyes, Mum. You shut yours."

On bad days we reassured each other frequently; on good days we played and replayed his often revealing games of list-making.

I remember one of these lists started out quite idly, a catalog of Matthew's past favorite possessions. As I sharpened a pencil and looked for a clean page in his writing book, he was feigning ennui, putting on the air of a jaded Philistine sated by a surfeit of worldly goods.

"Don't you want to play this game?"

"Got to, Mum. You start telling."

I took him back to his earliest years, reminding him of his velvet pig, Dido's Burl Ives records, his once so precious little blue pedal motorcar. He opened his eyes wide.

"*Never* little motorcar. Write it big."

I asked if he recalled his tricycle or any of the bicycles he had inherited, one after another, from Dido. He braced himself against his backrest, then jarred the murmuring quiet of the ward badly as he let out an almost perfect imitation of the clamorous ringing of his silvery blue bicycle bell, the bell which, because he was so enamored of it, we would transfer from one bicycle to the next.

"First time you impolite," called Giovanni.

"'S my bike bell done it."

"Let's hope your bike doesn't come riding through here again, then," growled Mr. Abrams.

That marvelous mimicry released a variety of recollections: the scissors which were kept in the art room, a tape measure that pinged back into its shell, a torch with many colored lights, his bomber jacket, Dido's camera, any number of calculators, and finally his collection of watches.

He no longer looked jaded or sated.

"Got to write Dad today now."

I gave him his writing book, and in a flourishing hand heedless of legibility he knocked off an urgent message to his father. By the time I arrived the next morning, Mr. Cohen had overseen the making of a somewhat fair copy. I did as Matthew asked and put it in an envelope which I later posted to Theo.

Someone from his school telephoned, offering to bring one or two of Matthew's friends to see him. "Do you feel like seeing anyone from Had-a-Home?"

"Nope." He looked very miserable.

"Perhaps Mark?"

"Nope."

"Anyone else?"

"Nope, not no one."

"That's quite all right, they shan't come. We can write them a letter if you like."

"Won't write letters no more."

He sat very still with his fists clenched against his chest, then all at once he shook himself. "Not going back no more, very nice here, live bit here, bit with you."

"I shall enjoy that."

"Have little cat on my bed, always. You push Dido's [old wheel] chair—when 'm tired."

"I'll do it gladly."

"You do cooking. Dido come in car. Dad come?"

"Of course."

A new patient, not yet fully adult, looking lonely and wretchedly ill, wandered over to sit with us. He told us he was about to have heart surgery. "How old are you?" he asked Matthew.

"Going to be twenty-six—p'raps."

"You are five years older than me." The young man gave a sigh and moved away, leaving Matthew considering the matter.

"Very old now, aren't I? May twenty-sixth coming soon, Mum?"

"It's still July, it goes August, September..." I recited the months as I had done so often before. "All those months have to pass before it will be May again."

"Go other way."

"Backwards? June, May; your birthday was barely two months ago."

"'S shorter that way." Matthew smiled. "Have my birthday party then."

The next morning when I arrived at his bedside, he had his writing book and pencils out, ready for me to write.

"May twenty-six; Matthew's twenty-six birthday; twenty-six best friends in party." Overnight Matthew had devised a framework, a motif, for his ultimate list. For the next few days, when neither hospital life nor televised sport distracted him, Matthew focused his daydreams on the number 26. He perceived it as a consummately beautiful number, possessing a symmetry that gave him intense satisfaction.

"Twenty-six, twenty-six May. Write proper, Mum."

"Write what?"

"Twenty-six people for party—ter . . . wenty six."

So we set about compiling his last inventory. What he composed over the next days was a testament; a list of all the companions and comrades he had loved during the fourteen years in which he had been part of the MacIntyre community. This testament, which he titled "Great Twenty-Six Party of Mr. M. Crosby," was surprisingly far-reaching. The recollection of one friend frequently begot that of another. He was able to bring to mind names and memories of houseparents and teachers who had been patient enough to bring about, in conjunction with his own doggedness, this capacity to recall . . . a kind of matriculation—a rondo.

It was in this hospital, of all places, that he was at last able to see himself as a man among men, albeit a dying man among dying men. Here he found himself hardly more handicapped than those about him.

MATTHEW GESTURED THAT I hand him the writing book. He laid it on his knees and, selecting a clean page and using his set square, he drew a rather fragile looking one-roomed house. Within its walls he ordered me to write Dido's, Robert's and the dog's names. On the lines below came others: Auntie Gladys, Fred, Our Lil, and further down, Mr. Theo and Mrs. Anne, "little writing, please, Mr. Roger R." Here he appeared to hesitate. Wondering if he wanted to be fair, I asked if he wanted me to put Livie's name on the same line.

"She got to wait 'n see."

Finally he named not Livie but "Davie Sylvester."

I teased, "What sized writing for him?"

"Nice fat."

"Why are we all in a house, Matthew?"

"Different bit 'f party; can have whiskey in Hamsmith house."

We both laughed. Matthew found it so painful that we never dared laugh that way again.

As the days passed and Theo did not come to the hospital, Matthew instructed me to separate his father's name from mine and write it "smally," and the next day, "very smally." While working on his party list one afternoon, Matthew fell asleep. I tidied away our work and decided to take a stroll out of doors. While I was gone Matthew wakened to find a most original and carefully bound bunch of flowers lying across the foot of his bed, tight little red roses circled by Marguerite daisies, fringed by masses of blue scabious. As I passed the sluice room, a young probationer beckoned me. She was thrusting this posy into a glass vase.

"Your son rang his bell and told me his flowers were thirsty. While he was asleep a gentleman came. You were nowhere about, and so he just laid the flowers on the bed, gave your son a kiss and went away. Oh, he said for you to telephone."

I did not have to ask for a description of the "gentleman." I knew it was Theo. I took the vase to Matthew's bedside. When he understood his father had been and gone, Matthew turned his face away from the bouquet and waved me away, so I went in search of the telephone trolley. By the time it was our turn to use it, he would not let me call his father. Not wanting to upset him further, I wheeled the trolley back into the corridor and talked to Theo myself. He said he would come again and promised to rouse Matthew if he found him asleep.

The next morning Matthew had recovered his good humor. He forbade me to kiss him good morning. "No kisses. Busy man, m'writing." He was rejoining Theo's name to mine. He looked at me and smiled. "Red, white, blue flowers smell divine."

CHAPTER FORTY-FOUR

Two Handkerchiefs

As the pace of his decline accelerated, Matthew dispensed with his already fragile awareness of the passing of time. He issued invitations to companions who had died in his childhood and to friends long gone from his life, among them the little girl whom he had adopted during his first weeks at Mount Tabor House. He also enjoyed barring old enemies: the lad who prevented him from using the lavatory so long ago, the girl who "snatched and scratched and *could* help it," Hugo, the bully, and his old love, Sarah. His worst enemy, Simon, was never referred to.

When I pointed out that we had exceeded our limit of twenty-six guests, Matthew was gratified. "Have to hold hands."

"You mean your friends must come to your party the way the animals entered Noah's ark, two by two?"

"Yep, twenty-six bigger that way."

I told him I admired his cleverness.

"Yep, clever every day now."

But within a few days this was no longer so. He brought the game to a close, saying "'Nuff friends for party, got to put 'Ther End.'" He lay against his pillows for several minutes.

"Are you feeling very tired, Matthew?"

"Not clever no more. Pain there for bit now."

When I was sure he had fallen asleep, I went to report this to a staff nurse, who took it so seriously that she at once paged the Lady Doctor. After examining Matthew, she said, "He must have been experiencing serious pain for some days."

That evening I accompanied Matthew and a recently acquired friend, a large-bosomed training nurse, whom he had both embarrassed and endeared himself to while she was on night duty by whispering, "Like your front very much." We accompanied his stretcher down to the ground floor where Matthew was put through a series of wearying tests. We had wrapped him in the Japanese dressing gown Theo had given him; for most of the time he held its sleeve across his eyes to avoid seeing what was being done to him.

The drugs the doctor prescribed reduced Matthew's pain, but they also disoriented him, and this disturbed him profoundly.

"'S horrid in my head; sleep-awake—. You ask em, Mum, make me back being proper Matthew."

I was impressed that he recognized it was opiates that were dislocating him. "That stuff is being given to you to make your pain go away."

He answered me wearily, "Pain's all right."

Not daring to relax against his pillows for fear of being overpowered by the medications, Matthew sat in his now habitual cross-legged posture, swaying a little and looking pathetically ill at ease.

The person most able to bring Matthew out of this purgatory was Dido's friend, Robert. He had two or three times dropped by to sit with us. Though I doubt he was aware of it, his presence was an elixir to Matthew. Like an emissary from another country, he bore gifts, favors, and trivia relating to Matthew's darling football team, 'Evert'n 'Nited, or a couple of bottles of "pretend" beer, which the two ritualistically sipped.

One morning, with my sanction but to the astonishment of the nurses and the doctor, Matthew flatly refused to be dosed with any further narcotics. With amiable dignity, he three times repeated his axiom, "Pain's all right," until finally the doctor yielded. Now despite the pain, Matthew was again at one with himself.

Robert arrived that evening. Rather diffidently he offered Matthew the most desirable of all gifts—we were now in the month of August—a flamboyant blue-and-white-striped winter scarf, the Everton United football colors. Matthew was overcome with delight. Quite forgetting he should say thank you, he gave a soft little sigh and wound the scarf round his neck. He fell asleep with it draped across him. From then on it was his most favored possession, replacing in his affections the Japanese dressing gown from his father.

Each morning I arrived earlier and earlier. As I approached his bedside, I could divine to what degree Matthew was coping with his pain from the way he held his head or clenched his fists. He had always had a conviction that any suffering which came upon him was a part of his corporeal self, his to reckon with and to dominate as best he could. He had endured so much illness in his life that he saw it as something akin to the weather, his personal weather.

If on one of those mornings I caught Matthew in the grip of a battle with pain, he would whisper, "Quiet a bit, Mum." Later when he breathed more easily and I was putting a drinking straw between his lips or sponging his face and hands, he with a clownish gesture would wave the fringes of his scarf in my face.

"Wait. Do swearing first in a minute."

After spending twenty days observing the behavior of his fellow patients in the second bay of the Heart Unit, Matthew knew it was good form to swear under one's breath after a "nasty turn." Taking a deep breath, he would embark on his little litany of bad words, his voice and his spirit strengthening with the delivery of each one.

"Blast, blood, stupid monkey. Mud, horrid-pudding. Scratch, biting, fart."

After this satisfactory discharge of favorite curses, Matthew sometimes fell into a doze. On one such morning Mr. Cohen beckoned me to his bedside. He wanted to know how Matthew had survived all those years "in an institution"—"Must be a bit like prison, after all"—without learning any more forceful expletives than the ones he had just uttered. I explained that it was the practice at Matthew's school to find substitute swear words to replace foul ones. Mr. Cohen looked doubtful, and I found myself launching into a perhaps apocryphal tale of my mother's. She claimed that as she was mounting the steps of St. Paul's Cathedral one morning she came upon the bishop about to descend them. At the same moment, a flock of pigeons swooped down and splattered their droppings over the recently swept flagstones. An old verger rushed out waving a broom and shouting, "Bugger off, you lot." My mother overheard the bishop admonish him, "If you say, 'shoo, shoo,' they bugger off just the same."

Mr. Cohen shook his head. "So they apply the bishop's rule at your son's asylum, do they? Wouldn't work among real kids, would it, now?"

One afternoon, Mr. Cohen heaved himself out of bed and shuffled off to shave himself. When he came back he lay on top of his blankets, wrapped in his dressing gown, waiting for Mrs. Cohen to bring him his clothes. He announced to Matthew he was going home.

"Can't go. You live next us."

"Not any more, Sonny. Perhaps your mum is going to take you home soon."

"Nope."

"That's right. You stay here till you are properly well."

"You stay too."

"Mrs. Cohen needs me."

Matthew's tears were an embarrassment to both of them.

"You've got your friend Giovanni over there and Abrams isn't going anywhere just yet."

When he was dressed, Mr. Cohen came to Matthew's bedside and gently shook his hand.

"You've been an education to me, my friend. I've enjoyed our time together." He put into Matthew's hand a large, well-ironed white handkerchief with his initials emblazoned across one corner.

"Now you can't forget me."

Matthew carefully unfolded the handkerchief and blew his nose loudly. Mrs. Cohen stroked his forehead.

"I've left plenty of little comforts in the fridge for you, Matthew. Mind you, be a good boy and eat them up."

Matthew looked at her fondly. "Sweet nothings 'gain?"

She kissed his cheek.

Seated in a wheelchair, making a gesture reminiscent of an army salute, Mr. Cohen was propelled out of our lives by a hospital orderly.

When two nurses began to strip his friend's bed, Matthew was devastated.

"Mustn't do it, might come home t'night."

I mopped his tears away with the new handkerchief. A staff nurse came over and perched herself beside him, leaning against his pillows. She put her arm about him.

"Don't worry. We'll put clean sheets on Mr. Cohen's bed and keep it ready for him for a day or two in case he comes back. You calm down now, we don't want you to be too tired to go on your ride with the night nurses, do we?"

Later, when Matthew was more peaceful, I asked him to tell me about the rides.

"At hot drinks 'n pill time I ride in chair."

"Who pushes your chair?"

"'Mm choose ... like one who baths me best."

As I was leaving the ward, I went to say goodnight to Giovanni, who was looking very ill and was spending more time with us.

"'E shouldn't 'ave left. 'E discharged hisself, says 'e wants to die at 'ome. I think 'e wants to smoke 'is cigarettes also."

IT WAS NOW rare that anyone came to visit us. Very occasionally a friend of mine might appear, but after a sympathetic glance in Matthew's direction, they usually declared they had only come to say a quick hello and leave a little present. I used to wonder if these people were aware—or if they were aware that I was aware—that they had really come to say goodbye.

Joan, Matthew's social worker, bustled through the arch one day. Only for a second, as she caught sight of Matthew's dark eyes and spent air, did she allow her expression to betray her dismay. Her step did not falter, but was on tiptoe by the time she reached his bedside. With the blandest of smiles she exclaimed how sweet Matthew was looking. She was right; in a curiously delicate way it was so. She presented him with a get-well card, then drew up a chair and murmured that her dog would be envious when she told him she had seen his friend Matthew. He smiled continuously as she chatted with him. When she and I shook hands she gripped mine painfully.

Despite Matthew's refusal to see anyone from Had-a-Home, the very instructor who had wondered if Matthew was being "piggy" in the bakery materialized one afternoon, accompanied by a lad who I knew used to intimidate Matthew dreadfully. They brought with them a present. Someone had carefully transposed one of Matthew's car paintings onto a piece of cross-stitch canvas. A range of pretty-colored wools and two huge needles were included in the package. After I had found chairs for these two, the instructor unrolled this piece of handwork and spread it on the bed. Matthew confounded him by refusing even to glance at it.

"It's something for you to do to help pass the time."

"Don't want passing time."

Brushing aside this softly said but significant statement, the instructor, who knew when he must show forbearance, proceeded to boom out snippets of news from Had-a-Home. Matthew appeared bored.

Meanwhile the once-intimidating lad slipped lower and lower in his seat and turned his head in an attempt to hide his tears. He looked so woeful that I reached for his hand.

"You know, Matthew is extra tired today. He will be better when he has had a little sleep."

The lad straightened his back, took a rasping breath, and demanded loudly, "Is that why Matthew isn't wearing his glasses?

Is he going to sleep?" Matthew gave the slightest of nods and waved his scarf in his direction.

That same evening, Theo strolled into the ward. He pulled up a chair and made himself at ease before he leaned over and planted a light kiss on Matthew's forehead.

I was not certain that Matthew's reciprocal nonchalance was not a mere reflex, an application of his old stratagem, that of paying his father in his own coin. After giving him the briefest of smiles, Matthew readjusted his shoulders against his backrest and closed his eyes. I turned a little away from the two of them and opened my newspaper.

"Hasn't much to say to me, has he?"

"Matthew has become very economical with words lately."

In his most facetious tone, Theo drawled, "How wise... Before you go to sleep, Matthew, I must tell you I got your letter. It was very nicely written, but you mustn't expect me to go out and buy all those things you asked for."

Matthew kept his eyes tightly shut. I was nettled on his behalf. "For God's sake, Theo, Matthew isn't going to need any of those things ever again." I was aghast that I had spoken in such a way within Matthew's hearing. I continued lamely, "The letter to you was a spinoff from one of his list-making games." I stood up. "Now you have your Dad here, Matt, shall I go and read my paper in the corridor for a while?"

Matthew fluttered his eyelashes, a gesture I knew as tantamount to a wink, and said in a serene voice, "'S right, Mum, got t' read paper."

A bare five minutes passed and Theo came and threw himself on the bench beside me. "Has it crossed your mind that you are being a little too attentive to our darling son? Surely the hospital does not require that you remain at his side every minute of the day? From what I can see they aren't short of nurses."

In his determination not to recognize that Matthew was dying, Theo had, a few minutes before, put me in mind of the well-insulated instructor from MacIntyre Schools. Now so forlornly slumped on the bench beside me, he seemed more like the once-intimidating lad. With a weary and to me infinitely appealing gesture, he removed his spectacles and rubbed his eyes, then taking out a bright red handkerchief he polished and repolished the spectacles. His vexation entirely dissipated; he reached for my hand.

"Do you remember, Theo, how the doctors kept telling us that Matthew was doomed to a very short life, and how ambivalent our feelings were as to whether this was good or bad news?"

"Now you mention it, I do. I also seem to recall that they extended his life expectancy every time they examined him."

"But not forever."

"No." Theo sighed and looked at his watch. "Pity I haven't got more time." He did not sound entirely sincere. "You know, I quite forgot to bring him a present. What shall I have sent to him?"

"If you can manage the rest of the day without it, I bet he'd like that handkerchief. You know how pleased he always is when you lend him one and then say he'd better keep it now he's messed it up."

"Do I say that? Well, if you think it will do, I'll give it to him."

We sat for a moment longer, then Theo replaced his spectacles, folded the handkerchief and walked back to the ward.

When I joined them some minutes later, Theo and Matthew had Mr. Cohen's and Theo's handkerchiefs spread out upon the bed.

"Matthew tells me he'll use one in the day and the other at night. I say they both need to go to the laundry. By the way, why does he have to wear a scarf? Isn't it a bit hot for that?"

"No, Dad. 'S Everton."

Theo kissed Matthew goodbye tenderly. He held onto his hand for a moment. "You telephone me when you think it's time for another visit. Your Mum has all the relevant numbers."

"Might do, Dad."

Matthew was able to sleep for several hours during the night. In the morning he told the doctor he felt "big 'n strong today." He told her he was "going to do walking."

"We'll decide that tomorrow."

Despite his declared vigor, we passed a dull day. Matthew made me uneasy by frequently referring to his projected walk.

"Next time Dad like me walking 'bout."

"Your Dad liked you just as much resting in your bed. You saw how much he liked you yesterday."

"Yep. Got handkerchief. Done 'nough resting. Got to go through arch 'n shake hand at Mr. Peter tomorrow."

"We'll see what the doctor has to say."

A while later, "Dad likes me better better."

"He loves you however you feel."

CHAPTER FORTY-FIVE

Here Comes the Champ

As if the August summeriness of the world outside was a restorative for failing hearts, no new patients came to fill the empty beds in Matthew's ward. There was a continuous Sunday-like serenity, an absence of doctors and technicians, and of orderlies transporting patients to and from clinics. The glaring sunlight that poured through the windows flattened and blanched all the shapes around us and contributed to Matthew's and my feelings of being cut off from the world.

He lay supported and cushioned to alleviate his pain. As the day wore on, a probationer and I plumped pillows, lowered and raised Matthew's backrest, sampled television programs, adjusted and readjusted the curtains to prevent the sunlight from being "too loud." We fed him a variety of yogurts, but we were not able to calm his increasing restlessness. His limbs twitched, and unfamiliar expressions surged across his face.

The sister on duty, not sure whether all this activity was caused by pain, came several times to take Matthew's temperature and pulse. She stroked his forehead and reminded me that "narcotics as needed" was still scrawled across his prescription sheet.

As if he could wait no longer, admonishing himself to "get on with it" and "get going, M. Crosby," Matthew raised himself to a sitting position and using both hands heaved first one then the other skeletal leg over the side of the bed. Perhaps sardonically, he muttered, "Here comes the champ."

I hurriedly interceded. "Wait while I find your dressing gown and slippers." I pressed his bell. Curtains were half drawn round the few occupied beds, patients were somnolent. There seemed to be no nurse to answer my call.

"Do you want me to find a wheelchair?"

"Walking now this time."

I helped him into his dressing gown so reluctantly that he frowned at me, "You no good."

I pushed each foot into a slipper and helped him raise himself.

"Go say 'How do do' to Mr. Giovanni."

"He has gone to sit in the garden."

"Say to Mr. Abrams, p'raps?"

With a kind of formal shyness he placed a shaking hand on my shoulder. I grasped his waist and was startled by his dry, overheated boniness. He reminded me of a sun-warmed gastropod shell. As if setting out on a treacherous journey, Matthew slid one foot the tiniest bit forward, sighed, and repeated the movement with the other, glad the art of walking had not deserted him. "'S working, Mum, let's go." He hauled himself along a sleeping Mr. Abrams's bed rail, and from there we managed to shuffle through the arch and reach the empty armchair beside the Crusader's bed. I lowered him into it. He seemed to be shivering. When he regained his breath he patted the Crusader's pillow. "Good af'noon, come to say how do do."

The Crusader's whisper was faint. "Glad to see you."

"Can't see; your eyes too shut."

"I know who you are all the same."

"'S clever."

"Better go back to bed now." The Crusader's whisper was stronger and very solicitous.

"Yep."

"You sit still, Matt, I'll fetch a chair."

The Crusader was already pressing his bell. A nurse left her desk and was immediately at his side. With an almost imperceptible movement of his head the Crusader indicated Matthew. "Him." He opened his eyes just for a second, "Goodbye, my friend."

The nurse wheeled Matthew to his bed and together we fussed about trying to get him settled. I pleaded with him to sip some water. He allowed me to put the drinking straw between his lips. After one token swallow, he asked, "You better now, Mum?"

Before going to sleep, he mused, "Did walking proper, do 'nother when Dad be there."

I examined his greenish skin, his blue lips, his swelled eyelids, and the unrelenting pulsation of a newly visible vein at his throat, and wondered if the time had come to ask Dido to return to London.

I was making a little drawing of Matthew's head. "He's asleep as usual." Theo loomed over us. I leaned over and stroked Matthew's cheek. "Wake up, Matt, your Dad's here, he's come to see you."

Matthew appeared indifferent to this piece of news. "You all right, Dad?"

"I've brought you some grapes."

"Don't need 'em, thank you." He rolled his head from us and closed his eyes.

"He tried to walk this afternoon. I don't know why I let him."

"He doesn't seem to be going to wake up in a hurry. I think we should leave him to it. What about Chez Ciccio's?" He named our favorite restaurant of long ago.

I demurred a little and Theo laughed. "Same old Anne, duty first. I've already told the sister I am taking you out."

She came forward. "Enjoy yourselves. We'll keep an eye on him."

Chez Ciccio's was gone, a hairdressers' emporium having taken its place. We drove about Notting Hill Gate till we came upon Chez Some-other-Italian-restaurateur. We ate pasta, and our talk was pleasantly remote from our immediate realities, but before we had properly finished our meal my thoughts flew back to Matthew.

I drove us back to the hospital a little too fast. Leaving Theo to his more leisurely pace, I ran up the stairs and along the corridors, then walked quietly into the ward. Matthew's bed was empty. I spun round. Giovanni pointed toward the nursing station. There the sister told me, "I am afraid Matthew woke up almost as soon as you and his father were gone. His Italian friend sat with him for a while, then he rang for our help. He thought Matthew was dangerously upset. It seems he was worried that his father might not come back. We tried to reassure him, but we could not convince him that you both would be back very soon. His agitation continued so we paged his doctor. She has had him removed to a side ward. I'll take you to him."

Theo was hovering in the corridor. "This way, Mr. Crosby." She led us into an area that consisted of three cubicles within one large room. The wall behind Matthew's cubicle was filled with formidable-looking machines each displaying all kinds of screens and dials. He was sitting upright on a high bed, taking little gulps from an oxygen mask. When he saw, us he pulled the mask from his face. A nurse reached forward and gently removed it from his grasp. She stroked his hair from his eyes, and in lilting Jamaican cadences reassured him, "There now, your Mumma and Dadda are here to be beside you. You show them how this toy makes you breathe easy."

I put my arms round Matthew. "We were away for too long. I'm sorry, Matt, so sorry."

"'S all right, Mum."

"Your Dad's come to say goodnight."

"I don't suppose you two need me around. I'll only get in the way. I'd better be off."

"Not just yet, Theo. Matthew must have his kiss goodnight."

Theo took a few steps forward and put a hand on Matthew's shoulder. Matthew looked up at him and smiled. I had the impression that the spontaneity of that smile was what released Theo from his restraint. With reciprocal brio he bent over and picked up Matthew's hands and placed them on each side of his own neck. He then kissed his forehead. "Shall I come and say 'Hallo' before I go to work tomorrow morning?"

"Yes, Dad."

Retrieving a gesture from our past, he came and rubbed his hand between my shoulder blades so that I reflexively straightened my back.

"Telephone me when you've got him sorted out, perhaps in an hour or so." He kissed me too and was gone.

Someone had dimmed the light over Matthew's bed to a moonlike glow. The Jamaican nurse gave him a cursory wash and dressed him in the inevitable hospital gown. In the faintest of voices he protested, "Don't want it."

"Such a fine young gentleman you look wearing it." He seemed to be getting the hang of the oxygen mask. He sniffed at it whenever he found himself gasping. Telling us the doctor would be along shortly, the nurse left the cubicle and made herself comfortable in an armchair that stood by a desk in the outer part of the room.

I took off my shoes and climbed onto the bed. I shifted Matthew over a little till we shared his backrest.

"Wetted tee shirt bit." He tried to giggle but doing so aggravated his pain.

"Shhh. I'll bring you a clean one tomorrow. Does it hurt very badly?"

"Much bigger."

The doctor came in and beckoned to me as the nurse moved to sit beside Matthew. Too flustered to locate my shoes, I followed the doctor out to the nursing station barefooted. She talked rather formally. "I telephoned my chief to describe your son's sudden deterioration. He says he will come if you feel you need a second opinion."

"Tell me the first opinion, yours."

Her voice softened. "He's suffering badly. We can relieve that right away by performing the same procedure as we did last time."

"But that relief turned out to be temporary."

"I am afraid it did."

"Wouldn't it be even more so this time around?"

"I think it might."

"So one way or another, Matthew is doomed to die soon, isn't that what we are saying?"

Her "yes" was almost inaudible.

She took a breath and said the word again. "Yes, your son is in severe heart failure and is inevitably going to die, fairly soon."

"Is there any possibility that a second opinion could tell me anything different?"

"I am certain it couldn't."

We stood together. "Would it contravene some law or another if I forbade you to make him go through that torture all over again?"

"You go back and sit with him while I make another call to my chief, then I'll be able to tell you his thoughts on the subject."

She returned to us in a very short time. "I have a message from my chief, Mrs. Crosby. He asked me to tell you that if he were in your shoes he would want what you want, that is, to let Matthew's life come to its natural conclusion without further suffering. He told me to reassure you that, since Matthew's heart failure is now so acute, there is little point in trying to prolong his life. He salutes your courage."

We both smiled, though I felt like weeping.

"I must ask my husband if he agrees."

The doctor gestured toward one of the telephones that stood on the nurses' desk. "Make all the calls you like. I'm not in a hurry."

I dialed Theo's number. He sounded sleepy.

"How's it going? Have they calmed him?" I gave him a précis of the discourse between the doctor and myself. "So now Matthew is about to be encouraged to die?" he asked. Before I could draw breath to object to what sounded like a jibe, he continued, "Don't feel bad. It's the best thing we can all do for him. Goodnight, love."

I dialed the Wiltshire number. Dido listened to all I had to say in silence. "How long will it take? How much time have we got till…"

I repeated her question to the doctor; she shrugged her shoulders. "Perhaps not more than two days, probably less."

I repeated these words to Dido adding, "I think you should come as soon as you can."

"I'll ask Robert to put me on an early train tomorrow. He can stay and look after the dog."

YET ANOTHER TUBE was being attached to Matthew, this one ending in a fine needle that was slipped under the skin just above the palm of his hand. By the time it was embedded and concealed by a bandage, enough morphine was flowing into his veins to quieten his protests. The mask fell from his hand, he gave a deep sigh and let his head flop against his pillows. The nurse was able to lower the backrest far enough so that for the first time in three weeks he lay at ease, no look of endurance on his face.

The nurse went back to the outer room, and I was left sitting in an armchair in our blue-lit cubicle. As I listened to Matthew's harsh, irregular breathing, I half-dreamed we were journeying together in a darkened railway carriage toward a destination we had no interest in. Matthew saved me from the dream by opening his eyes to ask if his spectacles were "ready." I put them in his hand.

"Evert'n scarf, please." Later he wanted to know if I was all right. I answered that I was and asked him the same question. "'S all quiet." Then we both fell asleep.

At three in the morning I wakened and watched the nurse as she sat Matthew up, rubbed his back and offered him, first a chance to urinate, then a drink of water, both of which he refused. She turned to me, "Not important; he's dehydrated, but he's on the drip. Now, Mrs. Crosby, your son is not likely to wake up for several hours. His vital signs are satisfactory, and I shall be by him until another nurse takes my place. You go off home and get some rest, too."

I ARRIVED AT Matthew's bedside early next morning to find him, not as I anticipated, almost comatose, but propped up being washed by the night nurse.

"Good morning, Mrs. Crosby. Your Matthew slept through most of the night. He hasn't managed to pass water. Can you remember when he last went?"

"I don't think he has asked to since about midday yesterday."

"I'll put that in my report."

After we had helped him into the clean tee shirt I had brought with me, I asked, "Shall I try to get him to do one now?"

"I don't think we need bother him again just yet."

"Doesn't come out, Mum." Matthew swayed back and forth as he spoke. "Evert'n scarf, please. Lying down time now."

"Before you lie down, can you tell me if you are hungry?"

"You say, Mum."

"A yogurt, perhaps?"

"Yellow nice." I hurried to fetch one from the little kitchen. He would not allow me to feed it to him. He looked very small and intent, as with a wavering hand he tried to aim the spoon toward his mouth.

As I scrutinized him, I could not determine why he appeared so young, until I realized that his face had become puffy during the night. As the night nurse was winding his backrest to an almost flat position, Matthew was falling back to sleep. "Shall I put your scarf round your neck and your glasses under the pillows?"

"Mum, hold 'em."

A cup of tea was brought to me. I drank it gratefully, then I carried the cup back to the tea trolley, which was being trundled round the ward. Our former neighbors seemed to need to avoid looking at me and gave the merest of nods to my greetings. When I returned to the room, I found Theo standing just inside the door and again bringing flowers.

"Is he unconscious?"

"No, he has just had a wash, and he ate a pot of yogurt." This news seemed to dispel Theo's diffidence. I pushed a chair close to Matthew. "Stay with him till I get back, won't you? I am going to find a jar for your marvelous flowers."

"You like them? I bought them outside the tube station."

"So early in the morning? How surprising."

We were embarrassed by our commonplace words. Theo handed me three tightly bound bunches of anemones; their concentrated luminosity quickened my eye muscles, a feeling so intensely pleasurable that for a moment I was ashamed of my frivolity.

I lingered in the sluice room, rinsing a flower vase again and again to pass the time. When I returned, I found Theo stooped over Matthew, possibly in prayer. He rose at once. Unable to hide his eagerness to quit the room, he beckoned me after him. As I followed him, the young male nurse who had taken the night nurse's place silently rose from his chair and went to sit beside Matthew.

"Call me at any time." After kissing me goodbye, in a pitiable effort to apply his old disguise, he called over his shoulder, "Keep up the good work."

I was sitting in a stupor nearly as deep as Matthew's when suddenly a small, wiry figure darted across the room to kneel on the floor on the further side of Matthew's bed. In his gray pinstriped suit, his dark shirt and tie, and pointed black shoes, he looked the very picture of a member of the Chicago mafia. With his hands folded before his face as he whispered a prayer; I supposed him to be an eccentric priest. It was not until he rose to his feet and picked up his hat from the end of the bed that I recognized Giovanni. He was in tears.

"I leave the 'ospital, go 'ome till it is over and 'e is gone. I want not to be 'ere losing my little friend. I lose so many. I bless 'im an' 'is good little mama. I say goodbye." He clutched my hand convulsively, then hurried from the room.

Giovanni had given me no time to say anything. I wished I had thanked him on Matthew's and my own behalf and found the words to tell him how much we valued his sweetness.

I saw Giovanni's evanescent visit as an admonishment, a reminder to yield to heartache while Matthew was still there beside me and not postpone or stifle my responses to his dying.

Twice during the morning the doctor came to check on Matthew. Later on, the young male nurse slipped away to eat a quick meal, and I was brought a luncheon tray. I ate a slice of bread and some custard; they tasted exquisite.

The doctor came again. "We may need to insert a catheter soon."

"Those things frighten Matthew terribly."

"Then we'll leave it a while longer. If he shows signs of discomfort, tell the nurse at once, won't you?"

"Of course."

Matthew stirred and I asked him if he was hungry or thirsty and if he thought he could pee. To all these questions he shook his head. There were moments when he seemed to be looking for me. Then I would move closer to him and tell him I loved him and say how brave and honorable I had always found him, and how good he was for me and for a lot of people.

I wondered why Dido had not come. I went to ask the nurse if there had been a telephone message. There had not.

Toward four o'clock in the afternoon Matthew was restless. I called the nurse to come in. "Do you think it is time for the catheter?"

"Perhaps I should go and get it."

At that moment Matthew opened his eyes wide. He struggled to sit up. The nurse came to his other side and arranged the backrest and pillows so as to support him. "I'll get the catheter; be back in a minute."

Matthew fluttered his eyelids and reached out his left hand.

"You want your spectacles?" I leaned over to give them to him. He pushed them aside. Then he took a long calm breath and looked at me very intently. I slipped my arms round him and brought his head close to mine. He gazed at each part of my face as if committing it to his memory; he seemed to need to stare and stare. I returned his concentration until I saw his eyes very slowly withdraw their focus. He gave a little sigh and his head fell back into the palm of my hand.

Postscript

M atthew had always been a virtuoso of silent exchanges. The most purposeful, the least equivocal of them had just taken place. I marveled that no accident of mistiming or mismanagement had robbed me of it. I lowered Matthew's head till it once more rested against the pillows. I dabbed his eyes closed, placed his arms in their habitual position, then pulled my chair close to the bed. I watched his face slowly, slowly lose its eloquence.

The doctor interrupted my absorption. She whispered that she had to verify that Matthew was "gone." Later she reappeared to tell me that a death certificate was ready. Not knowing what to say, I shook her hand and we said goodbye.

The young male nurse came in and asked if there was anyone I wanted to contact. He offered to make some phone calls on my behalf.

I realized I ought to tell Theo his son was dead. I went over to the desk and dialed his office number. His secretary told me she could not put me through to him because he was "in the middle of a ticklish meeting" and had asked not to be interrupted. When she understood that Matthew had died, she said she would get him to call me back. I reminded her of the telephone number.

The nurse stood over me once more. "I'm afraid there are some things I have to do for your son. If you like they can wait a little longer."

Only a few minutes passed before he returned, pushing a chrome-plated trolley. "I must lay him out, you know."

"Perhaps I could help."

"I think that would be OK. It is not a very complicated procedure, though there is one part you might not wish to ..."

350

He was quick and discreet as he performed the only intimate part of the ritual. The functions I participated in were much like the usual assistance I had been used to giving Matthew. I was pleased to be doing them, until the nurse prized open a plastic package and drew from it a crisp and ugly paper robe. The idea of Dido seeing Matthew dressed in that horrified me. "Can't he wear his dressing gown instead?"

"It's the regulation shroud, the morgue expects him to arrive in it."

"Then I'd like to cover it with his dressing gown."

"I don't see why not."

He helped me place the Everton scarf around Matthew's neck, and I put his spectacles in his hand. We spread a clean sheet on the bed and arranged his still faintly warm body on it, in as restful a position as we could devise. Then I sat down again on my chair.

In the course of the next hour the nurse brought me two messages. He told me that Dido had been delayed but was now on her way and that Theo would be with me as soon as his meeting was over. He then asked if I minded being left alone while he went on his tea break. He came back carrying a cup of tea and shyly reminded me that he could not go off duty till he had escorted Matthew's body down to the morgue. He said he was now on overtime, but he did not mind.

Matthew's corpse resembled a small, solemn effigy. It had taken on a dull yellowish quality, which made it appear quite untouchable. I wished I could prevent Dido and Theo from having to look at it. I got up from my chair and started to walk toward the window. At that very moment Theo appeared. I hurried to meet him, meaning to somehow absolve him from having to do something I knew he would hate. I was about to take him by the arm and lead him away when I saw Livie. She had a camera slung from her neck and was flourishing a cellophane cone of flowers. She strode past the two of us and proceeded to switch on every available light and then unwrap kindly-meant but calamitous-colored carnations which too nearly matched Matthew's skin. She placed some of the flowers around his face and laid the rest haphazardly about his body. Next, she climbed onto the chair I had just vacated and started snapping photographs. Theo and I stood watching blankly; we had not even exchanged a greeting. There was no need for him to tug at my sleeve to make me comply when Livie directed us to stand one on each side of Matthew's corpse. I was already obeying her.

A clamor resonated from somewhere beyond the outer room. Our nurse darted to my side and slipped his hand beneath my elbow to maneuver me out of the cubicle.

"What is it?"

"Your daughter. She's . . . well, she's upset." Dido had arrived at last, but to my horror she was hurrying away. I ran to catch up with her.

"Dido, don't go, it's all right."

"No, it's not. How can you and Dad just stand there and let her take photographs of Matthew dead among those awful carnations!"

Her voice was thrumming with intensity; she was in tears.

I reached out to lift her heavy satchel from her shoulder, but it was Theo's hand that grasped it. He gave it to me, then swept Dido under his arm and propelled her along the corridor to a bench. I watched them settle onto it.

A feeling of disengagement welled through my body. I strolled back to the cubicle. It didn't interest me that Livie was still clicking her camera round what remained of Matthew. She came to a standstill.

"Where have Theo and Dido got to? I want to take a couple more photographs . . . Ah, there you are; come and stand . . ."

Foreseeing another anguished outburst, I made a feeble move to intercede, but to my surprise Dido said nothing whatsoever. Livie patted her shoulder.

The nurse's patience and time had run out. He entered the crowded cubicle, accompanied by an orderly who was pushing a wheeled stretcher. Their presence was an irrefutable signal.

The nurse gave me a sweet and totally unnecessary apologetic smile, and I smiled back.

WE LEFT THE hospital. Livie and Theo rode in her motorcar, Dido and I in mine. We had one last duty to perform. Theo had told us we must come and have supper at Whitechapel; he said Livie had the meal all ready and prepared. Dido was loath to comply, but I persuaded her. "The offer is meant kindly, Livie and Theo think it fitting, and anyway we have got to get through the evening somehow."

As we drove through the twilight, Dido recounted how, because of an IRA bomb warning, she was trapped for the whole afternoon in a stopped underground train. After having been instructed on how to avoid brushing against the central electric rail, she and her fellow passengers were led by torch-waving guards in slow single file through more than three-quarters of a mile of tunnel to the next station. Since she was not carrying enough money to pay for a taxi, she had had to catch first one, then another bus, to arrive at the hospital much too late.

In return I told her how dreadfully I regretted that, through those days leading up to Matthew's final crisis, I had suspended any honest reckoning of how close he was to dying. It was I, as well as the IRA, who robbed her of her right to say goodbye. Toward the end of our drive across London, our conversation grew lighter. I quizzed Dido as to how she had managed to remain silent when Livie asked her to participate in her photo session.

"Oh, Dad said it was mostly his fault she was taking all those photographs. He needed them because he planned to make a sculpture of Matthew."

"Why, when he has plenty of photographs of Matthew alive, does he need any of him dead, especially with us posing beside the body?"

THE NEXT TIME I was invited for a drink at Theo's office, I expected to have to discuss our long overdue divorce. As he poured me a glass of whiskey and water, he ordered me to sit down and open his briefcase. I pulled out a large envelope sealed with sticky tape in a fashion that reminded me of Matthew's careful packaging.

"Don't unseal it."

"The divorce document?"

"No, you'll get that from my lawyer. The photographs...you know...the ones of Matthew."

"Aren't you going to use them?"

"No, and in case you are going to ask, neither is anyone else. The negatives no longer exist."

I waited to open the envelope in Dido's presence. We took a horrified peek at the contents. She suggested I tear them up at once, but I did not. In the early hours of the next morning, I took the photographs out of the envelope. This time I pored over them. His skin, as it had when he came into this world, again looked marbly, but rather than a sea-blue, this was a marble of no specific color. With his eyes closed and his mouth set, in the face which was once Matthew's I saw nothing but absence.